Interpreting the Russian Revolution

Interpreting the Russian Revolution
The Language and Symbols of 1917

Orlando Figes and Boris Kolonitskii

Yale University Press
New Haven and London

Set in Goudy by Print Line, New Delhi
Printed in Great Britain by Redwood Books, Wiltshire

ISBN 0–300–08106–5
Library of Congress Catalog Card Number 99–63582

A catalogue record for this book is available from the British Library.

10 9 8 7 6 5 4 3 2 1

Contents

Illustrations

Acknowledgements

The authors would like to thank Steve Smith and Raj Chandavarkar for reading and commenting on individual chapters; Vladimir Cherniaev for his general comments; and Daniel Beer, Helen McNamara and Laura Pieters Cordy for helping with the preparation of the manuscript.

Abbreviations

BA	Bahhmetieff Archive, Columbia University, New York
GAKO	Gosudarstvennyi Arkhiv Kuibyshevskoi Oblasti
GARF	Gosudarstvennyi Arkhiv Rossiiskoi Federatsii
OR IRLI	Otdel Rukopisei Instituta Russkoi Literatury (Pushkinskii dom)
OR RNB	Otdel Rukopisei Russkoi Natsional'noi Biblioteki
PRO	Public Record Office
RGA VMF	Rossiiskii Gosudarstvennyi Arkhiv Voenno–Morskoi Flot
RGIA	Rossiiskii Gosudarstvennyi Istoricheskii Arkhiv
RGVIA	Rossiiskii Gosudarstvennyi Voennyi Istoricheskii Arkhiv
SPARAN	Sankt-Peterburgskoe Otdelenie Arkhiva Rossiiskoi Akademii Nayk
TsGAIPD	Tsentral'nyi Gosudarstvennyi Arkhiv Istoriko-Politicheskikh Dokumentov (St Petersburg)
TsGASP	Tsentral'nyi Gosudarstvennyi Arkhiv Sankt Peterburga

Introduction

This is a book about the ways in which language was used to define identities and create new meanings in the politics of 1917. Language is defined in the broadest sense – songs and texts, symbolic flags and emblems, pictures and monuments, banners and slogans, common speech and rumour, dress and body language, ritualized demonstrations by the crowd, parades and other ceremonies to represent and show allegiance to the idea of 'the revolution'.

All these systems of symbolic meaning defined and separated the competing sides of the political struggle. Indeed, at one important level they were the object of the fight itself, the symbolic battlefield of the revolution, in so far as each side competed for the ascendancy of its own political symbols within the political culture of 1917. Some wanted to hoist the red flag, others to rally behind the national one. Some wanted to sing the 'Marseillaise', others to march with the 'Internationale'. Some spoke the language of the populist tradition, others the language of the Marxist one. The political struggle between the socialist parties was to a large extent defined by the struggle to establish the common symbols of the revolutionary tradition. Each faction fought to control the symbolic system of the revolutionary underground (the red flag, the 'Marseillaise', the key words and slogans of liberation, and so on) which dominated the political culture of 1917 and alone was capable of mobilizing mass support. Whoever mastered the red flag, or monopolized the meaning of its lexicon, was in pole position to become the master of the revolution too.

But to control the language of the revolution was not so simple or straightforward. The whole of society was rapidly politicized by the February Revolution, and it was impossible for official media (government and party newspapers, pamphlets and so on) to determine all the meanings and uses of its language within society. Individual statements could take on meanings within several different fields of discourse simultaneously, or they could combine to produce new meanings unanticipated by their original authors.

The whole of the revolutionary period could in this sense be conceived as one of near chaos in which the political actors competed with each other to fix public meanings, yet ultimately lost out to the power of a language that each proved unable to control. The new words and symbols of the revolution floated off the page or from committee rooms and out on to the streets, into shops and taverns, schools and churches, factories and barracks, towns and villages, where they were interpreted and used in many different ways. Some words took on a real symbolic meaning and power for a time – only to retreat into the background just as suddenly or to burst like a bubble. Others saw their meanings or their connotations change as time passed or political circumstances altered.

The language of the revolution contained many different idioms and dialects, then, which greatly complicated politics in 1917. Key words and symbols could mean different things, or imply different strategies, to the members of a single party organization. Many rank-and-file Bolsheviks, for example, continued to sing the 'Marseillaise' in 1917, seeing it as a song of solidarity with all socialists, although Lenin himself considered it a 'bourgeois' anthem and preferred to sing the 'Internationale' as a more exclusively Bolshevik song. Such differences of interpretation were a result of the cultural traditions of the revolutionary underground in which the various sections of the Social Democratic movement had developed. It was no easy matter for the leadership to get them to give up their particular traditions and unite on the basis of a single (centralized) symbolic system. All the major parties were confronted with this problem during 1917.

In this sense the struggle for power was not just defined by the competition between rival symbolic systems. It was also defined by the struggle within them. Each side struggled to unite and mobilize its own diverse supporters, and to convert others, under its own symbols of the revolution. Flexibility was a cardinal advantage in this symbolic battle: the party whose political language was able to accommodate the greatest number of different idioms and dialects, and yet unite them all in a common understanding which had real significance for people's daily lives, was likely to attract the most support and dominate the revolutionary discourse. This was the key to the remarkable success of the language of class, for example, which dominated the political discourse during 1917. It was a language that could express a wide range of identities (the 'labouring people', the 'proletariat', the 'working class', loyalties to factory or trade, etc.) and could equally articulate many different ideals of social justice (moral reform, workers' rights and so on), yet always managed to unite these different idioms in a common discourse of political struggle that was capable of appealing to anyone who felt excluded from society.

In the highly fragmented political culture of 1917 the power or effectiveness of any word or symbol was likely to be increased by its flexibility.

Wo₁ds and symbols united diverse groups only in so far as they allowed each one of these groups to project its own meanings and values on to them. The ambivalence of these words and symbols was the basis of their power. Take the red flag, for example. It was a universal symbol of the revolution. Being able to fight under it was a crucial advantage for the Bolsheviks in the civil war, enabling them to claim (however unjustifiably) that they alone were the true defenders of 'the revolution'. Yet the key to its symbolic appeal was the polyvalent nature of the red flag: many groups could project their own revolutionary ideals on to it. The Kronstadt sailors, the striking workers, and the peasant rebels of 1921 all fought under the red flag, as if to reclaim 'their' revolution from the Bolsheviks who had captured it.

So language was itself a complicating factor, if not quite an independent actor, in the politics of 1917. Words and symbols acted as a code of communication, whose signals served to sanction and legitimize the actions of the crowd, to define the revolution's common enemies, to uphold principles and generate authority for certain leaders. Yet in the process of communication this code could be changed, its signals could be reinterpreted or used for different purposes by local activists. The effect was often to exacerbate political and social conflicts, as we shall explore in the following chapters.

This is the first book to pay such close attention to the role which language played in shaping the political identities and discourse of the Russian Revolution.

Chapter 1 examines the role of rumours and political pornography (cartoons and pamphlets disseminating scandals of the Tsarina's 'affairs' with Rasputin and her alleged 'spying' for the German High Command) in turning public attitudes against the monarchy and fostering the belief throughout society that to overthrow the Tsar would be a patriotic act.

The next chapter argues that the February Revolution was organized around a symbolic overturning of the old order – the public conquest and recasting of symbolic sites and monuments, the destruction of the old state emblems and their replacement with new symbols of the revolution, the renaming of names, the changing of the forms of personal address – which assigned public meanings to the revolutionary events and sometimes even acted as a substitute for them.

In some ways the language of the revolution served as a bridge to the past. The February Revolution was based upon widespread political rejection of the monarchy. It promoted the cult of democratic ways. Yet a popular 'monarchical psychology' (expressed in the refrain: 'Long live a republic! Let's elect a good Tsar!') remained a potent force in the political discourse of 1917. This was reflected in the cult of the leader – of Kerensky, Kornilov and Lenin – which is discussed in Chapter 3.

The next two chapters focus on the ways in which the political languages and symbols of the revolution were interpreted and used by different groups in society. This in itself can tell us a great deal about how these groups identified themselves, how they saw their place in society, and how they conceived their moral and political ideals. Chapter 4 discusses the constant tension and ambivalence between, on the one hand, the moral idiom of universal human rights and, on the other, the class-exclusive idiom of workers' rights in the political language of the urban masses. Chapter 5 examines the ways in which the peasants constructed their own moral visions of the new political and social order through their interpretation and appropriation of the revolution's language in the towns.

If the revolution can be viewed as a struggle between competing symbolic systems, each attempting to mobilize and unite its followers behind its own symbols of identity, then the image of 'the people's enemy' played a crucial role in it. This is the subject of Chapter 6, which focuses on the changing image of the enemy and the ways in which it combined common phobias (of the foreigner, the Jew, the bourgeois and various 'dark forces') in a language and mentality of mass terror.

The chapters in this book are exploratory, and most of their conclusions are rather tentative. We do not apologize. This, as we have said, is the first book of its kind. Nor do we apologize for the methods which this book has been obliged to use in order to excavate the political language of 1917, even though they may be questioned by our critics. The texts which we have cited (letters, petitions, resolutions, slogans, songs, etc.) are by definition selective, and others could easily be found from which different inferences and conclusions might be drawn. It might be argued that our texts are themselves distortions of the views which they are supposed to represent: that, for example, the literate scribe, in setting down the views of his illiterate peasant clients, might have imposed his own views or language on them. We have been painfully aware of such methodological problems, but we have been careful to draw our conclusions from the balance of the evidence. In the main we have worked on the assumption that where the ideas contained in these texts are also expressed in public actions, they are likely to have been more widely held than ideas which remained – well, just ideas.

The history of the 1917 Revolution has traditionally been written as a conflict between rival social classes, political parties and ideologies. These social and political identities were usually assumed to reflect social and political realities. Thus it was assumed that class identities were more or less directly a reflection of the relations of production, and that political identities and allegiances were basically a reflection of social class.

The social history of the revolution, which dominated the field in the 1970s and 1980s, began to approach these material categories with greater sophistication, drawing on the study of *mentalités*, in particular, and on social anthropology, in general, to question what these forms of social and political identification actually meant to collective groups such as the workers, the soldiers, national groups or the peasantry.[1] But the pre-existence of these categories was still taken for granted. And rightly so, for these groups existed and their existence was socially defined.

In recent years, however, historians have begun to place more stress on the role of language in defining social and political identities. They have emphasized the degree to which the latter were cultural constructions rather than reflections of reality. Classes and ideologies were created, in this view, through a language or symbolic discourse, whose purpose was to give a collective meaning or interpretation to the life-experience of social groups and unite them on this basis politically.

This 'linguistic turn' – looking at the ways in which language contributed to the formation of social and political identities as well as to the exercise of power – has had a strong (and mainly beneficial) influence on Russian labour history, particularly in the late Imperial period.[2] It has also (and more controversially) influenced the study of Soviet social history.[3] But

1. See e.g. D.P. Koenker, *Moscow Workers and the 1917 Revolution*, Princeton, 1981; S.A. Smith, *Red Petrograd: Revolution in the Factories, 1917–1918*, Cambridge, 1983; D.P. Koenker and W.G. Rosenberg, *Strikes and Revolution in Russia, 1917*, Princeton, 1989; A. Wildman, *The End of the Russian Imperial Army*, 2 vols, Princeton, 1980, 1987; R.G. Suny, 'Nationality and Class in the Revolutions of 1917: A Re-examination of Categories', in N. Lampert and G. Rittersporn (eds), *Stalinism: Its Nature and Aftermath*, London, 1992; O. Figes, *Peasant Russia, Civil War: The Volga Countryside in Revolution (1917–1921)*, Oxford, 1989.

2. See e.g. M. Steinberg, 'Stories and Voices: History and Theory', *Russian Review*, 1996, vol. 55, no. 3, pp. 347–55; C. Emerson, 'New Words, New Epochs, Old Thoughts', ibid., pp. 355–65; also the essays (on the Imperial and Soviet periods) in L.H. Siegelbaum and R.G. Suny (eds), *Making Workers Soviet: Power, Class and Identity*, Cornell, 1994.

3. The tendency to see the popular appropriation and subversion of Soviet official discourse as dispersing and diluting the state's power is particularly questionable, for although this language could be used to legitimize resistance to the state, the regime's power did not depend on language, but on coercive force, and could thus not be challenged to any real effect through the subversion of its official discourse. Other historians, while acknowledging the state's hegemony (mainly over the control of linguistic meaning), have emphasized that the appropriation of the official discourse opened possibilities of popular resistance to the state, or at least some form of autonomy from it within highly localized or semi-private habitats. See e.g. S. Fitzpatrick, *Stalin's Peasants: Resistance and Survival in the Russian Village after Collectivization*, Oxford, 1994; Fitzpatrick, 'Signals from Below: Soviet Letters of Denunciation of the 1930s', in S. Fitzpatrick and R. Gellately (eds), *Accusatory Practices: Denunciation in Modern European History, 1789–1989*, Chicago, 1997, pp. 85–120; D. Hoffman, *Peasant Metropolis: Social Identities in Moscow, 1929-1941*, Ithaca, 1994; S. Kotkin, 'Coercion and Identity: Workers' Lives in Stalin's Showcase City', in Siegelbaum and Suny, *Making Workers Soviet*, 274–310; J. Rossman, 'The Teikovo Cotton Workers' Strike of April 1932: Class, Gender and Identity Politics in Stalin's Russia', *Russian Review*, 1997, vol. 56, no. 1, pp. 44–69; S. Davies, '"Us against Them": Social Identity in Soviet Russia, 1934–41', *Russian Review*, 1997, vol. 56, no. 1, pp. 70–89. Other historians have stressed the degree to which individuals were trapped within the official discourse, even when critical of the regime, and this had the effect of paralysing potential opposition: J. Hellbeck, 'Fashioning the Stalinist Soul: The Diary of Stepan Podlubnyi (1931–1939)', *Jahrbücher für Geschichte Osteuropas*, 1996, vol. 44, no. 3, pp. 454–63; I. Halfin, 'From Darkness to Light: Student Communist Autobiography during NEP', *Jahrbücher für Geschichte Osteuropas*, 1997, vol. 45, no. 3, pp. 344–73. See also J.

surprisingly it has yet to inspire many studies of the revolutionary period.[4] Surprising because the revolution itself – like all revolutions – involved a symbolic overturning of all political identities and sources of authority. It was based on its own linguistic turn.

This contrasts starkly with the study of the French Revolution, where the influence of the new cultural history has been very strong for many years. As long ago as the early 1980s historians such as Roger Chartier and Jacques Revel (fourth-generation Annales historians) were arguing that *mentalités* – 'representations of the social world' – were a primary determinant of historical change.[5] Linguistic theorists such as Michel Foucault and Pierre Bourdieu have influenced several historical studies since the 1980s which have set out to show how the eighteenth-century state and its institutions, as well as the public culture which opposed them, were 'discursive objects' rooted in the political language and cultural constructions of the time and could thus be studied and interpreted as discourses or texts.[6] Other historians were inspired to much the same purpose by the cultural theorist Clifford Geertz, whose seminal collection of essays *The Interpretation of Cultures* (1973) encouraged them to interpret or 'read', as symbolic 'texts', the ritualized actions of the crowd.[7] François Furet's classic history of the revolution, which presented it as a cultural creation, similarly stressed the role of symbolic language and rhetoric. The revolution, Furet argued, was above all a moment of political imagination, when people could choose what they would be, and language was an essential creative tool for this.[8] A similar approach can be seen in many other

Hellbeck and I. Halfin, 'Rethinking the Stalinist Subject: Stephen Kotkin's "Magnetic Mountain" and the State of Soviet Historical Studies', *Jahrbücher für Geschichte Osteuropas*, 1996, vol. 44, no. 3, pp. 454–63.

4. See e.g. P. Holquist, 'A Russian Vendée: The Practice of Politics in the Don Countryside', Ph.D. diss., Columbia University, 1996; E. Landis, 'Anti-Bolshevism and the Origins of the Antonov Movement: The Tambov Countryside through Revolution and Civil War', Ph.D. diss., University of Cambridge, 1997; D.J. Raleigh, 'Languages of Power: How the Saratov Bolsheviks Imagined Their Enemies', *Slavic Review*, 1998, vol. 57, no. 2, pp. 32–49.

5. R. Chartier, 'Intellectual History or Sociocultural History? The French Trajectories', in D. LaCapra and S. Kaplan (eds), *Modern European Intellectual History; Reappraisals and New Perspectives*, New York, 1982, p. 30. See further L. Hunt, 'French History in the Last Twenty Years: The Rise and Fall of the Annales Paradigm', *Journal of Contemporary History*, 1986, vol. 21, pp. 209–24.

6. L. Hunt, *Politics, Culture and Class in the French Revolution*, London, 1984; L. Hunt (ed.), *The New Cultural History*, Berkeley, 1989; D. Outram, *The Body and the French Revolution: Sex, Class and Political Culture*, New Haven, 1989; K. Baker, *Inventing the French Revolution: Essays on French Political Culture in the Eighteenth Century*, Cambridge, 1990; R. Chartier, *Les Origines culturelles de la Révolution française*, Paris, 1990; L. Hunt, 'The Virtues of Disciplinarity (History and the Study of the French Revolution)', *Eighteenth-Century Studies*, 1994, vol. 28, no. 1, pp. 1–7.

7. Robert Darnton, *The Great Cat Massacre and Other Episodes in French Cultural History*, New York 1984. This approach was also pioneered (before Geertz) by E.P. Thompson (*The Making of the English Working Class*, London, 1963) and (post-Geertz) by Natalie Zemon Davies (see her article, 'Anthropology and History in the 1980s: The Possibilities of the Past', *Journal of Interdisciplinary History*, 1981, vol. 11, pp. 267–75).

8. F. Furet, *Penser la Révolution française*, Paris, 1978. See also Furet and M. Ozouf (eds), *The*

studies of the revolution's political culture. Some have focused on the 'cultural construction of the citizen'.[9] Others have studied the imagery and symbolism of the revolution and its festivals and cults.[10] Others still have focused on the dissemination of the revolution's political language as a function of the cultural and political integration of the nation after 1789.[11]

If there is a weakness in the literature on the French Revolution, it is that it says comparatively little about the reception of the revolution's language, its interpretation and appropriation, among different groups in society. This is a dimension one can hardly miss in a study of the Russian Revolution, since its leaders at the time were painfully aware of the gulf between their own political discourse and its common understanding in the streets.

The leaders of the February Revolution saw their task as no less than the construction of a democratic culture, a new nation based upon the concepts of democracy. Their political philosophy was rooted in the Enlightenment ideals and values of 1789 and the nineteenth-century European revolutionary tradition, whose cultural system they adopted in the underground. After the February Revolution this republican tradition dominated the political culture. Its system of political values (civic rights and duties, the rule of law, the sovereignty of the Constituent Assembly, etc.) was propagandized with the missionary zeal of the revolutionary underground. There was an explosion of newspapers, many with a circulation of millions,[12] brochures, song books and dictionaries on political themes. In Petrograd alone the socialist presses published over 550 pamphlet titles, with a total run of nearly 29 million copies, during 1917, while the 'bourgeois' press published over 250 titles with a run of 11 million copies.[13] There were public festivals and celebrations modelled on the French revolutionary ones. In all their efforts the leaders of the revolution built upon a base of popular cultural media – cinema and theatre, music hall and cabaret,

French Revolution and the Creation of Modern Political Culture, 3 vols, Oxford, 1989.

9.   S. Schama, *Citizens: A Chronicle of the French Revolution*, London, 1989.

10. See e.g. M. Agulhon, *Marianne au combat: l'imagerie et la symbolique républicaines de 1789 à 1880*, Paris, 1979; Agulhon, *Marianne: les visages de la République*, Paris, 1992; M. Ozouf, *Festivals and the French Revolution*, trans. A. Sheridan, Cambridge, Mass., 1988. See also L. Mason, *Singing the French Revolution: Popular Culture and Politics, 1787–1799*, Cornell, 1996.

11. See e.g. M. de Certeau, D. Julia and J. Revel, *Une Politique de la langue: la Révolution française et les patois*, Paris, 1975.

12. In July–August 1917 the total press run of the 'bourgeois' newspapers in Petrograd alone was approximately 1.5 million. The SR and Menshevik papers sold up to 750,000 in the capital. For further details see B.I. Kolonitskii, 'Bor'ba s petrogradskoi burzhuaznoi pechat'iu v dni kornilovskogo miatezha', in *Rabochii klass Rossii, ego soiuzniki i politicheskie protivniki v 1917 godu: Sbornik nauchnyh trudov*, Leningrad, 1989, pp. 297–304.

13. Calculated from *Knizhnaya letopis'*, 1917, nos 1–50; Tsentral'nyi Gosudarstvennyi Voenno-Istoricheskii Arkhiv, f. 13251, op. 2, d. 25, l. 3; OR RNB, f. 601, op. 1, d. 1580, ll. 1–2; *Sovetskie arkhivy*, 1967, no. 3, p. 39.

workers' clubs and tea-rooms, taverns and people's houses (*narodnye doma*) – that had rapidly developed since the turn of the century.[14]

There was a huge popular demand for access to the new language of the revolution after February 1917. Soldiers at the Front, factory workers and inhabitants of remote villages wrote to the authorities in their thousands appealing for more printed words. Among them there was a groping understanding that language was a source of power, and a general sense of mistrust and resentment that the educated classes had mastery of it. 'We cannot defend our interests,' one peasant complained to a village teacher in 1917, 'because the masters have a silvery tongue and we can't match their words.'[15] A similar distrust often characterized popular attitudes towards the political parties, especially if the latter were perceived to be talking down to the 'simple people' from an intellectual eminence. This greatly complicated the parties' task of propagandizing their democratic political culture after the February Revolution. More than that, however, the parties were aware that the language which they used to disseminate these values would be taken over and translated by the common people to uphold and legitimize popular political traditions and ideals, which were often very different from their own. The intelligentsia's very source of power – its creation of the political language of the revolution – was at the same time a cause of its own fragility in the Russian Revolution of 1917.

14. R. Stites, *Russian Popular Culture: Entertainment and Society since 1900*, Cambridge, 1992; A.M. Konechnyi, 'Shows for the People: Public Amusement Parks in Nineteenth-Century St Petersburg', in S.P. Frank and M.D. Steinberg (eds), *Cultures in Flux: Lower-Class Values, Practices, and Resistance in Late Imperial Russia*, Princeton, 1994, pp. 121–30; G. Thurston, 'The Impact of Russian Popular Theatre, 1886–1915', *Journal of Modern History*, 1983, vol. 55, pp. 237–67; H. Jahn, *Patriotic Culture in Russia during World War I*, Cornell, 1995.
15. *Narodnyi uchitel* ', 1917, no. 25–6, p. 7.

1

The Desacralization of the Monarchy: Rumours and the Downfall of the Romanovs

The Russian monarchy had always based its power on divine authority. It was more than the 'divine right of kings'. In his propaganda – and the minds of many of his peasant subjects – the Tsar was more than a divinely ordained ruler: he was a god on earth. Popular belief in the sacred nature of the Tsar underpinned the monarchy's authority until this belief collapsed, quite suddenly, in the final decade of its existence. Two events were at the heart of that collapse: the 'Bloody Sunday' massacre of 1905, which profoundly shook, if it did not quite destroy, the popular belief in the 'benevolent Tsar'; and the various rumours of sexual corruption and treason at the court which swept through Russia in the First World War. As we shall argue in this chapter, these rumours played a major role in bringing down the Russian monarchy.

That at least was the considered view of many at the time. A detailed survey commissioned by the Temporary Committee of the Duma, based upon the reports of its provincial agents for the first five months of 1917, concluded that the spread of 'licentious tales and rumours' about Rasputin and the 'German' Empress had done more than anything to puncture the belief of the peasantry in the sacred nature of the monarchy.[1] The Romanovs themselves were of the same opinion.[2] It no doubt suited them to blame their catastrophe on the spread of false and malicious gossip, since this made their downfall appear both unnecessary and beyond control.

Rumours played a more important role in the February Revolution than most historians have so far acknowledged; or perhaps care to know. Indeed, this is probably the case in all revolutions. Rumours acted as a means of spreading vital information (and disinformation) where there were no other means. They created a 'mood' and helped to organize the

---

1. RGIA, f. 1278, op. 10, d. 11, l. 332.
2. See e.g. the comments by the Grand Duke Alexander Mikhailovich in A. Maylunas and S. Mironenko (eds), *A Lifelong Passion*, London, 1996, p. 529.

people in the streets (who generally believed what they wanted to believe). Hence there was a tendency to amplify those rumours, however false they were, which played upon the fears and prejudices of the crowd. Rumours could galvanize the crowd into decisive actions, from which otherwise they might have refrained. Would the Bastille have been stormed without the rumours – false, as they turned out, but playing none the less on the people's fears – that the authorities were filling it with soldiers and munitions to crush the Paris rising?

Recent historians of the French Revolution have shown how sexual gossip and pornographic satire stripped the Bourbon monarchy of all authority. The sexual decadence of the royal family – Marie Antoinette's uncontrollable libido, the king's 'impotence' – served as a metaphor for the moral and political degeneration of the old regime.[3] A similar political pornography robbed the Romanovs of their sacred image and authority. As pornography, it was much more tame than its French equivalent (there were, it seems, no explicit pictures and only innuendoes in the text) – a fact still remarked upon by S.P. Melgunov even for the period after February. It was no doubt a result of the relatively repressive publishing conditions that still obtained in Russia, despite the relaxations of the laws of censorship since 1905, and the stiff penalties that continued to be imposed for any defamation of the Tsar.[4] None the less, in the years leading up to 1917 there was a booming market for anti-dynastic political satires, mostly with a sexual cutting edge, and, just as in France, they had revolutionary consequences for the popular perception of the monarchy.

The Market-place for Rumours

The market was exploited in many different forms. Pornographic cartoons and verses circulated by hand. Home-typed copies of spicy stories such as 'The Restless Saint and Horse-Thief Grigorii' (written in December 1915) or 'The Holy Devil' by S. Trufanov (a.k.a. the monk Iliodor) were reproduced in their thousands.[5] Iliodor claimed that Rasputin was the real father of the Tsarevich, that he was the effective ruler of the country, and that he was responsible for starting the war. The monk tried to sell

---

3.   See e.g. Chantal Thomas, 'L'Héroine du crime: Marie-Antoinette dans les pamphlets', in J.-C. Bonnet et al. (eds), *La Carmagnole des muses*, Paris, 1988; Lynn Hunt, *The Family Romance of the French Revolution*, Berkeley, 1992, esp. pp. 105–6; S. Schama, *Citizens: A Chronicle of the French Revolution*, London, 1989, pp. 203–27.
4.   RGIA, f. 1405, op. 521, d. 476, l. 143.
5.   Ibid., f. 1101, op. 1, d. 1140, l. 9. The Public Library in St Petersburg has a copy of 'The Holy Devil' (call mark: 34.106.8.188). On its cover are the words: 'Purchased for 1 ruble in 1916'.

his story to the Germans, and there was talk of air-dropping copies of it to the Russian soldiers at the Front.[6] New and more daring stories and verses appeared after Rasputin's murder:

And rumour had it that at his grave
It was ordered to plant only a lily
And write an epitaph: 'Here lies
A member of the Imperial Family'[7]

After the February Revolution newspapers printed extracts from these tales and verses, satirical ditties and anecdotes. The more daring editors published documents, which were clearly forgeries, purporting to show the sexual liaisons between the Empress and Rasputin, or printed fabrications of her 'treacherous telegrams'.[8] Street traders grew rich from the sales of pamphlets such as 'The Secrets of the Romanovs', 'The Life and Adventures of Grigorii Rasputin', and 'The Tsarina and Rasputin', which sold between 25,000 and 50,000 copies each. There was even a best-selling 'historical' novel on the subject.[9]

Then there were the smutty postcards – drawings of the nude Tsarina lying with Rasputin;[10] the cabarets and circuses, satires, plays and farces, with such suggestive titles as 'Rasputin's Night-Time Orgies'. This had audiences laughing in the aisles at its sexual innuendoes (PROTOPOPOV: 'Rasputin has enormous talent'; MADAME VYRUBOVA: 'Oh, I know, an enormous talent') in two performances every day for nearly two months in 1917.[11] Alexander Blok, who attended one such play, noted in his diary on 1 June: 'Yesterday evening in the little theatre – a show about Rasputin and Anna Vyrubova. Cruel stuff from the streets. Despite the poor acting and coarseness, there was a grain of truth. The audience (there were a lot of soldiers) was hysterical with laughter.'[12]

As one would expect, the political pornography of 1917 was much more daring and expansive than that of the previous years. The myths it

6. Politisches Archiv des Auswärtigen Amts (Bonn), Der Weltkrieg, Russland, 104, no. 11c, R. 20984, A. 2587; R. 20985, A. 981; R. 20986, A. 3657, 3885; R. 20987, A. 6370. *Padenie tsarskogo rezhima*, 7 vols, Leningrad, 1924–7, vol. 1, p. 40.
7. RGIA, f. 1101, op. 1, d. 1140, l. 20.
8. S.P. Mel'gunov, *Sud'ba imperatora Nikolaia II posle otrecheniia*, pp. 147–8; BA, Raupakh Papers, Box 1, E. von Maiden, Roman Romanovich von Raupakh, p. 41.
9. S. Kshesinskii, *Sviatyi chert (Imperatritsa Aleksandra i Grigorii Rasputin: Istoricheskii Roman v 2 chastiakh)*, Moscow, 1917. Circulation figures from *Knizhnaya letopis* for 1917.
10. See *Vsemirnoi iumor*, 1917, no. 14, p. 2.
11. V. Bezpadov, *Teatry v dni revoliutsii*, Leningrad, 1927, p. 38; *Russkaia muzykal'naia gazeta*, 1917, nos 25–6, p. 420; A. Swift, 'Kul'turnoe stroitel'stvo ili kul'turnaia razruha?', in *Anatomia revoliutsii: 1917 god v Rossii*, St Petersburg, 1994, p. 403. Tamer and less popular plays, sometimes even on entirely different subjects, were reduced to competing with these farces by introducing extra 'scenes with Rasputin' at the end of their performances.
12. A.A. Blok, *Dnevnik*, Moscow, 1989, p. 211.

peddled, after all, had become almost part of the official version of events leading to the downfall of the monarchy in so far as, after the February Revolution, they were freely repeated by the press as 'facts', and to some extent believed by people such as Blok who sat on the Provisional Government's Extraordinary Commission of Inquiry into the malfeasance of the court (on which more below). However, the productions of 1917 took nearly all their plots and ideas, themes and motifs from the productions of previous years.

During the spring of 1917 there was an outpouring of scandal-mongering about Rasputin and the licentious royals. The cinemas were packed with audiences ogling at cheap-thrill movies such as *The Secrets of the Romanovs, The Secret Story of the Ballerina Kshesinskaia, The Shame of the House of Romanovs* and *Traitors of Russia*.[13]

To Russian public sensibilities, unused to the sort of cheap erotica that could be found in any back-street cinema or theatre in the West, much of this appeared like cheap pornography (which no doubt much of it was). There were frequent calls to ban performances, and sometimes scuffles broke out in cinemas and theatres. Cinema employees appealed to the Minister of Justice, Alexander Kerensky, to clamp down on 'shameless businessmen', who took advantage of the liberated people's joy to put out films, made in two or three days, on the filthy subject of the deposed monarchy. Censorship of films was introduced in a piecemeal fashion during 1917. Some of the most offensive scenes were cut – although, interestingly, this was often because the scenes in question had offended not just the sexual but the moral and political code. For example, the Provisional Committee for the Regulation of Theatrical Life in Moscow ordered the film company of I.G. Libkin to cut the scenes from its film *Dark Forces* in which Rasputin 'gave a lesson in humility' to a group of society ladies in the baths.[14]

This sort of censorship was an exception. There was little control of the media in 1917. In any case, it would have been impossible to censor more than a small fraction of all such productions in the press and journals, cinemas and theatres, throughout Russia. By 1917 there had developed an independent street culture that was simply too pervasive to control. Its purveyors claimed to know the truth about the court, and this gave the people, who believed them, a real sense of power – manifested, as is carnival, in mockery and defamation of the monarchy.

13. V. Rosolovskaia, *Russkaia kinematografiia v 1917 g.: Materialy k istorii.* Moscow and Leningrad, 1937, p. 57. The contemporary press provides a sketch of the relevant cinema screenings. See Zriachii, 'Grishka na ekrane', *Vsemirnaia nov'*, 1917, no. 21, p. 15.
14. *Proektor*, 1917, no. 7–8, p. 12; no. 9–10, p. 14; no. 13–14, p. 7–8; no. 17–18, p. 4.

Theme 1: Moral Corruption

The stories of sexual corruption at the court served as a metaphor for the diseased condition of the Romanov regime. The Tsarina, like Marie Antoinette, was accused of cheating on her husband. She had 'committed such debauchery', it was claimed in *The Secrets of the House of the Romanovs*, 'that she eclipsed the most depraved libertines [*rasputnikov i rasputnits* – word-plays on Rasputin] in the history of humanity.'[15] Various names of lovers were offered – from Orlov to Sablin – and sometimes the imagination was permitted to run wild:

In the Tsar's bedroom our dark little flower
Has opened up her petals of pleasure.
In the Tsar's tower our little Alexandra
Has been plucked by all the Guards.[16]

Most often, of course, it was claimed that the Tsarina was Rasputin's lover. Rumours of the affair spread throughout society. They were of particular concern to the military censors, who feared for the effects on soldiers' morale, and it was forbidden to show any films in the army's cinemas that might give rise to ribald comments about the Tsar's absence from his family. When the film was shown of Nicholas awarding himself the St George Cross, comments in the dark were sometimes heard: 'He's with George – and she's with Grigorii.'[17] After the murder of Rasputin one soldier told his officer: '. . . the peasant [Rasputin] was alright until that old woman came along, and of course the Tsarina is only a woman, and she needed it because her husband was at the front.'[18]

But it was not just the common people who believed the rumours. The poet Zinaida Gippius was equally convinced, as she wrote in her diary on 24 November 1915: 'Grisha is governing and getting his way with the ladies in waiting . . . And with Fedorovna [the Empress], as usual.'[19] As in pre-revolutionary France, the rumours were believed and disseminated by the malcontents of high society. A.N. Mandel'shtam, an official of the Foreign Ministry, claimed that he had at his disposal information 'proving an affair between the Empress and a "spiritual adviser"'. No objections or doubts were raised by his colleagues.[20] When the historian S.P. Mel'gunov

15. *Taina doma Romanovykh: favoritki Nikolaia II* (vyp. 1), Petrograd, 1917, p. 16.
16. *Trepach*, 1917, no. 1, p. 11.
17. V.V. Shul'gin, *Dni*, Leningrad, 1926, p. 108.
18. Ibid., p. 108; D.P. Os'kin, *Zapiski praporshchika*, Moscow, 1931, pp. 81–2.
19. OR RNB, f. 481, op. 1, d. 1, l. 62. This sentence was omitted from the published versions of Gippius's diary.
20. G.N. Mikhailovskii, *Zapiski: Iz istorii rossiikogo vneshnopoliticheskogo vedomstva, 1914–1920gg.*, kn. 1, *Avgust 1914–oktiabr' 1917g.*, Moscow, 1993, p. 149.

went before the censors for permission to publish fragments of Iliodor's pamphlet, 'The Holy Devil', he found the bureaucrats in full dress uniform poring like a group of dirty-minded schoolboys over its smutty tales about the Empress and Rasputin.[21]

After the February Revolution this topic became the favourite theme of the booming gutter press. The story of Rasputin's affair with the Empress was repeated so frequently that it came to have the status of an accepted truth. Even Blok was surprised to learn that it was not true when he questioned courtiers on the Extraordinary Commission of Inquiry. 'So it turns out, after all, that he lived neither with the Empress nor with Vyrubova,' Blok wrote in his diary on 8 June.[22] Anna Vyrubova – lady-in-waiting to the Empress and loyal follower of Rasputin – was a constant participant in the 'orgies' that were said to have occurred between the three (and more), even though this naive and dim-witted spinster was medically certified to be a virgin by the Extraordinary Commission of Inquiry in 1917. In some versions Vyrubova was the lover of Nicholas, while the Empress carried on with Rasputin, and this too was believed widely – even in intelligentsia circles. Blok, who was present at her interrogations by the Extraordinary Commission, wrote in his diary: 'She thought of herself as Orthodox, and firmly believed this. What an interesting combination, if, as they say, she slept with Nicholas.'[23]

The political effect of all these sexual scandals was manifold. The rumours served to tarnish the image of the court, to desacralize the monarchy and strip it of all claims to divine authority, let alone the respect of its citizens. Laughter and mockery deprived the Tsar of power; and this was symbolized by his sexual impotence, which, according to the stories, had driven the Tsarina into Rasputin's arms. A man who could not rule or satisfy his wife could not be taken seriously as a tsar.

Theme 2: Who Rules Russia?

Loss of manliness was the subtext of the question, 'Who rules Russia?' – the second major theme of this political pornography. The rumour was that the Empress was the real ruler of the country: 'The Tsar reigns but the Tsarina governs.' It offended the patriarchal (not to say misogynistic)

21. S.P. Mel'gunov, *Vospominaniia i dnevniki*, Paris, 1964, vyp. 1, pp. 201, 214.
22. Blok, *Dnevnik*, p. 213. Blok had evidently not considered the rumours regarding a liaison between the Empress and the 'holy man' as necessarily untrue.
23. OR IRLI, f. 654, op. 5, d. 6, l. 10; L. Zhdanov, *Nikolai 'Romanov' – poslednii tsar': Istoricheskie nabroski*, Petrograd, 1917, p. 95; G.P. (G.G. Peretts), *V tsitadeli russkoi revoliutsii (Zapiski komendanta Tavricheskogo Dvortsa, 27 fevralia – 23 marta 1917 g.)*, Petrograd, 1917, p. 109; S. P. Mel'gunov, *Sud'ba imperatora Nikolaia II*, p. 130.

attitudes of the peasants and upholders of tradition to see the Tsar relinquish power to his wife. Tsarist power was growing weak because it was being feminized.

The belief that the Tsarina was the country's real ruler was almost universal. Even the British Ambassador, George Buchanan, claimed in a despatch to London on 5 February 1917 that she was in fact running the country.[24] The widespread belief that Alexandra liked to compare herself to Catherine the Great served as the pretext for satires such as this:

Oh, how I've made so many plans
To become a new 'Catherine'
And for so long I have wanted
To call Petrograd Hesse.[25]

Once mention of Catherine had been made, it was but a short step to conclude that Alexandra, like her German predecessor, was preparing a palace coup to name herself as regent and promote the Germans at her court. Many people believed in this rumour, coming as it did from a lady close to B.V. Stürmer, President of the Council of Ministers. It was said that Alexandra would name Stürmer the 'Premier of Her Royal Highness'.[26]

According to some rumours from the yellow press, Alexandra even planned to murder her husband. She was supposedly intending to bring about a 'revolution with the help of German bayonets'. Peasants bluntly said that Nicholas had gone into a monastery, that the country was being ruled by the 'German woman' and her lover Rasputin, and that the Tsar 'had given Grishka the deeds of the kingdom'.[27]

Rasputin himself was deemed to be the dark force behind the government. He was the 'Chancellor of the Russian Empire', the 'uncrowned king', 'Gregory the First'. Iliodor called him 'the unofficial Russian Tsar and patriarch'. Of course Rasputin, by his constant boasting of his influence at court, helped to spread these rumours.[28]

According to the liberal opposition, it was the circulation of such rumours in the popular press that undermined the monarchy's authority among

24. G. Buchanan, *My Mission to Russia and Other Diplomatic Memoirs*, 2 vols, London, 1923, vol. 2, p. 56.
25. *Chto teper' poet Nikolai Romanov i ego Ko.*, Kiev, 1917. p. 1.
26. A.I. Spiridovich, *Velikaia voina i fevral'skaia revoliutsiia, 1914–1917 gg.* New York, 1960, kn. 2, p. 106; M. Paleolog, *Tsarskaia Rossiia nakanune revoliutsii*, Moscow, 1991, pp. 208–9, 228.
27. S. Kshesinskii, *Sviatoi chert*, pp. 25, 159; S. Iakolev, *Poslednie dni Nikolaia II* (Ofitsial'nye dokumenty, rasskazy ochevidtsev), Petrograd, 1917, p. 24; Mikhailovskii, *Zapiski*, kn. 1, *Avgust 1914–oktiabr' 1917 g.*, p. 149.
28. V.E. Burdzhalov, *Vtoraia russkaia revoliutsiia: vosstanie v Petrograde*, Moscow, 1967, p. 67; I. Trufanov, *Tainy doma Romanovykh*, Moscow, 1917, p. 135; *Kazn' Grishki Rasputina*, Petrograd, 1917, p. 13; Iliodor (S. Trufanov), *Sviatyi chert: zapiski o Rasputine*, Moscow, 1917, p. 94; S.S. Ol'denburg, *Tsarstvovanie imperatora Nikolaia II*, St Petersburg, 1991, pp. 577–9.

the lower classes of society.[29] But the rumours were seemingly confirmed by the testimony of high-placed officials and dignitaries, generals and politicians, which gave them credence in the popular mind. In November 1915, for example, the Minister of War, A.A. Polivanov, claimed in public that Rasputin was 'ruling Russia'. Further evidence of this widespread conviction in the government was given to the Extraordinary Commission of Inquiry in 1917 when M.S. Komissarov, the General of Police, told it that Rasputin 'was the Chancellor'. General I.G. Erdeli quoted General Diakov in a private letter of November 1916: 'I see that Russia will perish, everything is moving to collapse and ruin, the German organization is playing its part . . . There is nothing surprising about all these evils, given that the country is being ruled by Grishka Rasputin.'[30] Moreover, the image of Rasputin as the country's secret ruler was exploited by the propaganda of the revolutionary opposition and this too gave credence to the various rumours on the widest scale.[31]

Whatever their credentials, the effect of all these rumours was revolutionary. The Tsar's authority, as the divine and omnipotent sovereign, was completely undermined by the popular belief that the Empress and Rasputin were ruling in his stead. Gossip turned these stories into 'facts', coarsening and simplifying them in the process. Nicholas was said to be a 'degenerate', 'an alcoholic like his father', and a 'puppet in the hands of the corrupt peasant, Rasputin, and his own ambitious German wife'.[32] Among the peasant soldiers, in particular, it was widely held that the Tsar had been deceived and exploited by his wife, who was cheating on him with the 'filthy Grigorii'; and that Nicholas was blind to everything. A front-line soldier wrote in 1916: 'Our father-tsar cannot live by the light of this world, since he has no eyes, the Germans plucked them out, and covered up his holes with black glasses' (inside the letter was a portrait of the Tsar with his eyes scratched out).[33]

In all these popular versions, Nicholas was weak-willed and impotent. He had 'degraded himself', in the words of one mass-circulation pamphlet of 1917, 'by passively surrendering his throne to Rasputin – and not just

29. *Burzhuaziia nakanune fevral'skoi revoliutsii*, ed. B.B. Grave, Moscow, 1927, p. 64.
30. A. Iakhontov, 'Pervyi god voiny (iiul' 1914- iiul' 1915 g.): Zapisi, zametki, materialy i vospominaniia byvshego pomoshchnika upravliashchego delami Soveta Ministrov', in R.Sh. Ganelin and M.F. Florinskii (eds), *Russkoe proshloe: Istoriko-dokymental'nyi al'manakh*, St Petersburg, 1996, kn. 7, p. 326; P.E. Shchegolev, 'Padenie tsarskogo rezhima: Stenografich. otchety i pokazaniia, dannye v 1917 g.' in P.E. Shchegolev (ed.), *Chrezvychainoi sledstvennoi kommissii, Vremennogo pravitel'stva*, Leningrad, 1925, t. 3, p. 166.
31. Cited in Mel'gunov, *Sud'ba imperatora Nikolaia II*, p. 148. V.I. Lenin, *Polnoe sobranie sochinenii*, 5th edn., Moscow, 1958–65, vol. 31, pp. 12, 297; V.V. Lapshin, *Khudozhestvennaia zhizn' Moskvy i Petrograda v 1917 gody*, Moscow, 1983, p. 88.
32. See e.g. L. Zhdanov, *Sud nad Nikolaem II*, Petrograd, 1917, pp. 28–9, 31, 33, 42 and *passim*.
33. *Tsarskaia armiia v period mirovoi voiny i fevral'skoi revoliutsii (Materialy k izucheniiu istorii imperialisticheskoi i grazhdanskoi voiny)*, Kazan, 1932, pp. 108–9.

his throne but his wife as well'.[34] He lived 'in terror' of his 'manly wife'– to the extent, in the words of one best-selling pamphleteer, that 'when she appears in the study of the Tsar, he – and I am not exaggerating – literally jumps under his desk to hide from her'.[35] Foreigners and criminals were rumoured to have the 'weak-willed little Nicholas under their thumbs' and, in some of the wilder versions of the tale, kept him 'plied with drugs'.[36] Yet such was the climate of opinion in the final months of the dynasty – when everything was rumoured and nothing known – that even this was believed within the highest circles. The British Ambassador, in a despatch to the Foreign Ministry on 30 April, reported, as if fact, a rumour he had heard from Felix Yusupov and the Grand Duke Dmitry Pavlovich that Rasputin's hold over Nicholas was, indeed, maintained with the help of drugs. Lord Hardinge, the Deputy Foreign Minister in London, noted the report as 'extremely interesting'.[37]

Once again, as with the stories of sexual corruption, it was Nicholas's 'unmanliness', his pitiful relinquishing of power to his wife, that undermined his image and set the people's mood on the eve of the February Revolution. The pathetic figure of Nicholas did not correspond to the patriarchal ideal of the autocrat in official propaganda or the peasant mind; and this was a huge relief to the people, inviting them to laughter and mockery. Peasant soldiers poked fun at the 'hen-pecked Tsar who had been cuckolded by the peasant Grigorii'. The army medic (and future Soviet writer) D.A. Furmanov noted in his diary in 1917 that the peasants' attitudes towards the Tsar were nearly always 'mocking', based on their belief that he was an alcoholic, that he was commanded by his 'evil German wife', and that he was powerless to prevent her and Rasputin from doing what they liked. 'Their basic image of the Tsar was of a simpleton, a man forever drunk and unhappy, ensnared in a net, deceived and intimidated by his wife.'[38]

It is ironic that Nicholas was mocked for failing to live up to the model of the 'real Tsar' in the peasant consciousness, because this was the image he projected through his own propaganda in the final years of the dynasty.[39] He was not the patriarchal Tsar traditionally expected and revered. Indeed, it was a paradox that the Tsar should fall victim to the peasants' anti-monarchism in this way, for it was itself a 'monarchical' expression of the peasantry's ideals. This 'monarchical psychology' could coexist with anti-

34. *Nikolai II-oi Romanov: Ego zhizn' i deitel'nost', 1894–1914 gg. (Po inostrannym i russkim istochnikam)*, Petrograd, 1917, p. 72.
35. *Tainy tsarskogo dvora i Grishka Rasputin*, Moscow, 1917, p. 12; Iliodor, *Sviatyi*, p. 93.
36. *Tainy tsarskogo dvora i Grishka Rasputin*, pp. 4, 5.
37. Cambridge University Library, Manuscript Division, Harding Papers, Sir George Buchanan to Lord Hardinge, vol. 31, p. 214; vol. 33, p. 249.
38. P. V. Kupriianovskii, *Neizvestnyi Furmanov*, Ivanovo, 1996, pp. 51, 100.
39. See O. Figes, *A People's Tragedy: The Russian Revolution, 1891–1924*, London, 1996, pp. 1–24.

monarchism in the peasant consciousness, as we shall explore further in Chapter 5.

Theme 3: Treason

Treason was the third major theme of all these rumours, and perhaps the key in unifying all the opposition forces against the monarchy. The idea of treason in high places, which started in 1915 with the Miasoedov Affair[40] and the Great Retreat, gained momentum in 1916 as rumours spread of the existence of a 'Black Bloc' at court, which was said to be seeking a separate peace with Berlin. The large number of German names at court, Stürmer's rise, in particular, to the status of virtual 'dictator' of the government, and Rasputin's well-known sentiments against the war all helped to fuel such speculation. But 'the German woman' was the focus of these rumours. It was said that she was a German spy, that she told the Kaiser of her husband's military plans, and that she 'rejoices when our soldiers die and cries when the enemy is killed'.[41] In some wilder versions of these tales Bismarck had arranged the Tsarina's marriage so that she could act as a German spy.[42]

Rumours such as these were widely circulated -- often in much coarser forms – by soldiers at the Front, resulting in huge problems of discipline. Judging from the letters home, demoralized soldiers and officers were prepared to believe that the Empress did not speak a word of Russian; that the Grand Duchess Maria Pavlovna (the elder) and the ballerina (and mistress of the Tsar) Mathilde Kshesinskaya both passed on military secrets to the Germans; that Stürmer had been paid by the Germans to starve the Russian people to death; that Count Fredericks, the Minister of the Imperial Court, had agreed to sell the western half of Russia to the enemy; and that Rasputin was a German agent.[43] People unfortunate enough to share Rasputin's name were equally suspected of treachery. A rifleman of the 80th Siberian Regiment, L. Rasputin, appealed to change his surname for this reason: 'I am mistrusted in a war situation,' he wrote to the Temporary

40. Miasoedov, an officer in Sukhomlinov's Ministry of War, was dismissed, tried and executed on charges of spying. There is no evidence to prove his guilt.
41. RGIA, f. 1405, op. 521, d. 476, l. 106.
42. I. Kovyl'-Bobyl', *Tsaritsa i Rasputin*, Petrograd, 1917, pp. 5–6.
43. 'Russkaia armiia nakanune revoliutsii', *Byloe*, 1918, no. 1 (29), p. 153. It is indicative that the Marshal of the Nobility of Samara, A.N. Naumov, asked a courtier, before the Empress, 'May a Russian marshal speak in Russian at an audience with the Empress?' A.N. Naumov, *Iz utselevshikh vospominanii, 1868–1917*, New York, 1954, t. 2, p. 40. *Taina doma Romanovykh: favoritki Nikolaia II*, p. 16; *Dnevnik b. velikogo kniazia Andreia Vladimirovicha*, p. 75; 'Russkaia armiia nakanune revoliutsii', p. 154; *Blagorodnaia zhertva fevral'skoi revoliutsii 1917 g. student V. I. Khlebtsebich*, Syzran', 1918, p. 60. Kshesinskaya was suspected of passing the secrets of the Russian artillery to the enemy.

Committee of the Duma on 21 March 1917. 'My comrades don't trust me to watch the trenches or to watch the activities of the enemy.'[44]

No one ever managed to discover any proof of Rasputin's collaboration with the German secret services. Samuel Hoare, head of British military intelligence in Petrograd, carried out a special investigation to uncover links between Rasputin and the enemy, but found no evidence.[45] However, there were suspected spies in Rasputin's entourage, and it is possible that German agents picked up information from his table-talk, which was always loud and boastful. He regularly dined at the house of a Petrograd banker whom the French Ambassador believed to be the leading German agent in Russia.

None the less, the point of all these rumours was not their truth or untruth, but their ability to unify and mobilize an angry public against the monarchy. And here there was an astonishing degree of acceptance at all levels of society that the treason allegations were already proved.

Even the most educated believed them. Zinaida Gippius noted in her diary in September 1915: 'In the final analysis the government is not even fighting the Germans – it does not care about Russia. . . . The Tsar is a traitor . . .' Academician V.A. Steklov called the Tsar a 'German lackey and traitor' in his diary. And A.N. Rodzianko (the wife of the President of the State Duma) wrote in hers on 12 February 1917: 'It is now clear that it is not just Alexandra Fedorovna who is guilty of treason – the Tsar is even more criminal.'[46] Politicians were equally convinced. A.N. Khvostov, the former Minister of the Interior, was the source of many of the rumours about Rasputin as a German spy – and this lent them credence among other politicians and diplomats.[47] Kerensky, for one, the moving force behind the Provisional Government's Extraordinary Commission of Inquiry, initially believed the treason allegations against the Romanovs. N.K. Murav'ev, the Commission's chairman, thought that the Empress had foiled her husband's plans to launch a new offensive against the Germans by giving details of the Russian troop movements to the Kaiser.

The same notion was widely circulated in the newspapers after February. Indeed, after the revolution such rumours became the 'public property' of the tabloid press. *Russkaia volia*, for example, reported that the Empress

44. RGIA, f. 1412, op. 16, d. 531, l. 1; d. 103, l. 2.
45. Cambridge University Library, Manuscript Division, Templewood Papers, S. Hoare, 'A Watchman Makes his Rounds', XXI: I, p. 52.
46. OR RNB, f. 481, op. 1, d. 1, l. 55. The text, which was placed in inverted commas, did not appear in the published edition of the diary. Compare E.N. Gippius, *Siniaia kniga: Peterburgskii dnevnik, 1914–1918*, Belgrade, 1929, p. 38. SPARAN, f. 162, op. 3, d. 168, l. 58. 'Zapis' za 17 marta. K istorii poslednikh dnei tsarskogo rezhima (1916–1917 gg.)', *Krasnyi arkhiv*, 1926, t. 1 (14), p. 246.
47. Spiridovich, *Velikaia voina i fevral'skaia revoliutsiia*, New York, 1960, kn. 2, pp. 47, 48, 64; *Padenie tsarskogo rezhima*, t. 1, p. 30.

and her 'Germanized husband' were building up a 'nest of treason and espionage' at the court. Interviews with disaffected Romanovs and courtiers lent even greater credence to these theories. 'I have asked myself on numerous occasions whether the Empress is an accomplice of the Kaiser Wilhelm,' the Grand Duke Kirill Vladimirovich confessed to one journalist, 'and each time I have tried to drive this awful thought from my mind.' Then there was the gossip of high society, which was also picked up by the press, that the Empress was to blame for Lord Kitchener's death: it was said that she had informed the Germans of the route to be taken by his ship when it was sunk in May 1916 (Rasputin may have been the source of this rumour when he shocked a dinner party with his view that Kitchener's death was a blessing since he might have brought harm to Russia).[48] It was even asserted in the press that there was a secret radio-telegraph station at Tsarskoe Selo which the Empress used to pass on information to Germany. Counter-espionage officials made several efforts to locate the station at the palace but were always stopped by the palace commandant. Of course there was no radio apparatus. Yet such was the power of the myth that for many years after the revolution, when the palace was turned into a museum, visitors would ask to be shown it.[49]

The conviction of Russia's political élite that the court was engaged in treachery was passed on to foreign diplomats – and by them to foreign governments. The British Ambassador George Buchanan was only too aware of the court's 'pro-German sympathies'. He complained to the Duma President, M.V. Rodzianko, in November 1916 that he found it difficult to get an audience at court, and expressed his view 'that Germany is using Alexandra Fedorovna to set the Tsar against the Allies'.[50] Elsewhere, however, Buchanan stated his view that the Empress was 'the unwitting instrument of Germany'.[51] The English MP, Major David Davies, who visited Petrograd in January 1917, wrote in his report to the British king and cabinet: 'The Tsarina is thought to be, correctly or incorrectly, an agent of the German government.' He recommended that every possible measure should be taken to persuade her to leave the country until the cessation of the war.[52] Similar rumours – of Allied plans to kidnap the

48. Spiridovich, *Velikaia voina i fevral'skaia revoliutsiia*, pp. 92, 106, 169.
49. A.W.F. Knox, *With the Russian Army*, London 1921, vol. 1, p. 577; Columbia University Library, Bakhmatieff Archive, Raupakh Papers, Box 1, E. von Mahdel, 'Roman Romanovich von Raupakh', p. 40; Trufanov, *Tainy doma Romanovykh*, pp. 53. 128–31; Mel'gunov, *Sud'ba imperatora Nikolaia II*, pp. 68, 69, 146–7.
50. K istorii poslednikh dnei tsarskogo rezhima (1916–1917 gg.)', *Krasnyi arkhiv*, 1926, t. 1 (14), pp. 242, 246.
51. Buchanan, *My Mission to Russia*, vol. 2, p. 56.
52. Trinity College, Cambridge, Wren Library, Layton Papers, Box 28-14, Allied Conference at Petrograd, January–February 1917. Report on Mission to Russia by Major David Davies', pp. 1–3. Davies added: 'there is no doubt that the enemy is constantly informed of any troop movements and planned operations. As a result, no serious information can be kept secret and

Tsarina and send her into exile – circulated in Russian high society. It was said to be all the talk in fashionable salons, army headquarters and guards regiments.[53] The rumour spread throughout the Allied world. Lord Bertie, the British Ambassador in Paris, for example, wrote about the Empress immediately after the February Revolution: 'The Empress is not only a Boche by birth but in sentiment. She did all she could to bring about an understanding with Germany. She is regarded as a criminal or criminal lunatic and the ex-Emperor as a criminal from his weakness and submission to her promptings.'[54]

The immediate concern of the Allied governments was the impact of these rumours on the morale of the Russian army. The signs were not encouraging. Soldiers said it was useless fighting while the court was on the side of the enemy. German propaganda leaflets, dropped by aeroplane to soldiers at the Front, reinforced this message with a picture of the Kaiser supported by the German people, while the Tsar was resting against Rasputin's private parts.[55] Among the soldiers it was widely held that the Empress was betraying military secrets to the Germans; that she was withholding shells, food and medical supplies from the army; and that she had brought the country to the brink of starvation by secretly exporting Russian bread to Germany. In their imagination the Tsarina appeared as the patroness of a huge smuggling operation. They said that she had secured the release of all the German prisoners of war and had sent them home to Germany where they returned to the army's ranks.[56] Soldiers also made her the evil machinator of their conspiracy theories about the war. They said that she was forcing Nicholas to enter into negotiations with the Germans for a separate peace; that the whole war had been a Romanov conspiracy to enslave Russia to Germany. German propaganda officers noted other rumours of this type during their brief spells of

this has to be contiually borne in mind in any negotiations with the Russian leadership.'
53. Shul'gin, *Dni*, p. 108; V. N. Voeikov, *S tsarem i bez tsaria: Vospominaniia poslednogo dvortsovogo komendanta gosudaria-imperatora Nikolaia II*, Moscow, 1995, pp. 166–7; A.F. Kerensky, *The Kerensky Memoirs. Russia and History's Turning Point*, London, 1965, pp. 147, 150, 159, 160.
54. Cambridge University Library, Harding Papers, Lord Bertie to Lord Harding, vol. 31, p. 165.
55. K.K. Zvonarev, 'Agenturnaia razvedka', in *Germanskaia agenturnaia razvedka do i vo vremia voiny 1914–1918 gg.*, t. 2, Moscow, 1931, p. 146. This was possibly a reference to a cartoon mentioned by M. Lemke in correspondence dated 21 February 1916: Wilhelm was depicted measuring the length of a German shell, and Nicolas, sizing it up, is 'kneeling on Rasputin's member'. M. Lemke, *250 dnei v tsarskoi Stavke (25 sent. 1915–2 iiulia 1916)*, Petrograd, 1920, pp. 561, 683.
56. 'K istorii poslednikh dnei tsarskogo rezhima (1916–1917 gg.)', pp. 242, 246; Mikhailovskii, *Zapiski: Iz istorii*, kn. 1: avgust 1914 – oktiabr 1917 g., Moscow, 1993, pp. 142, 143; 'Russkaia armiia nakanune revoliutsii', pp. 152, 155–6; 'Oktiabr'skaia revoliutsiia v Baltiiskom flote (Iz dnevnika I. I. Rengartena)', *Krasnyi arkhiv*, 1927, t. 6 (25), p. 34; P.G. Kurlov, *Gibel' imperatorskoi Rossii*, Moscow, 1991, p. 243; *Tsarskaia armiia v period mirovoi voiny i fevral'skoi revoliutsii*, pp. 150–2; *Vsemirnyi iumor*, 1917, no. 12, p. 11; J.W. Long, *From Privileged to Dispossessed: The Volga Germans, 1860–1917*, Lincoln and London, 1988, p. 229; F. Koch, *The Volga Germans in Russia and the Americas*, University Park, Penn. and London, 1977, p. 240.

fraternization with the Russian troops. The effect on the morale and discipline of the soldiers could be catastrophic, especially when these rumours came on top of months of supply shortages and dashed expectations of an end to the war. Soldiers refused to take up their positions or to obey officers who sought to defend the Tsarina – especially those with German names. 'What's the use of fighting if the Germans have already taken over?', many soldiers said.[57]

But the officers themselves were becoming just as hostile to the court, blaming it for the reverses at the Front. Many of them were beginning to talk openly of politics, calling for a more patriotic government. A special report of the military censors in the early weeks of 1917 noted that most officers attributed the poor performance of the army to the actions of the 'German party' at the court. Many of them condemned the Tsarina as a German agent – and did not hide their feelings from the lower ranks. 'Alexandra Fedorovna is in effect the ruler of the country,' wrote an officer of the naval intelligence in his diary in January 1917. 'It is said that she has definite German sympathies. The scoundrels! What are they doing to the motherland?'[58]

Even some of the highest-ranking officers were convinced of the Tsarina's treachery. When she visited General Headquarters special steps were taken to conceal all military documents from her; yet it was still said that after every visit the Russian army suffered a defeat. General Alexeev claimed that the Tsarina had a secret map showing the location of the Russian forces, although there were only supposed to be two copies of the map – one held by the Tsar and the other by himself. General Brusilov for the same reason declined to answer questions from the Empress concerning the timing of attacks. A senior commander of the Guards claimed (as early as 1915) that the war could not be won 'until the traitors at the court are rooted out'. And even the Guards officers at Tsarskoe Selo sympathized with speeches 'exposing' the treachery of the Empress. The general mood of the senior command was summed up by one unnamed general, who told an English officer: 'What can we do? We've got Germans everywhere.'[59]

The Allies' concern about the adverse impact of these rumours on the Russian army must have been a factor behind their decision not to oppose

57. Burzhuaziia nakanune fevral'skoi revoliutsii, p. 78; Tsarskaia armiia v period mirovoi voiny i fevral'skoi revoliutsii, pp. 150–1, 152; Bayerisches Hauptstaatsarchiv (Munich), Abt. IV: Kriegsarchiv. 2 Bay. Landw. Div., Dand 5, Akt 9, 11; A. Wildman, The End of the Russian Imperial Army: The Old Army and the Soldiers' Revolt (March–April 1917), Princeton, 1980, pp. 110–15.

58. 'Oktiabr'skaia revoliutsiia v Baltiiskom flote (Iz dnevnika I.I. Rengartena)', Krasnyi arkhiv, 1927, t. 6 (25), p. 34.

59. N.A. Epanchin, Na sluzhbe trekh imperatorov, Moscow, 1996, p. 471. OR IRLI, f. 654. op. 5, d. 2, l. 4; d. 9, l. 1; Dnevnik b. velikogo kniazia Andreia Vladimirovicha, Leningrad, 1925, pp. 84–5; Knox, With the Russian Army, vol. 2, p. 515.

the plans for a palace coup by Guchkov and others in the final weeks before the February Revolution, nor indeed to inform the Tsar of them. The Allies' disposition was against the monarchy. We know for sure that the Allied representatives in Russia were extremely anxious about the influence of the 'German party' in the court and government – and that they themselves generally believed the rumours that suggested this influence. Many of the Allied diplomats presumed that German agents were censoring the press, and this reinforced their trust in the rumours. The British Ambassador, George Buchanan, was particularly convinced of the German influence – a fact he could not hide in his last conversations with the Tsar (see Chapter 6). It is also possible that the Allied missions knew more about the plans to murder Rasputin than they let on.[60] If so, neither took any measures to inform the Russian government. By this stage all the rumours of treason had created such profound divisions within Russia's ruling circles – alienating much of the army command, officialdom, the aristocracy and society itself from the 'pro-German court' – that it must have seemed impossible for the Allies to continue with the war campaign in Russia until there was a government of national confidence.

Official Responses

Such divisions may help to explain the weak response of the Tsar's authorities to these subversive rumours of sexual corruption and treachery. There was an extraordinary lack of resolve or coordination in the government's attempts to stem the tide of slander against the monarchy – and this was no doubt because many senior officials half believed the tales themselves. The military and civilian censors, which were two separate bodies, pursued entirely different policies – with the military censors far more liberal than the main administration of the press. There were some arrests for spreading rumours – the police assumed quite rightly that the revolutionaries were putting out the rumours to undermine the monarchy – but the rumours continued to spread.[61]

The revolutionary underground used many of the rumours in its propaganda. Reacting to the charges of treason against Colonel Miasoedov, for example, the Petrograd Committee of the Bolsheviks proclaimed in a leaflet that there were 'no traitors among the Russian people . . .They are all high up, within the government, in the ministries and salons which shine with gold.'[62] The liberal parties of the Progressive Bloc were just as

60. Predictions of Rasputin's murder frequently appeared in the foreign press. See Buchanan, *My Mission to Russia*, p. 48; RGIA, f. 1470, op. 2, d. 101, l. 37.
61. See e.g. P.G. Kurlov, *Gibel' imperatorskoi Rossii*, Moscow, 1991, p. 160.
62. RGIA, f. 1405, op. 530, d. 1127, l. 1; See also, A.G. Shliapnikov, *Kanun semnadtsatogo goda. Semnadtsatyi god*, Moscow, 1992, t. 1, pp. 160, 170, 173.

ready to spread and even manufacture rumours of corruption and treason at the court.[63] It was often said – and is still repeated – that the Freemasons were responsible for a campaign of gossip against Rasputin and the court.[64]

In the Criminal Code there was a special penalty for disseminating 'insults against the Imperial family'. During the war, under prohibition, it was presumed by criminologists that the number of such prosecutions would decline; but in the event they rose – which reflected the fact that this hostility was a sober view – and from 1916 the Tsar ordered that such prosecutions must cease, presumably to forestall the possibility of demonstrations against the government.[65]

Official efforts at counter-propaganda were equally feeble. The activities of the Tsarina and her daughters in caring for the wounded at military hospitals were favourably viewed to begin with, but then public approval of them declined. In the end they were better publicized in the Allied press than they were in the Russian. In any case the popular perception of the nurse was so transformed by the experience of war that photographs of the Empress and Grand Duchesses in Red Cross uniforms became something of an embarrassment. The front-line soldiers either looked upon the nurses ('sisters of comfort') as sex objects (an image reinforced by the tendency of Russia's wartime prostitutes to work the streets in nurses' uniforms) or else as useless women ('sisters without mercy') who rode in the staff cars ('nurse carriers') but had no medicine or other means of helping the soldiers. Any mention of nurses automatically gave rise to dirty jokes among the ranks. The news, for example, in November 1915 that the Tsar was awarding medals to a group of nurses resulted in the rumour that they were being rewarded not just for their professional service but for other kinds of service as well.[66] Indeed, it was thought by many peasant soldiers, in the words of one, that the Tsar and the Tsarina had 'built hospitals for their own debauchery – and they travel round in them'.[67] Finally, the attempt to democratize and popularize the image of the Tsarina by presenting her as a simple nurse could prove counter-productive in so far as it took away from the mystique of the monarchy. 'The Empress,' recalled the police chief A.I. Spiridovich, 'having cared for the wounded and the sick, having washed the feet of soldiers, lost all her majesty from their perspective. She became no more than an ordinary nurse, a simple hospital functionary.'[68]

63. V.S. Diakin, *Russkaia burzhuaziia i tsarizm v gody pervoi mirovoi voiny (1914–1917)*, Leningrad, 1967, pp. 251–3.
64. O.A. Platonov, *Zhizn' za tsaria (Pravda o Grigorii Rasputine)*, St Petersburg, 1996, pp. 97, 231 and *passim*. B.I. Nikolaevskii, *Russkie masony i revoliutsiia*, Moscow, 1990, p. 40.
65. See RGIA, f. 1405, op. 521, d. 476, ll. 4, 14, 34, 71, 74, 75, 80, 84, 86, 230 and *passim*.
66. Ibid., l. 390.
67. Ibid., l. 481.
68. Spiridovich, *Velikaia voina i fevral'skaia revoliutsiia*, kn. 3, p. 74.

Unopposed by the authorities, the rumours of corruption and treason at the court achieved the status of factual truths. Without this 'atmosphere' – created out of gossip and half-truths, facts and fabrications, bits of information from the press which were then distorted into fantasies – it is impossible to understand the 'revolutionary mood' or the ways in which the revolution turned on the (mis)interpretation of hearsay and events. 'Rumours filled the lives of all inhabitants,' recalled a resident of Petrograd. 'They were believed more readily than the newspapers, which were censored. The public was desperate for information, for almost anything, on political subjects, and any rumour about the war or German intrigues was bound to spread like wildfire.'[69] What gave these stories political power and significance – the ability to motivate and inform the public's actions – was not to what extent they had any basis in fact (who knew, after all, what to believe?), but how far they accorded with the 'general mood' – and of course with previous rumours that had shaped that mood. Once a rumour, however false, becomes the subject of common belief, it assumes the status of political fact, informing the attitudes and actions of the public in a revolutionary situation. All revolutions are based in part on myth.

But what gave these rumours their potential as a unifying belief in the February Revolution was the fact that they were endorsed by the Duma leaders, and indeed even by conservatives. Miliukov's speech in the Duma on 1 November 1916 – in which he denounced the government's abuses, asking after each: 'Is this folly or treason?' – is certainly the best known but by no means the only case in point. That a statesman as cautious as Miliukov, and one, moreover, with such close connections to Allied diplomats, had openly used the word 'treason' was enough for the public to conclude that treason there had been. This had not been Miliukov's aim. To his own rhetorical question he himself would have answered 'folly'. Yet the public was so charged up with emotion from the rumours that by the time it read his speech it was bound to answer 'treason'. Moreover, because the speech was banned from the press and had to be read in well-thumbed typescripts passed from hand to hand people were even more inclined to reach this conclusion. Such was its revolutionary effect that in some versions of the typescript a particular social grievance would appear inserted into the middle of the speech (e.g. claiming that in addition to its other abuses the government treated teachers very badly). 'My speech acquired the reputation of a storm-signal for the revolution,' Miliukov recalled. 'Such was not my intention. But the prevailing mood in the country served as a megaphone for my words.'[70]

The fact that these rumours circulated among the upper classes gave

69. *Burzhuaziia nakanune fevral'skoi revoliutsii*, pp. 125–6.
70. Figes, *A People's Tragedy*, p. 287.

them even greater credence on the street. 'What is said in high society,' wrote V.I. Gurko, 'trickles down into the social circles of the two capitals, and subsequently, through the servants and caretakers, passes down to the masses, upon whom such rumours have a certain revolutionary effect.'[71] Gossip about Rasputin, in particular, circulated in conservative and reactionary circles of high society, where various 'dark forces', especially the Germans and the Jews, were blamed for the problems of the dynasty. According to Prince N.D. Zhevakhov, a senior official of the Holy Synod, Rasputin had been selected by the Jews and other 'agents of the Internationale' to bring down the monarchy.[72] Black Hundred ultra-nationalist organizations accounted for the political crisis by claiming that Nicholas had been 'hypnotized by the spiritual adviser' who was 'surrounded by foreigners and spies'.[73] It is telling that in many of the anti-Rasputin texts and rumours of this provenance individual members of the Romanov family appear as positive characters – the Grand Dukes Nikolai Nikolaevich, Dmitrii Pavlovich and Mikhail Aleksandrovich, for example, or the Dowager Empress Maria Fedorovna – as if the institution of the monarchy was not beyond salvation, provided it got rid of the evil in its ranks.[74]

It is possible that rumours such as this contributed to the popular perception that the Jews, like the Germans, were among those 'dark forces' undermining Russia in 1916–17. It was often said – by this soldier, for example – that 'Our Sovereign is as stupid as a calf – he is surrounded by Yids and Germans, who become his officers and commanders.'[75] On the other hand, the lower classes themselves gave their own expression and interpretation to such ideas, as we shall see in Chapter 6. The term 'dark forces', used increasingly in high society, had been current for decades in revolutionary circles. It could be used in different ways by different sections of society. For some it meant a clique of 'Rasputinites' at court. For others, it incorporated the whole dynasty. Rhetoric and actions against the 'dark forces' could thus take on many different political colours – anti-monarchical, anti-Semitic, anti-German, and anti-bourgeois – all at the same time.

71. V.I. Gurko, *Tsar' i tsaritsa*, Paris, 1927, pp. 70–1.
72. [N.D. Zhevakhov], *Vospominaniia tovarishcha ober-prokurora Sv. Sinoda kniazia N. D. Zhevakhova*, Moscow, 1993, t. 1, sentiabr' 1915 – mart 1917, pp. 184, 207, 240, 242–3, 246–53 and *passim*.
73. Burdzhalov, *Vtoraia russkaia revoliutsiia*, p. 67; V.A. Maevskii, *Na grani dvukh epokh*, Madrid, 1963, pp. 131, 220. Compare this with the statement of a shop steward in June 1915: 'Our sovereign is as stupid as a cow – he is surrounded only by Jews and Germans, who are his officers and governors' (RGIA, f. 1405, op. 521, d. 476, l. 1).
74. See e.g. *Tainy tsarskosel'skogo dvortsa*, Petrograd, 1917, p. 14; Trufanov, *Tainy doma Romanovykh*, pp. 23, 24.
75. RGIA, f. 1405, op. 521, d. 476, l. 1.

The Revolutionary Impact of Rumours

Rumours played a vital role in the February Revolution (even if that role has been neglected ever since). People believed what they heard, not what they read; and interpreted what they read in terms of what they heard. Rumours helped to organize different segments of society – to unite them against a monarchy that was perceived as corrupt and treacherous – and in the process they split the government. They acted as an important conduit of information for the people on the streets. They set the 'revolutionary mood'.

The 'people's side' defined itself and decided on its actions in response to the rumours on the streets. Bread queues were turned into food riots and demonstrations against the monarchy by tales of 'dark forces' – speculative traders, Germans and Jews, corrupt officials – conspiring to profit from the people's hunger. Rumours of the movements of the loyalist forces determined the movements of the crowd: people moved towards the Tauride Palace, the main railway stations, and the Peter and Paul Fortress, as rumours spread (and in each case they were false) that these were the main targets of the Tsar's remaining troops. There is also evidence that rumours of the court's intention to surrender to the Germans influenced the decision of many officers in the Petrograd garrison to join the people's side.

Such rumours served to give the people's side a sense of its own righteousness. It made it patriotic to oppose the Tsar. Or as someone put it: 'Now we have beaten the Germans here, we will beat them in the field.'[76] This sense of justice was a source of strength: by presenting their revolutionary opposition to the Tsar as a patriotic movement the demonstrators sought to legitimize their protests and win over the rest of society, particularly the soldiers and their officers, whose allegiance would be crucial to the insurrection – literally a matter of life and death. People in the streets harangued the soldiers with claims that the Tsar was on the Germans' side.

The rumours also gave the people confidence by debunking the myth that the Tsar was both divine and omnipotent. The idea that it was a heinous sin to oppose the Tsar appeared ridiculous to all but the most remote and superstitious peasants once it was believed that he had been cuckolded or that he was controlled by evil foreigners. The February Revolution was based on the belief that the monarchy had fallen into the hands of 'dark forces' – an image which ruled out the possibility of a restoration in the years to come. The spread of rumours made this belief commonplace.

Finally, one should not underestimate the extent to which these rumours stirred up violent hatred of the monarchy. The iconoclasm witnessed in

76. Figes, *A People's Tragedy*, p. 352.

the February Days – the burning of straw effigies of the Tsar, the pornographic pictures of the Empress and Rasputin, the tearing down of
emblems, the smashing of statues, the cutting out of eyes from Tsarist
portraits – was an expression of the mockery and anger hitherto embodied
and constrained by the rumours yet always waiting to explode. Once the
monarchy had been overthrown the effect of these rumours could be to
provoke an exceptionally violent and merciless contempt for the exposed
'traitors' – even from the most mild-mannered types. The mathematician
V.A. Steklov wrote in his diary on 10 March:

> The loathsome picture of filth and corruption within the court is gradually
> being exposed . . . A real Rome in the age of decadence. Even worse. One
> cannot speak of such bloody and evil deeds. The traitors! They are scum,
> not human beings. The new authorities are treating them with too much
> ceremony. They have abolished the death penalty. But they should be
> told that they'll all be executed by a public hanging, and they should be
> locked up in Tsarskoe Selo in constant expectation of their punishment
> until the torture makes them lose their mind. And then we should hang
> them all like worthless scum. And that would still be to let them off
> lightly![77]

Steklov was a man of very moderate views. Among the lower classes, the
soldiers and the workers with greater cause to detest the monarchy, there
were even louder calls for bloody retribution. Rumours of assassination
attempts on the Empress were heard every day before the revolution. The
most common claim was that she had been shot at by an officer while
recuperating from a mysterious illness in hospital. Some versions had it
that the bullet meant for her had wounded Vyrubova. Others had the
Empress wounded in the hand.[78] It would be idle to speculate whether
rumours such as these were cases of collective wishful thinking. Certainly,
there were frequent calls for the execution of the Tsar and the Tsarina
by workers, soldiers and sailors in 1917. This confirms the veracity of the
Soviet claim – confirmed by no less than the Patriarch of Moscow on 17
July 1998 – that the Russian people met the news of the murder of the
Tsar and his family with indifference.

Once the February Revolution was victorious the Russian monarchy
became the 'old regime'. The demonization of the old regime was a vital
means of legitimizing and enforcing unity around 'the revolution'. Indeed,
it was a necessary means inasmuch as the Provisional Government, without

77. SPARAN, f. 162, op. 3, d. 168, l. 47.
78. 'Oktiabr'skaia revoliutsiia v Baltiiskom flote', p. 34; *Tainy russkogo dvora*, vyp. 2: *Tsar' bez golovy*,
     Petrograd, 1917, p. 1; Trufanov, *Tainy doma Romanovykh*, vyp. 2, pp. 2, 6. 92; 'K istorii poslednikh
     dnei tsarskogo rezhima (1916-1917 gg.)', p. 246.

the mandate of a democratic vote, depended on the construction of this moral consensus to establish its own authority.

In this context, the continued propagation of the old myths about the Romanovs – which was guaranteed by the commercial explosion of books and pamphlets, plays and films exposing their 'dark secrets' – also served the interests of the new authorities. Equally, it was important that the rumours of corruption and treason were deemed true. Here the Provisional Government had a very useful tool. Its Extraordinary Commission of Inquiry, established under the chairmanship of N.K. Murav'ev on 8 March, acted as judge and jury of the charges against the old regime.[79] Exiled monarchists referred to it as 'the first Cheka'.[80] And it is true that Murav'ev was heard to remind its members that their slogan ought to be the words of Kerensky: 'We need a little bit of Marat within us.'[81] One wonders whether the Commission's members actually believed the rumours brought before it, or whether they discounted them but continued with their work to satisfy the public hunger, as the editors of *Sel'skii vestnik* put it, for the 'light of Truth to be cast in all the dark places of the old regime'.[82] The evidence suggests that they believed the rumours – because it was convenient for them to do so. Kerensky's insistence on interrogating the Tsarina himself was a reflection of the seriousness with which he took the charges of treason against her. Senator M.R. Zavadskii, the Commission's deputy chairman, recalled that 'Murav'ev was convinced of the possibility that the Tsar had intended to form a military alliance with the Germans, or that the Tsarina had given Kaiser Wilhelm information on the movement of Russian troops.'[83] This was indeed one of the Commission's main lines of questioning.

Yet endorsing rumours such as these was a dangerous game to play. The idea of a conspiracy, of treason and corruption in the ruling circles, was one the Bolsheviks deployed with much success against Kerensky and his Provisional Government. Indeed, as we shall see in Chapter 3, there was a striking resemblance between the fates of the last Tsar and Kerensky. If the old regime had been brought down in a 'flood of speech', to paraphrase Carlyle, the new government would find it just as hard to assert its political authority in the relaxed conditions for public debate after February 1917.

---

79. On the establishment of the Commission see R.P. Browder and A.F. Kerensky (eds), *The Russian Provisional Government, 1917: Documents*, Stanford, 1961, vol. 1, pp. 193–4. The testimony before the Commission was partly published as *Padenie tsarskogo rezhima.*
80. A.I. Spiridovich, 'Otkrytoe pis'mo redaktoru "Dnei"', *Vechernee vremia*, 19 Dec., 1925.
81. F.I. Rodichev, *Vospominaniia i ocherki o russkom liberalizme*, Newstonville, Mass., 1983, p. 126.
82. *Sel'skii vestnik*, 11 March 1917.
83. Columbia University, Bakhmatieff Archive, Raupakh Papers, Box 1, p. 40.

2

The Symbolic Revolution

It is impossible to imagine the February Revolution without the sound of the 'Marseillaise' or the image of the red flag. Yet we should not regard these simply as colourful adornments of the revolution. They were important political symbols and played a major role in defining the struggle. Indeed, there was a whole array of cultural symbols, rites and festivals that helped to make the revolution what it was. We should study these more closely as the instruments of revolutionary politics rather than as a passive reflection of them.

This perspective has informed the study of the French Revolution for many generations. As early as 1904, one of the renowned fathers of French revolutionary historiography, Albert Mathiez, published *Les Origines des cultes révolutionnaires*, a self-consciously Durkheimian study illustrating how the French Revolution developed its own symbolic system, with oaths and festivals, to unite the nation and sacralize itself.

The precedent is apt. For the leaders of 1917 consciously adopted the symbolic traditions of the French Revolution.[1] They compared themselves to the heroes of 1789. Kerensky, for example, was frequently compared (and perhaps in private compared himself) to Mirabeau and, later, even to Napoleon. They looked for precedents for their policies, and for models for their institutions, in the revolutionary history of France. The socialists were often called the Jacobins, which is also how they saw themselves: there was rivalry between the socialists for the title of 'true Jacobins'. The Bolsheviks, in turn, called the liberals Girondins; and it was true that many of the moderates compared their own position to that of the Girondins. Practically everybody warned of the dangers of 'counter-revolution'. Left-

---

1. On this see O. Figes, *A People's Tragedy: The Russian Revolution 1891–1924*, London, 1996, p. 357; D. Shlapentokh, 'The Images of the French Revolution in the February and Bolshevik Revolutions', *Russian History*, 1989, vol. 16, no. 1. See further, Shlapentokh, *The French Revolution in Russian Intellectual Life 1865-1905*, London, 1996 and *The French Revolution and the Russian Anti-democratic Tradition: A Case Study of False Consciousness*, London, 1997.

wing parties worried about Bonapartism; but many others welcomed the idea of a 'Russian Bonaparte' to save the country from left-wing 'anarchy'. The 'provincial commissars', the soldiers' committees and army commissars, the provincial committees of public safety and the Constituent Assembly itself – all of them were copied from their French equivalents. The old deferential terms of address were supplanted by the terms *grazhdanin* and *grazhdanka* ('citizen' and 'citizeness') which had been used in a different context before 1917 (see pp. 60–2 below). The 'Marseillaise' – which the Russians mispronounced as the *Marsiliuza* – became the national anthem of the revolution. 'Marsovoe pole', the Champ de Mars, became the main public space of commemoration, the altar of the cult of the revolution, during and after 1917; and the choice was significant, reviving as it did the association with the French tradition. There were even plans for festivals to reproduce the events of the French Revolution on Russian soil: one envisaged the burning of the Lithuanian Castle, a political prison, in a holiday to mimic Bastille Day; a more ambitious plan of August 1917 proposed a 'grandiose carnival-spectacle honouring the epoch of the French Revolution in the Summer Garden . . . A prop city will be built depicting the Paris of that time. Actors will portray the artistic and theatrical bohemia of the late eighteenth century.'[2]

Historians of the French Revolution have reminded us of the role played by symbols, songs and festivals.[3] They unify the crowd, giving it a banner around which to rally in street battles with the police and other enemies. Sometimes these symbols themselves become the object of the fight. The clash between the crowds and the Petrograd police on Znamenskaia Square on 24–26 February is a case in point. Why did this square become the central point of the February Revolution – indeed its very symbol in later years when the Soviets renamed it the Square of the Uprising (*ploshchad vosstaniia*)? Firstly, it was an important intersection connecting the outlying industrial suburbs with Nevsky Prospekt, so workers marching into the centre of the city simply could not avoid it (a point to which we shall return). Secondly, once they found themselves on the square, the demonstrators were organized by the nature of its space: a huge open area with a statue in the middle, it was an ideal arena for a political meeting, a stage for the 'theatre of the Revolution', which brought in spectators too. But finally, and perhaps most crucially, the square itself was a symbolic challenge: for the monument in the middle was the huge equestrian statue of Alexander III, a symbol of autocracy, of its monolithic

2. J. von Geldern, *Bolshevik Festivals 1917–1920*, Berkeley, 1993, p. 23.
3. See e.g. M. Ozouf, *Festivals of the French Revolution*, Cambridge, 1988; M. Agulhon, *Marianne into Battle: Republican Imagery and Symbolism in France 1989–1880*, Cambridge, 1979; L. Hunt (ed.), *The New Cultural History*, Berkeley, 1989; K. Baker, *Inventing the French Revolution: Essays on French Political Culture in the Eighteenth Century*, Cambridge, 1990.

immobility and, at the same time, a reminder of the mounted police who came to the square to defend it. Both sides were determined to make the site their own – the crowd to conquer and defile a sacred place of the regime, the police to stop them. In towns throughout Russia the February Revolution was organized around the struggle for the control of such monuments. Symbols of authority were the prize itself.

Words and songs also had symbolic meaning for the crowds. The rallying cry of 'liberty', the emotional strains of the 'Marseillaise', strengthened their resolve. The red flag became an emblem of the people's struggle, embodying their anger and ideals.[4] People were prepared to die for these symbols. They would literally risk their lives to attach a red flag to a Tsarist building, or to take down the Romanov double-headed eagle, because for them, at that precise moment, that is what the revolution was about.

The ritualized dismantling of the old regime's symbols, and their replacement by revolutionary ones, itself became an aspect of the reconstruction of society. As Mona Ozouf has argued in her pioneering work on French revolutionary festivals, it was a question of recasting space and time. The revolution opened up the closed spaces of the old regime (palaces and prisons), adopted large and open public spaces (like the Champ de Mars) for its festivals, made new places sacred and renamed streets and squares. In terms of time, it adopted a new calendar, reclaimed public dates, and identified with historical and mythical traditions, such as Sparta and ancient Athens, whose values set them apart from the old regime. In Ozouf's analysis, the role of the revolutionary festivals was to ritualize this recasting of space and time – to reinvent the nation and rewrite its history.[5]

There was a large element of theatricalization in all of this, of course. The boundary between street theatre and revolution can indeed be blurred– not just because the struggle is a drama but because the protagonists themselves are prone to act out roles (the messenger, the hero, the martyr and so on) as if upon a stage. The carnival aspects of the crowd's behaviour were self-consciously theatrical: the acts of mockery and humiliation; the ritualized destruction of emblems of state power and authority; the self-assertive body language and dress of the soldiers (wearing their caps back

4.   The colour red has been a revolutionary symbol since 1789. But in Russia it was also associated with the idea of beauty: the word 'red' (*krasnyi*) was a synonym of 'wonderful' (*prekrasnyi*) and 'beautiful' (*krasivyi*) – from which is derived the idea of 'Red Square', meaning beautiful. Red was seen as benevolent and good. There was a proverb: 'reddest is the best' ('*prekrasnyi-samyi krasnyi*'). The colour red also had symbolic significance in Russian Orthodoxy: the main religious festival, Easter, was called 'Red Easter', and at this time the priests wore red robes (I. Kiblitskii, 'Nemnogo o tsvete, o krasnom tsvete', *Krasnyi tsvet v russkom iskusstve*, St Petersburg, 1997. pp. 6–7).
5.   See Ozouf, *Festivals of the French Revolution*, esp. pp. 126–7, 148–52, 267–70 and *passim*.

to front, or tilted to one side, as a sign of liberation, or wearing their coats and tunics unbuttoned in contravention of military regulations).

There was also a new pattern of revolutionary dress – improvised and proudly worn by individuals as a mark of their revolutionariness: red ribbons and flowers tied to epaulettes, red stripes added to uniforms, and so on. Each fashion statement of rebellion could create new conflicts with superiors who insisted on the old codes of dress. There were literally millions of these microcosmic revolutions, and at the time people saw them as important: some as statements of personal liberation; others as a sign of anarchy. The Marxist tradition was sensitive to the idea of the revolution as a 'festival of the oppressed and exploited'. To a large extent that is what February was. Or, at least, that is how it was commemorated almost from Day One. The dramatization of the revolution as a 'people's epic' was one of the effects of the festivals and cults promoted after February. The Bolsheviks commemorated their 'Great October' in the same way.[6]

At the root of this symbolic revolution was the idea of destroying in order to renew. Like the French revolutionary festivals, the iconoclasm of the February Revolution obeyed the law of the purge. It sought to sweep away the superfluity, the excess wealth and decadence of the monarchy, not just for the sake of an end to privilege but in an attempt to ensure the restoration of a purer and more simple model of society. There was said to be revolutionary virtue in the renunciation of luxury and rank – in the spartan fashion for the military dress of the common soldier (as worn by Kerensky and later by the Bolsheviks) or in the adoption of democratic forms of personal address ('Citizen-Minister', 'Comrade Kerensky' and so on). This simplification was more than just a democratic trend. It was a projection of the ideal republic on to the culture, the daily life and customs, of the revolution. All revolutions are sacralized. In the euphoria which they themselves create they are conceived as a spiritual renewal, a moral resurrection of the people, in which all sins vanish with the old regime and virtues are restored. This was the cult of the French Revolution – the holy trinity of liberty, equality and fraternity symbolized by the surrogate Madonna of Marianne.[7] 'The Revolution' itself became a sacred altar – a supreme authority demanding veneration and obedience from its citizens. The February Revolution and its symbols were to play a similar role.

6.   On which see von Geldern, *Bolshevik Festivals*; R. Stites, *Revolutionary Dreams: Utopian Vision and Experimental Life in the Russian Revolution*, Oxford, 1989.
7.   See Agulhon, *Marianne into Battle*.

The Symbolic Code of the February Revolution

During the February Days in Petrograd the crowds displayed an extraordinary level of self-organization and solidarity. 'The entire civil population
felt itself to be in one camp against the enemy – the police and the military,'
the Menshevik Sukhanov recalled in his memoirs. 'Strangers passing by
conversed with each other, asking questions and talking about the news,
about clashes with and the diversionary movements of the enemy.' The
London *Times* was equally impressed. 'The astounding, and to the stranger
unacquainted with the Russian character almost uncanny, orderliness and
good nature of the crowds are perhaps the most striking feature of this
great Russian Revolution.' The crowds on the streets seemed to act as
one.[8]

The cohesive ties were there for all to see. People wore red arm bands,
or tied red ribbons in their buttonholes, to display their support for the
revolution. Not to do so was to invite persecution as a 'counter-
revolutionary'. Bonfires were lit throughout the city so that people could
warm themselves during the long hours of street-fighting. Residents fed
the revolutionaries from their kitchens, and allowed them to sleep – in
so far as anyone slept – on their floors. Café and restaurant owners fed
the soldiers and workers free of charge, or placed boxes outside so that
passers-by could contribute towards their meals. One café displayed the
following sign:

> FELLOW-CITIZENS! In honour of the great days of freedom, I bid you
> all welcome. Come inside, and eat and drink to your hearts' content.

Shopkeepers turned their shops into bases for the soldiers, and into shelters
for the people when the police were firing in the streets. All sorts of
people volunteered to help the doctors deal with the wounded, or to run
as messengers or on other errands for the revolutionaries. It was as if the
people on the streets had suddenly become united by a vast network of
invisible threads; and it was this that secured their victory.[9]

This apparent cohesion of the crowd raises the question of its organization. If it seemed to act like a single body, were there leaders telling
people where to go, or did the crowd just organize itself? What is 'organized',
what 'spontaneous', when it is a question of the revolutionary crowd?
The historical debate has never been resolved.[10] The only way to do so

---

8.   N.N. Sukhanov, *The Russian Revolution: A Personal Record*, Princeton, 1984, p. 16; *The Times*,
     17 March 1917.
9.   S. Jones, *Russia in Revolution, Being the Experience of an Englishman in Russia during the Upheaval*,
     London, 1917, p. 127; V. Bulgakov, 'Revoliutsiia na avtomobiliakh (Petrograd v fevrale 1917
     g.)', *Na chuzhoi storone*, Berlin–Prague, 1924, no. 6, p. 28.
10. B.I. Startsev, 'Stikhiinost' i organizovannost' v fevral'skom vosstanii 1917 goda v Petrograde',

is to look at the cultural code by which the crowd was self-organized – for that is what is meant by its 'spontaneity'.

At the time the Tsarist authorities assumed the crowds had been organized. The Okhrana (secret police) reports on the February Days, for example, stressed the role of socialist agitators in the instigation of the workers' strikes. They spoke of a 'leading centre' issuing 'directives' to the movement and, while acknowledging the spontaneous origins of the demonstrations, assumed that they must have been organized by the 'revolutionary circles' to expand throughout the city the way they did.[11]

Others at the time thought the crowds were organized by the enemies of Russia. Some monarchists believed that they were led by various 'dark forces' – first and foremost the Jews and Freemasons. Miliukov accused the German government of instigating the disorders. Generals at Stavka (the army headquarters) suggested the unrest had been caused by 'German intrigues'.[12] Ironically, the Germans, in their own Russian-language propaganda leaflets, blamed the revolution on British agents supposedly intent on preventing a peace between the Tsarist government and Germany. The German press dubbed it the 'English Revolution'.[13]

From the 1930s Soviet historians were expected to stress the organizing role of the Bolsheviks – although from the 1960s, with the publication of E.N. Burdzhalov's revisionist study of the February Revolution, they were forced to admit that the party's influence had been minimal.[14] More recently historians have stressed the role of other socialist organizations, such as the Inter-District group, the 'United Front' of left-wing parties, or the Left SRs.[15]

But although their rank-and-file were present in the crowds, the socialist parties were completely unprepared to play an organizing role. 'The

in *80 let revoliutsii 1917 goda v Rossii* (Respublikanskaia nauchnaia konf.): *Tezisy, Doklady. i Soobshchenia*, St Petersburg, 1997, pp. 22–6.

11. R. P. Browder and A.F. Kerensky (eds), *The Russian Provisional Government, 1917: Documents*, Stanford, 1961, vol. 1, pp. 33–9.
12. 'Romanovy i soiuzniki v pervye dni revoliutsii', *Krasnyi arkhiv*, 1926, t. 2 (15), p. 47.
13. Even in their memoirs, German generals stressed the role of the Entente in the overthrow of the Tsar. See E. Ludendorf, *Moi vospominaniia o voine 1914–1918 gg.*, Moscow, 1924, t. 2, p. 9.
14. E.N. Burdzhalov, *Russia's Second Revolution: The February 1917 Uprising in Petrograd*, trans. and ed. D.J. Raleigh, Indiana, 1987 (see the excellent 'Translator's Introduction' on the Burdzhalov Affair). The edition cited in the notes to this chapter is E.N. Burdzhalov, *Vtoraia russkaia revoliutsiia: Vosstanie v Petrograde*, Moscow, 1967, abbreviated as Burdzhalov, *Vtoraia*. Also: G.L. Sobol'ev, 'Fevral'skoe vosstanie rabochikh i soldat v Petrograde: psikhologiia kollektivnogo povedeniia v ekstremal'snykh usloviakh', in *80 let revoliutsii*, p. 3.
15. M. Melancon, *The Socialist Revolutionaries and the Russian Anti-War Movement*, Columbus, Ohio, 1990; Melancon, 'Who Wrote What and When?: Proclamations of the February Revolution in Petrograd, 23 February–1 March 1917', *Soviet Studies*, 1988 vol. 40, no. 3, July 1988; J. White, 'The February Revolution and the Bolshevik Vyborg District Committee (in Response to Michael Melancon)', *Soviet Studies*, Oct. 1989, vol. 41, no. 4; D.A. Longley, 'The Mezhraionka, the Bolsheviks and International Women's Day: in Response to Michael Melancon', ibid.

revolution found us, the Party members, fast asleep, just like the Foolish Virgins in the Gospel,' recalled Mstislavsky, one of the SR leaders, in 1922.[16] Much the same could be said for the other revolutionary parties in the capital. 'There were no authoritative leaders on the spot in any of the parties,' Sukhanov recalled. 'They were all in exile, in prison, or abroad.'[17] In their absence the task of trying to lead – which in fact meant following – the revolutionary crowds fell on to the shoulders of the secondary leaders: but none of them was a natural leader.

However, the fact that the party leaders were unprepared to organize the crowds in the February Days should not lead us to conclude that the whole thing was 'spontaneous'. This is the received view of many historians. Yet it ignores the self-organization of the streets. It forgets that the crowd had its own mechanisms, its own leaders and cultural codes of protest, which directed it into organized channels.

The street generated its own leaders: students and workers (who may or may not have belonged to one of the revolutionary groups); soldiers who brought their military knowledge and organization to the battle on the streets; and especially sergeants, like Timofei Kirpichnikov, who led their regiments into mutiny. Their names, for the most part, have remained hidden from the history books. During the first weeks after February their portraits were displayed in shop windows – often with the heading 'Heroes of the Revolution'. There was one of Kirpichnikov, for example, in the windows of the Avantso department store.[18] But then these people's leaders faded from view and were gradually forgotten.

The fact that most of the people in the crowd had previous experience of strikes and demonstrations also added to its organization.[19] The Petrograd workers, in particular, had a long tradition of activism in the trade unions, and most had memories of the 1905 Revolution. Many of the strike leaders of 1905, young men in their twenties, had become experienced and perhaps skilled workers by 1917, often occupying leading positions in the factories. This would have helped them to bring others out, especially the aggressive teenage militants, who play an active part in all revolutions but who looked to these older workers as keepers of the revolutionary tradition. Their elders, after all, knew the codes and customs of the revolutionary protest tradition – they knew the words of revolutionary songs, how to make a banner, and how best to fight with the police.

16. S. Mstislavsky, *Five Days Which Transformed Russia*, London, 1988, p. 23.
17. Sukhanov, *Russian Revolution*, p. 21.
18. BA, Finland Regiment Collection, Box 10, D.I. Khodnev, 'Fevral'skaia revoliutsiia 1917 g. i zapasnyi battalion leib-gvardii finlandskogo polka', p. 63.
19. See A.V. Zhdankov, 'Ulichnye demonstratsii v sisteme politicheskoi kul'tury proletariata nakanune fevral'skoi revoliutsii', *Rabochii klass Rossii, ego soiuzniki i politicheskie protivniki v 1917 g.*, Leningrad, 1989, pp. 103–12.

CULTURAL GEOGRAPHY

The cultural geography of the capital also helped to give direction to the crowds. There was a long-established spatial-cultural code of street demonstrations in the capital with a number of clear points of orientation (e.g. the Kazan Cathedral) which stretched back to the student demonstrations of 1899. Petrograd's industrial suburbs were physically separated from the affluent governmental downtown district by a series of canals and rivers. Marching into the centre thus became an expression of working-class solidarity and self-assertion, a means for the workers to claim the streets as theirs.[20] This cultural dimension of the protest tradition may help to explain the carnival aspects of the crowd: the destruction of symbols of wealth and power; the verbal abuse of the well-to-do; the smashing of shop windows, and so on.

Nevsky Prospekt was the obvious focal point for the crowd. It was the backbone of the capital, the main public avenue connecting the industrial suburbs with the downtown administrative area, and for this reason was heavily policed. In the February Days the police's strategy was to defend the Nevsky; the crowd's to capture it. From the first day of the demonstrations, on 23 February, the strikers' aim, in the words of one of them, was to 'break through to the Nevsky and march down to the bourgeois quarters of the capital'.[21]

Znamenskaia Square was another vital focal point in the February Days – mainly on account of the equestrian statue of Alexander III. There was a huge rally in the square on 24 February. Revolutionary orators climbed on top of the 'Hippopotamus', as the workers liked to dub the statue of the Tsar, and made speeches to the crowd calling for an end to autocracy. The statue was covered with red flags and ribbons and the word 'Hippopotamus' engraved in large letters on its plinth. These actions bore the character of a demonstrative defiance of the law, a sticking-up of two fingers at the dynasty. Imperial laws stipulated severe punishments for insults to the Imperial family – in any form. There were cases of people being prosecuted for verbally abusing a monument.[22] It was here, on Znamenskaia Square, that the shootings of 26 February took place.

The square in front of the Kazan Cathedral had a special symbolic significance. Russia's first public demonstration, organized by the Populists, had taken place here in 1876, and from that moment on the square became a focal point for all demonstrations. In an attempt to prevent

20. See J. Neuberger, *Hooliganism: Crime, Culture, and Power in St Petersburg, 1900–1914*, Berkeley, 1993.
21. V.N. Kaiurov, 'Dni fevral'skoi revoliutsii', *Krushenie tsarisma: Vospominaniia uchastnikov revoliut-sionnogo dvizheniia v Petrograde (1907 – fevral' 1917g.)*, Leningrad, 1986, p. 240.
22. See *Ulozhenie o nakazaniiax ugolovnykh i ispravitel'nykh 1885 g.*, Petrograd, 1916, p. 338.

the crowds from assembling there, the authorities constructed a public garden, with large shrubs; but this merely confirmed the place's special status in the public mind.[23] The square became a quasi-sacred site. Protesters gathered there, as if calling on the Cathedral's protection. Sometimes they hid inside it from the police.

The urge to legitimize their uprising also influenced the route of the marching soldiers on 27 February. They headed for the Tauride Palace, hoping it would confirm the patriotic character of their movement and justify their actions.[24] Earlier calls to march to the Duma had not met with a positive response, but now the action of the soldiers and the presence of the Menshevik defensists released from jail strengthened the resolve of the demonstrators. Confident that they would not be fired on within view of the parliament building, they marched to the Tauride Palace with a sense of justice in their cause.

From then on the Tauride Palace became the residence of the new competing centres of power – the Temporary Committee of the State Duma and the Petrograd Soviet. It was the 'Temple of Democracy', the altar of the revolution as a cult. Contemporaries were struck by the parallels with Easter: 'The Tauride Palace,' wrote G.P. Peretts, 'is burning with the light of thousands of electric lamps . . . like Easter night. This was the night of the resurrection of Russian life.'[25] The Tauride Palace was the sacred site of the revolution in the popular imagination. Its image appeared on every possible kind of postcard and poster, frequently illuminated by that other icon of the revolution, the Sun of Freedom, as a ray of light and hope. Its picture featured on the Provisional Government's liberty bonds as well as on the new 1,000-rouble notes (people called them 'Duma notes').[26] Many people thought of the palace not only as a symbol, but also as the seat of the government itself – indeed the seat of power – to the extent that some petitioners addressed their greetings or complaints 'to the Tauride Palace'.[27]

All these sites influenced the movements and actions of the crowds. Everybody knew that they should go to the Nevsky Prospekt, or to the Tauride Palace, because these were the places that demonstrators went. The movements of the crowd were not 'spontaneous': they followed a long-established tradition, a spatial-cultural code of protest in the capital.

23. The site remains a focal point for demonstrations today.
24. Burdzhalov, *Vtoraia*, p. 202.
25. G.P. Peretts, *V tsitadeli russkoi revoliutsii: Zapiski komendanta Tavricheskogo dvortsa*, Petrograd, 1917, p. 45.
26. A.I. Malyshev, V.I. Tarankov and I.N. Smirennyi, *Bumazhnye i denezhnye znaki Rossii i SSSR*, Moscow, 1991, pp. 78–9, 81–2, 96.
27. O. Figes, 'The Russian Revolution of 1917 and its Language in the Village', *Russian Review*, 1997, vol. 56, no. 3, p. 325.

REVOLUTIONARY SONGS

Songs and flags were equally important in the self-organization of the revolutionary crowd. Songs had an important symbolic role in events from the very start of the February Days. The Menshevik A.E. Diubua recalled that 'a crowd of several hundred workers moved down Nevsky singing songs and carrying red flags'.[28] Songs were mentioned not only in the memoirs of demonstrators, who might be expected to romanticize their role, but also in the reports of the police.[29]

In the government's official reports of 24–26 February, even to the Emperor, the singing of revolutionary songs was frequently mentioned. According to memoirs, the demonstrators' singing became increasingly provocative and defiant: 'the endless sea of heads drones ever more threateningly, and seethes ever more powerfully and insistently. In one place they sing the "Marseillaise", in another the "Varshavianka", in a third "Bravely Comrades Keep Together". With the arrival of the Cossacks all falls silent and then they start to sing again.' Foreigners were reminded of a 'gigantic circus'. Marguerite Bennet, a Scottish governess turned office worker in Petrograd, wrote home to her family on 15 March: '[The crowds] were singing the "Marseillaise" and when they weren't doing that they were asking for "bread! bread!"'[30]

Singing was the signal for a demonstration. It gave the protesters a sense of purpose and confidence and, perhaps most importantly, lifted their spirits. The leaders of the singing were the focus of the crowd in the February Days. The sound of the crowd drew other people on to the streets and hence into 'the revolution'. By joining in with the singing, spectators turned into participants in a matter of moments. Songs united the demonstrators, giving cohesion and a collective identity to diverse groups and classes.

Both the singing and the songs themselves made revolutionary statements. Revolutionary songs were part of the popular tradition of protest, their words and tunes instantly recognizable. Of the various anthems, the 'Marseillaise' is mentioned most frequently in both police reports and the memoirs of contemporaries. E.N. Burdzhalov, the pioneering historian of the February Revolution, had good reason to assert that the victory of the revolution was underscored by the rhythm of the 'Marseillaise'.[31]

In fact there were two different versions of the 'Marseillaise' in Russia

28. International Institute on Social History, Amsterdam, A.E. Diubua Papers, 'Revoliutsiia v Petrograde', p. 1.
29. A.G. Shliapnikov, *Semnadtsatyi god*, Moscow, 1992, pp. 72, 83, 85, 96, 97, 101, 106–8; A. Blok, *Poslednie dni imperatorskoi vlasti*, Petersburg, 1921, p. 64.
30. T.K. Kondrat'ev, 'Vospominaniia o podpol'noi rabote', *Krushenie tsarizma*, p. 280; H. Pitcher, *Witnesses of the Russian Revolution*, London, 1994, p. 13; Diubua, 'Revoliutsiia v Petrograde', p. 3.
31. Burdzhalov, *Vtoraia*, p. 454.

during 1917. The one that was played by orchestras, alone, was the French version. But the one that was sung in streets was P.L. Lavrov's version, originally published in the newspaper *Vpered* ('Forwards') in 1875. 'Let's renounce the old world', as Lavrov called his version, was sung at the first public demonstrations in Russia the year following its first publication. During the 1905 Revolution this 'Russian Marseillaise' replaced the 'Dybinushka' as the main song of protest. Foreigners who did not know of its existence took it to be a slow caricature of the 'Marseillaise'. In fact the song digressed from the melody of the French original, and followed a different beat. It was essentially a separate work.[32] Some accounts of the February Days mention the so-called 'Workers' Marseillaise' but this was also Lavrov's version of the French original.[33]

The meaning of the Russian version also differed significantly from that of the French. Whereas the original 'Marseillaise' was an assertion of national unity, the 'Workers' Marseillaise' – i.e. Lavrov's version – was a song of social protest. It belonged to the socialist tradition – appealing to the 'working people' and the 'hungry people' in its cry for class war:

To the parasites, to the dogs, to the rich!
Yes and to the evil vampire-Tsar!
Kill and destroy them, the villainous swine!
Light up the dawn of a new and better life!

The songs of February were revolutionary symbols that transcended party divisions. A song sung by Mensheviks was willingly taken up by anarchists. SRs might rally behind a red flag raised by the Bolsheviks. It is significant that the 'Internationale' was very rarely sung in the February Days, despite its status as the party anthem for socialists. It was not yet widely known. The common cultural traditions of the revolutionary underground united people on the streets, regardless of party. If someone without party ties sang a protest song, he or she was presumed by activists to be one of them. Conversely, revolutionary symbols and songs were

---

32. There was a suggestion that Lavrov should write the words of a 'new song' based upon the 'Marseillaise' in which the concluding part would incorporate the popular song of Robert Schumann, 'Two Grenadiers'. In any case, a concert version of this song was performed during demonstrations, often with the public singing along with a professional singer. It is possible that Lavrov's text was influenced by various 'Workers' "Marseillaise"'s, widespread in both France and Germany. See E.N. Gippius and P. Shiriaeva, 'Rabochaia marsel'eza', *Biografiia pesen*, Moscow, 1965, pp. 54, 65, 67; also: F.I. Shalianin, *Stranitsy iz moei zhizni*, Leningrad, 1990, p. 310. There were also various 'national' versions of the 'Marseillaise' in the Russian Empire in 1917, as well as national versions of the 'proletarian' verses. See N.I. Mironets' and T. G. Soltanovs'ka, 'Frantsuska politichna pisnia v revoliutsinomu rusi Rossii', *Ukrains'kii istorichnii zhurnal*, 1985, no. 11 (269), p. 94.

33. *Proletarskii gimnii i drugie pesni svobody*, Moscow, 1917, pp. 10–12; *Pod krasnym znamenem: Sb. revoliutsionnykh pesen*, Arkhangel'sk, 1917, vyp. 2, pp. 5–6; *Pesni revoliutsii i svobody*, Moscow, 1917, vyp. 1, pp. 19–21; *Pesni truda i bor'by*, vyp. 1, pp. 26–8.

appropriated by others, such as the student movement. They became a part of the general urban protest culture.

FLAGS AND EMBLEMS

Red flags and emblems were central to the organization of street demonstrations in 1917. Standard-bearers were a focus for the crowd, and a target for police. The struggle between the people and the police was in many cases determined by the flags, their defence or their capture.

Flags and emblems were sometimes made in advance and sometimes hastily improvised. The flags were usually prepared, often by the underground. Activists purchased red material, used velvet tablecloths, or even a red skirt.[34] Some flags were made directly on the streets. As early as 23 February there were reports of flags and emblems fashioned out of red shawls and left tied to street railings when the crowds dispersed in the evening.[35] National flags were hijacked and commandeered into use as revolutionary banners. The demonstrators – as they had done in 1905 – tore off the white and blue horizontal stripes, leaving only the red piece. Narrow red flags, faded and tattered, hung for weeks and even months on the streets of Petrograd.

Various red objects acquired the status of revolutionary symbols. On 25 February, in the first symbolic battle of the revolution, the crowd was brought to a halt by a squadron of Cossacks blocking their way near the Kazan Cathedral. A young girl appeared from the ranks of the demonstrators and walked slowly toward the Cossacks. Everyone watched her in nervous silence: surely the Cossacks would not fire at her? From under her cloak the girl brought out a bouquet of red roses and held it out towards the officer in charge. There was a pause: the bouquet was a symbol of both peace and revolution. Then, leaning down from his horse, the officer smiled and took the flowers. With as much relief as jubilation, the crowd burst into a thunderous 'Oorah!'[36] The acceptance of the flowers was interpreted by the demonstrators as a sign of solidarity from troops who had previously always been faithful to the regime. Red ribbons were plaited into the tails and manes of the Cossacks' horses.

By 25 February many of the streets of Petrograd were under the control of the demonstrators. They echoed with the sound of their songs and were festooned with their flags. There were numerous improvised meetings, processions and demonstrations – the capital had become one gigantic street

34. T. Hasegawa, *The February Revolution: Petrograd, 1917*, Seattle, 1981, p. 249.
35. I. Mil'chik, *Rabochii Fevral'*, Moscow, 1931, p. 64.
36. Hasegawa, *The February Revolution*, pp. 252–3.

party.[37] This carnivalesque atmosphere, 'like a bank holiday with thunder in the air', drew people out on to the streets. Spectators became confused with participants. The crowds assembled in the same places as they would for city festivals and holidays before the revolution. 'The first night of the revolution was like Easter,' wrote Tatiana Gippius on 26 March. 'One had the sense of a miracle close by, next to you, around you.' Diaries and memoirs make the same comparison, both consciously and unconsciously.[38] It was as if people needed these familiar rituals to express their emotions about such strange and extraordinary events. A teacher recalled meeting with her colleagues: 'I saw many of my comrades, the first after the break. Shaking hands with them and embracing them, I said to each of them: "Christ has risen!" and kissed each one three times.'[39] During these euphoric days strangers – even soldiers – kissed each other in the streets.

The shootings of 26 February completely changed the situation. The mood darkened. It was no longer a 'holiday'. The element of theatre was still there – but the 'battle with the dark forces of the enemy', of which they had only sung in their revolutionary songs up to that point, now became a terrible reality. 'There behind a line of soldiers, on the Nevsky,' recalled one eyewitness, 'they were mercilessly shooting at the workers.' The spirit of the revolution could still be felt – the vast crowd of demonstrators, the singing of revolutionary songs and, to one side, an orator is speaking to the crowd. The idea of the struggle for life and death expressed in the songs was carried out in real life on the streets of the Russian capital.[40]

The mutiny which the shootings triggered was a decisive and (demonstrative) violation of authority carried out with regimental discipline. That day small red flags began to appear on the soldiers' bayonets.[41] Insurgent soldiers – once relieved of their officer – devoted much of their attention to the military ritualization of the mutiny. It was as if they needed this to make up for the military discipline previously instilled by their officers. The presence of the regimental orchestras was a vital aspect of this ritualization

37. See the interesting, if controversial, article by I. Arkhipov, 'Karnival "Svobodnoi Rossii" (Zametki o "bleske i nishchete" rossiiskoi polilticheskoi kul'tury obrastsa 1917 goda)', *Zvezda*, 1996, no. 1, pp. 182–91.
38. OR RNB, f. 481, op. 1, d. 174, l. 18. See also K. Oberuchev, *V dni revoliutsii: Vospominaniia uchastnika Velikoi russkoi revoliutsii 1917-go goda*, New York, 1919, p. 49; P.A. Sorokin, *Chelovek. Tsivilizatsiia. Obshchestvo*, Moscow, 1992, p. 228; G.A. Kniazev, 'Iz zapisnoi knizhki russkogo intelligenta vo vremia voiny i revoliutsii 1915–1922 g.', *Russkoe proshloe*, 1991, no. 2, p. 114; O Mitrov, 'Khristos Voskrese', *Russkaia Volia*, 10 March 1917; S. Pushkin, 'Paskhalnyi zvon', *Soldat-grazhdanin*, 1 April 1917; *Lukomor'e*, 1917, no. 9/10.
39. Cited in O.N. Znamenskii, *Intelligentsia nakanune velikogo oktiabria (fevral'–oktiabr' 1917 g.)*, Leningrad, 1988, p. 117.
40. Kaiurov, 'Dni fevral'skoi revoliutsii', p. 246.
41. A. Knox, *With the Russian Army*, London, 1921, vol. 2, pp. 554–5.

of the mutiny. It was the orchestras that led the soldiers out on to the streets. Kirpichnikov, who organized the mutiny of the Volynsky regiment, remembered: 'Then the sappers quickly joined us with music as well. The music was sent out ahead and the rest of us joined later at the tail. We went to the Znamenskaia Square – and met the remaining units of the regiment which were also marching with a band playing the "Marseillaise".'[42]

The inclusion of the military orchestras was of great psychological importance for the soldiers. Music ritualized and regimented the everyday life of the regiment. Its sound on the streets – now with rebel songs – formalized the actions of the insurgents and raised their spirits, giving them the confidence they needed for the coming battles with the police. 'You see,' recalled Sukhanov, 'we were not even used at that time to the sound of the "Marseillaise" and it affected me for a long time. The military band . . . and military homage to an "illegal" hymn of freedom.'[43] It united the civilian and the soldier in a common purpose and identity.

During the February Revolution these symbols of rebellion – the revolutionary songs and the red flags – engaged the crowd. They determined where the demonstrators went, what they attacked and what they defended. This cannot be said of the October Days. The Bolsheviks attacked strategic institutions – bridges, telephone and telegraph stations, banks and buildings – that had a military rather than symbolic significance.

Festivals of Freedom

The revolution occurred differently in the provinces. Armed uprisings took place in Kronstadt, Helsingfors and other towns. Elsewhere there were spontaneous demonstrations strongly reminiscent of events in Petrograd, leading to the collapse of the authorities and the assumption of power by various *ad hoc* public committees. In the more remote regions the revolution spread by telegraph. 'We gained freedom by the post,' claimed the leader of the Georgian Mensheviks.[44] In many places news of the revolution in Petrograd became the occasion for a public holiday.

One eyewitness recalled the celebrations in a village of Riazan province at the end of March: 'The youths and soldiers made some red flags and sang the "Marseillaise" with shouts of "Hurrah". Then they paraded down the streets of the village . . . There was radiant joy on all their faces. They frequently halted as the people embraced and kissed one another in jubilation. Everybody said: "Here it is at last, the triumphant Easter

42. Kirpichnikov, Vosstanie' I-go Volynskogo Polka v fevrale', *Byloe*, 27–8, 1917, p. 311.
43. N.N. Sukhanov, *Zapiski o revoliutsii*, Moscow, 1991, t. 1, kn. 1, p. 166. See also pp. 260, 263.
44. N. Zhordaniia, *Moia zhizn'*, Stanford, 1968, p. 73.

has arrived". They were all smartly dressed, as if for a big holiday.'[45] As in the capital, the Easter tradition of celebration became confused with the revolutionary festival.

In most of the provincial cities there were monster rallies for the revolution called 'festivals of freedom'. Leaflets and pamphlets were handed out, printed with 'hymns of freedom' for all to learn and sing. In some cities almost the entire population took part in the demonstrations. The character of the festivals reflected the revolutionary balance of power in the provinces and the local preoccupations of the organizers. Like the French revolutionary festivals after 1789, there were ritualized and highly symbolic displays of allegiance to the civic values of the new order. Yet they also followed distinct Russian patterns of celebration and adopted common signs and practices from popular tradition. The Orel correspondent of the Moscow newspaper *Soldat-Grazhdanin* ('Soldier-Citizen') noted the survival of these old traditions in the 'festivals of freedom'. The military orchestra played the 'Marseillaise' but, as he noted, the atmosphere was reminiscent of a traditional regimental parade and festival. People joined the celebrations as they would have done in Tsarist days – as if on an order from above, and their own 'songs of freedom could not be heard'.[46] Indeed, singing marked a different level of involvement in the political process – the singers became active participants in events, and the constant repetition of the 'hymns of freedom' helped to revolutionize their consciousness.

Even though festivals of freedom were arranged on the model of the old, the military orchestras played new melodies. Again, the 'Marseillaise' was predominant but the revolutionary funeral march ('You Fell Victim') was also popular in the weeks and months following the February Revolution. At the Riga festival the 'Internationale' (unusually for this time) was played. This can be explained by the fact that the organizers of the demonstration were Latvian Social Democrats, for the 'Internationale' was the favoured song of the Marxist tradition.[47]

The ritual of the festival allowed a symbolic revolution to be carried out. During the celebrations there was often a ritualized purge of the old state symbols and a welcoming in of the new. The national tricolour was destroyed in elaborate rituals. Eagles and portraits of the Tsar were destroyed. Sometimes the celebrations took place under the old flag, however. 'The population paraded around the city with national flags and returned to work,' reported one newspaper. In some cases, the red and national flags were carried side by side.[48] Elsewhere, however, one can

45. *1917 god v derevne: Sb. vospominanii krest'ian*, Moscow, 1929, p. 14.
46. *Soldat-grazhdanin*, 23 March 1917.
47. A. Ezergailis, *The 1917 Revolution in Latvia*, London, 1974, p. 14.
48. *Rabochaia gazeta*, 22 March 1917; *Amurskoe ekho*, 23 April 1917; OR RNB, f. 152, op. 3, d. 168, l. 3.

see a micro-revolution in the rituals of these festivals. During the Irkutsk festival, for example, there was a military parade by the troops of the local garrison: after it had marched by, one of the commanders of the military units moved away from the other officers and took up a position next to the members of the Committee of Public Organizations, which led the revolution in the town. The soldiers understood the significance of this demonstration and greeted it with shouts of 'Hurrah'. From that point on, all the other officers of the garrison took up the same stance, in defiance of their military superiors, who were subsequently dismissed.[49] The military ritual had provided an opportunity for symbolic protest and political reform. If officers in remote garrisons initially prevented the soldiers from singing revolutionary songs and even forbade them to wear red ribbons or other symbols of the revolution, then the 'festivals of freedom' legitimized the adoption of revolutionary symbolism, or at least provoked a battle between pro- and counter-revolutionary forces for its place in the order of things.

The experience of the revolution and its theatrical realization in the ceremonies of these festivals took many different forms in regions across Russia. Even a month after the revolution had been victorious, a delegate from the Romanian front declared: 'I have come from a front, where the regimental aide-de-camp to this day beats the musicians about the face for playing the "Marseillaise".' None the less, the 'Marseillaise' was becoming institutionalized and became a part of daily ritual within the ranks. It was heard at morning and evening prayers in many regiments, and the swearing in of new troops was increasingly accompanied by the playing of it.

During the festivals of freedom it was common for the regiments from the local garrison to swear their allegiance to the revolution. These oath ceremonies were also conducted to the sound of the 'Marseillaise'. It provided an opportunity for the expression of this new revolutionary symbolism. Imperial emblems were covered up on banners. In some cases troops refused to take the oath under the old flag and demanded its replacement by a red one.[50]

In the capital itself the revolution was theatricalized and relived in numerous city and district festivals. Every possible kind of demonstration took place, almost on a daily basis, throughout March, all of them accompanied by music and singing. Seemingly unconnected events served as a pretext for these festivals, including the restoration of the tram service after the interruptions of the February Days. The resumption of normal service was celebrated with great pomp – as if this too was a miracle of

49. V. Voitinskii, *Gody pobed i porazhenii*, Benson, Vt., 1990, pp. 18–19.
50. Burdzhalov, *Vtoraia*, p. 133; *Russkoe slovo*, 19 March 1917; *Pravda*, 19 March 1917; D.P. Os'kin, *Zapiski praporshchika*, Moscow, 1931, p. 109.

the revolution: carriages were decorated with red flags and the 'Marseillaise' was sung.

The holiday atmosphere of February continued with the establishment of the Provisional Government. March was an extraordinary month – like one uninterrupted street party. There were jubilant processions to the Tauride Palace, triumphant parades, rallies and meetings. 'Both in Moscow and in Petrograd,' recalled the sociologist P.A. Sorokin, 'the populace rejoiced and enjoyed itself as if it was Easter . . . "Freedom! Sacred Freedom!" – they shouted everywhere and everywhere they sang their songs of liberty.'[51]

As politics had become high drama, so the theatre itself became politicized. On 13 March the theatres of the capital were reopened after the disturbances of the February Days. By popular demand – and the people were aware that the programme was no longer dependent on the patronage of the Tsar – the choir and the orchestra in the Marinsky Theatre performed the revolutionary songs 'In Memory of the Fallen', 'Hey Let's Cry Out', and of course the 'Marseillaise'. On 15 March ballet performances were resumed. Here too the audience demanded the 'Marseillaise' and stood up as it was played. In many theatres the first performances after February developed into political demonstrations. Scenes from the revolution were inserted into new productions and revolutionary songs added to scenes of plays within the existing repertoire.[52]

The burial of the victims of the February Revolution provided the stage for by far the most elaborate 'festivals of freedom'. Triumphal parades and civic funeral ceremonies for the 'freedom fighters' took place in towns throughout Russia. Martyrs of the people's cause – who had either fallen in the February Days or were still remembered as the heroic victims of 1905 – were buried or commemorated with great pomp. Here was an exhibition and a confirmation of the new symbolism: the services were a hybrid of religious rites and a new revolutionary ritual – the funeral march with the sacred symbols of the people's cause, the red flag and the 'Marseillaise'.

The funeral of the victims of the February Revolution in Petrograd was distinguished by its size and character. Members of the Provisional Government and the Soviet were in attendance, although there were no priests or religious rituals, both having been prohibited by the Petrograd Soviet. Their absence at what was, by tradition, a religious ceremony

51. P.A. Sorokin, *Dolgii put': Avtobiograficheskii roman*, Syktyvkar, 1991, p. 89.
52. V. Bezpadov, *Teatry v dni revoliutsii*, Leningrad, 1927, pp. 39, 41; Sukhanov, *Zapiski o revoliutsii*, pp. 263–4; *Amurskoe ekho*, 8 April 1917; *Russkaia muzykal'naia gazeta*, 1917, no. 17–18, p. 358; no. 19–20, p. 380; E. Swift, 'Kul'turnoe stroitel'stvo ili kul'turnaia razrukha? (Nekotorye aspekty teatral'noi zhizni Petrograda i Moskvy v 1917 g.)', in *Anatomiia revoliutsii (1917 god v Rossii: Massy, partiia, vlast')*, St Petersburg, 1994, pp. 394–405.

caused great offence to some believers.[53] The Cossacks of the garrison in Petrograd refused to take part in the funeral for this reason. However, traditional funeral rites did influence the burial, and the hybrid of revolutionary and religious rituals which resulted from this event became a sort of template for other ceremonies in towns throughout Russia. The Petrograd authorities were acutely conscious of the ceremony's significance, and this was reflected in the large number of photographs, postcards and film documentaries it commissioned to inform the rest of Russia about the event.

The significance of the occasion was in the act and ritual of the burial itself. The identity of the corpses was of secondary importance. It is unlikely that all the 184 people buried in the Champ de Mars were opponents of the old regime: no one checked the revolutionary credentials of the corpses taken from the city morgues (and indeed many of the revolution's victims were buried earlier by relatives and comrades). Some were undoubtedly 'fallen heroes' of the people's side, but in all probability others were accidental victims of the revolution: spectators or policemen whose corpses were unclaimed from the morgues by their families for fear of reprisal.

From 1918 to 1944 the Mars Field was called the Square of the Victims of the Revolution; the name reflected the situation perfectly. The communal graves became a sacred site of pilgrimage, of homage to the people's 'freedom fighters', in the revolutionary tradition. The cultural and political topography of the capital was recentred around the Champ de Mars. The site was a centre of events on the crucial dates of the revolution – on 18 April (1 May in the new calender), in the June crisis, the July Days and finally on 5 January 1918 – the day the Constituent Assembly was convened. On all these occasions people came to the Champ de Mars to demonstrate their allegiance to the revolution. From 1917 the ritual of civic demonstrations and marches always included a march past its graves. Protests were legitimized by gathering on the graves of February's victims: as if this confirmed the 'revolutionary character' of the protesters' own actions and placed them in the tradition of the 'people's cause'.[54]

The burial of the victims of the February Revolution was a significant symbolic victory for the new order. The day before the ceremony there had been widespread panic in the capital. There were rumours of pogroms by the forces of the counter-revolution, threats of violence to disrupt the funeral, and even fears that the bodies might be exhumed. Nevertheless these threats failed to materialize and the festival was a brilliant success. Despite estimates (possibly exaggerated) that up to a million people took part in the procession, there were no violent incidents. The whole day

53. Filosofov, 'Dnevnik', *Zvezda*, 1992, no. 2, p. 198; OR RNB, f. 322, op. 1, d. 44, l. 80.
54. P.K. Kornakov, 'Simvolika i ritualy revoliutsii 1917g.', in *Anatomiia revoliutsii*, p. 365.

passed reasonably peacefully, considering the number of people involved. Contemporaries proclaimed it the most harmonious public ceremony in world history. 'Hundreds of thousands of people,' wrote Gorky, 'felt for the first time and almost tangibly – yes the Russian people has achieved this revolution, and now is joining in the world's great cause – the construction of new and ever freer forms of life!'[55]

Iconoclasm

In the absence of any obvious counter-revolution – without a real enemy to fight against – the destruction of the symbols of the old regime was, at least for the revolutionaries, the destruction of the old regime itself. Iconoclasm was a central part of February. Demonstrators attacked the visible incarnations of Romanov power: the double-headed eagle; the national flag; portraits and statues of the Tsar; monuments and symbols of Imperial power; and prisons, symbols of its tyranny.

For the crowd in 1917 the two-headed eagle symbolized Imperial rule, so taking control of the image of the eagle was a potent sign of the people's victory. The initiative for this symbolic revolution came from below. As early as 28 February, people had been 'roasting eagles' – a popular joke referring to the setting alight and melting down of Tsarist monograms. Several of the US eagles were also taken down and destroyed by crowds. In a desperate attempt to save their emblems from a similar fate, foreigners attached billboards to their statues and buildings with pleas such as: 'This eagle is Italian.' But it did not deter the crowds. Shop assistants knocked down the eagles from the signs of pharmacists and other retailers who supplied the court. Rags and soldiers' greatcoats were thrown over eagles too large to remove. The eagles on the gates and railings of the Winter Palace were covered with red material. The physical and symbolic removal of the Romanov double-headed eagle was perceived by some to be a sign of the actual establishment of a republic.[56]

By the end of April this symbolic revolution had become institutionalized to the extent that, according to a British colleague, Russian diplomats were 'obliged to suppress all Imperial emblems, strip off eagles from the gates and the façade of the building, hide the Emperor's portrait, strike out "Imperial" from visiting cards and official stationery, etc., and drop all these paraphernalia of Empire which count for much in a country like

55. *Aleksandr Benua razmyshliaet*, Moscow, 1968, pp. 57–8; M. Gor'kii, *Nesvoevremennye mysli: Zametki o revoliutsii i kul'ture*, Moscow, 1990, p. 80.
56. Pitcher, *Witnesses of the Russian Revolution*, p. 47; *Novyi satirikon*, 1917, no. 11, p. 3; G.N. Mikhailovskii, *Zapiski: Iz istorii rossiiskogo vneshnopoliticheskogo vedomstva, 1914–1920*, Moscow, 1993, kn. 1, p. 253.

this where adulation of royalty is counted next to godliness.'[57] As a symbol of authority, the eagle was totally removed in the course of the February Revolution. But it lived on in the state coat of arms adopted by the Provisional Government, albeit without its Imperial embellishments. The eagle's crowns, its sceptre and orb, the St Andrew's Cross and the emblem of the regions of Russia – all these disappeared. The new eagle assumed, as it were, the Byzantine aspect of its original forebear. I. Bilibin, the artist chosen to design the state's new coat of arms, produced sketches of an uncrowned eagle which was to remain the government's official emblem until the Constituent Assembly. It appeared on medals and on money, including the celebrated 'Kerenky' (the name given to 20- and 40-rouble notes printed after August). It was also depicted on the many postcards produced to commemorate the revolution and its government in 1917.[58]

This de-coronation of the double-headed eagle angered monarchists. In a symbolic demonstration against it the graduates of the élite Naval Academy commissioned the production of memorial medals with the old Imperial coat of arms.[59] Most people, however, saw the uncrowned eagles as symbols of the old regime, despite the insistence of the Provisional Government to the contrary. People simply did not draw the distinction between crowned and uncrowned eagles. Consequently hostile crowds continued to attack the offending birds, whether they were symbols of the old or new regime. On 16 March the Special Conference for Artistic Affairs appointed by the Provisional Government felt the need to declare: 'In view of the continuing destruction of eagles on the façades of public buildings, the militia must make it clear that depictions of the double-headed eagle (without crowns) do not represent the coat of arms of the Romanovs.' On the following day the conference declared that 'the destruction of state coats of arms inside former Imperial theatres' was to be prohibited. Contrary to the instructions of the conference, however, the destruction of all types of eagles continued to occur inside the theatres. Some were covered with red material. The eagle printed on the cover of the old programmes was replaced with a lyre.[60]

In Petrograd the state coat of arms was removed from all buildings. A popular pamphlet published by the Socialist Revolutionaries exposed the 'predatory eagle of autocracy' and declared that 'its time has passed . . . Another sign, another symbol will be chosen by the future Great Russian

57. Cambridge University Library, Manuscript Division, Hardinge Papers, vol. 32, p. 168.
58. N.A. Soboleva and V.A. Artamonov, *Simvoly Rossii*, Moscow, 1993, p. 143; *Ivan Iakovlevich Bilibin: Stat'i. Pis'ma. Vospominaniia o khudozhnika*, Leningrad, 1970, p. 308; Malyshev et al., *Bumazhnye i denezhnye znaki Rossii i SSSR*, pp. 81–3, 87.
59. V.D. Dotsenko, A.D. Boinovich and V.A. Kupriukhin, *Znachki i zhetony Rossiiskogo imperatorskogo flota, 1696–1917*, St Petersburg, 1993, pp. 26–7.
60. GARF, f. 6834, op. 1, d. 8, l. 9; Bezpalov, *Teatry v dni revoliutsii*, p. 39.

republic. It will appear before the whole world, not in the form of a bloodthirsty predator, but as two sisters – Land and Liberty.'[61]

The claim that the October Revolution signalled the beginning of an unprecedented 'war with the eagles' is unfounded.[62] The battle with the old coat of arms certainly continued under the Bolsheviks, but many documents of the early Soviet period were stamped, like those of the February system, with the double-headed eagle. There are 'democratic' uncrowned eagles on Bolshevik posters and official signs of the period. The double-headed eagle, crowned by the red star and gripping the hammer and sickle in its claws, even featured in some of the designs for the new state emblem.[63] It stood out vividly on the first Soviet banknotes next to the signature of the Bolshevik G.L. Piatakov, who for a while directed the State Bank. For their rouble notes, the Bolsheviks used the design of the Provisional Government (similar state credit notes were issued at the beginning of 1921).[64] But it was not until 3 August 1918 that the Soviet government prohibited the use of the eagle in the stamps of official institutions.[65]

The public's attitude to the national flag was, if anything, even more hostile than its attitude to the double-headed eagle. To begin with it was not completely hostile, particularly outside the capital where some festivals of the revolution took place under the old flag. But, in time, the same situation as with that of the double-headed eagle emerged in relation to the national flag – with the Provisional Government declaring that it was not a symbol of the old regime and the people continuing to see it as such.[66] Attempts to organize patriotic demonstrations under the old flag were perceived as counter-revolutionary and, at times, were abruptly cut short. For example, the rightist newspaper *Kievlianin* led a campaign for the restoration of the national flag. Two demonstrations were organized which attracted many students and military cadets. But the Left demanded 'decisive measures' to suppress the demonstrations. The workers' section of the Soviet even threatened to deploy 'armed detachments'. The liberal press joined in the opposition – claiming that the demonstration 'was being used by the Black Hundreds'.[67]

Similar sentiments were expressed by soldiers with regard to their regimental banners. In the main this took the form of refusing to kiss the

61. S.I. Barykov, *Slova i dela Nikolaia II*, Moscow, 1917, p. 32.
62. V. Lebedev, *Derzhavyi orel Rossii*, Moscow, 1995, p. 45.
63. Soboleva and Artamonov, *Simvoly Rossii*, p. 143; P.K. Kornakov, 'Kraski voiny', *Rodina*, 1990, no. 10, pp. 26–8, 34, 50–1.
64. Malyshev et al., *Bumazhnye i denezhnye znaki Rossii i SSSR*, pp. 86, 103–4.
65. *Dekrety sovetskoi vlasti*, Moscow, 1964, t. 3, p. 167.
66. *Russkoe slovo*, 29 April 1917.
67. V.V. Shul'gin, '1917–1919', *Litsa: Biografich. Al'manakh*, Moscow, 1994, vyp. 5, p. 144; *Kievlianin*, 23 March; 23, 24, 30 April 1917; *Russkie vedomosti*, 4 May 1917.

old Imperial banner after they had sworn their oath of allegiance to the Provisional Government. The soldiers argued that 'the monograms of the sovereigns – of our immemorial bloodsuckers – were present on the banners'. Old symbols were covered up with red material sewn on to the banners. During a parade in Moscow on 4 March one militia brigade marched under a banner with the inscription 'For Faith, Tsar and Fatherland' replaced with the help of a red strip by the new inscription 'For Faith and Fatherland'.[68]

The sailors of the navy were, ironically, more faithful to the old state symbolism, their revolutionary attitudes notwithstanding. Flying the red flag from the masts of battleships was their expression of solidarity with the revolutionary cause. But this did not extend to destroying the old emblems or the naval (Andreevskii) flag, which was generally left intact to fly at the stern. This had a precedent in 1905, incidentally, when the sailors of the *Potemkin* had carried out their mutiny under the Andreevskii. In 1917 individual sailors and their political organizers, including the radical Tsentrobalt, spoke out in favour of keeping the old flag. The *Aurora* and other ships which supported the Bolsheviks proudly bore its sign. It is true that sailors expressing their dissatisfaction with the policies of the Provisional Government sometimes raised the old flag with a red stripe or replaced it altogether with a red flag. But the Andreevskii, in principle and practice, continued to remain the official flag of the navy until 18 November, when a congress of the naval fleet resolved: 'To raise . . . instead of the Andreevskii – the flag of the "Internationale" as symbol of the fact that the entire Russian Navy is coming, as if one, to the defence of the people's sovereignty in the Soviet of Workers', Soldiers' and Peasants' Deputies'.[69] Subsequently the raising of the old flag was taken as a declaration of protest against the Bolsheviks. It was also flown by sailors on ships loyal to the Whites.

The national anthem was the one symbol consistently associated with Imperial authority, unlike the double-headed eagle or the national flag. When, on various occasions during and after the February Revolution, the old national anthem was sung, it gave rise to bitter divisions of opinion. On 9 March the Commander of the 12th Army at Riga issued special instructions categorically prohibiting its performance.[70] Various attempts were made to compose new words to the old tune – with 'God Save the People' rather than 'God Save the Tsar' – but none proved popular.

68. *Revoliutsionnoe dvizhenie v voennykh okrugakh (Mart 1917 – mart 1918 g.)*, Moscow, 1988, p. 38; Burdzhalov, *Vtoraia*, p. 52. Even school banners had their eagles torn out. See E. Levitskaia, 'Stranichka iz dnevnika', *Proletarskaia revoliutsiia*, 1923, no. 13, p. 257.
69. V. Milanov, 'Andreiskii flag', *Morskoi sbornik*, 1992, no. 5–6 (1746–7), pp. 65–6.
70. *Russkii invalid*, 11 March 1917; *Rabochaia gazeta*, 10 March 1917; A. Wildman, *The End of the Russian Imperial Army*, vol. 1, *The Old Army and the Soldiers' Revolt March–April 1917*, Princeton, 1980, p. 225.

Counter-revolutionary demonstrations made a point of performing the old anthem. 'Opposition to the revolution found expression among the young officers simply in the singing of "God Save the Tsar",' remarked a naval commander in Sevastopol during the summer of 1917.[71] The Imperial anthem assumed the status of a rebel song.

Given this iconoclastic climate, the question arose of what should be done with medals bearing Tsarist insignia. It was a dilemma for the government. Some priests gave up pectoral crosses that had been distributed in honour of the last Tsar's coronation. Soldiers scratched off the picture of Nicholas on their medals, or wore them back to front. This process was subsequently centralized, with thousands of medals from the army in the field being returned to the Mint where the image of the Tsar was replaced by the St George's Cross.[72]

The revolution was also reflected in visual changes to the soldiers' uniforms, once themselves a sign of the Imperial regime. Students of the College of Mines removed from their uniforms the epaulettes and Tsarist insignia awarded to them 'for military service to the needs of defence'.[73] The uniforms of state officials also changed. This was the cause of some confusion. A foreign correspondent walking down the Nevsky was baffled by the appearance of large numbers of casually dressed young people carrying briefcases. It was some time before he realized that these were in fact the officials of the Provisional Government. Such casual attire was not universally approved of. When the Social Democrat N.D. Sokolov, appointed as a senator in 1917, refused to wear full dress uniform – with, as he put it, its 'emblems of slavery' (in this case buttons embossed with eagles) – and appeared for the first time in the Senate dressed in normal civilian clothes, there were cries of protest from his new colleagues.[74] Some vestiges of bureaucratic dress-pride survived the revolution, it would seem.

The question of epaulettes, especially those of the senior officers, took on a special significance from the beginning of the revolution. When the former Minister for War, Sukhomlinov, was taken to the Tauride Palace in the February Days, the enraged soldiers, who considered him a traitor, were prevented from lynching him only by the timely intervention of Kerensky. The soldiers, however, satisfied their anger by tearing off Sukhomlinov's epaulettes in a heavily symbolic ritual (Sukhomlinov later claimed to have removed the epaulettes himself). It symbolized the removal of his power and the fact that, as a traitor, he no longer deserved the

71. Mikhailovskii, *Zapiski*, kn. 1, p. 482. On the demonstrative singing of 'God Save the Tsar', see Burdzhalov, *Vtoraia*, pp. 45, 295.
72. *Russkoe slovo*, 21 March 1917; *Russkii invalid*, 24 April 1917.
73. *Rech'*, 27 April 1917.
74. Pitcher, *Witnesses of the Russian Revolution*, p. 101; V.D. Nabokov, 'Vremennoe pravitel'stvo', *Arkhiv russkoi revoliutsii*, Moscow, 1991, t. 1–2, pp. 70–1, 125.

distinction of his stripes.

Increasingly, soldiers refused to obey officers wearing Tsarist monograms on their epaulettes. To maintain military discipline the Commander-in-Chief, M.V. Alexeev, ordered the removal of such monograms from the uniforms of generals and senior officers on 8 March. This was extended to the lower ranks on 4 April. Soldiers sometimes improvised their own epaulettes to show solidarity with the revolution.[75] They pinned red bows to their shoulders or sewed red material around the edges of their epaulettes.

Later the soldiers came to view all epaulettes as symbols of the old regime. They went against the spririt of Order No.1, which many soldiers saw as the fundamental document of the revolution. As one officer wrote in his diary, paraphrasing his soldiers' interpretation of the order: 'Saluting acknowledges epaulettes which were created by the Tsar: the Father Tsar is no more, so there is no need for epaulettes, and no need to salute.'[76]

Disagreements about the meaning of epaulettes reflected different views on military authority in general and, as such, were both the cause and focus of many conflicts. This was particularly true in the navy. The naval command and ministry were forced to resolve the situation. On 16 April the Minister of the Navy (A.I. Guchkov) issued a decree abolishing all forms of epaulettes. They were replaced with stripes on the sleeve rather like the signs of rank in the British navy. For a time the middle of the cockade, part of the peaked cap, was painted red. But eventually such caps were replaced altogether with a 'soft hat' in the American style. Buttons embossed with the eagle were exchanged 'when possible' with buttons decorated with an anchor. The attitude of the naval officers to these reforms varied considerably. Some threatened to resign as a mark of protest but many seemed to prefer the new uniform.[77] It fitted in perhaps with the Anglophilia in the navy's senior ranks. These reforms almost certainly prevented any major conflicts in the navy. However, some individual officers improvised their own reformed uniforms, with elements of the old and the new, and this often caused more disciplinary problems than it avoided. Further complications arose from miscommunications – both from the capital and between the ranks. In some cases sailors found out about the Guchkov decree earlier than their officers, whom they persecuted as 'counter-revolutionaries' for continuing to wear their epaulettes. In Revel on 16 April, for example, a group of unsuspecting officers had their epaulettes torn from their shoulders in the middle of the street.

Reform in the navy had implications for the army. Soldiers sometimes

75. Burdzhalov, *Vtoraia*, p. 146; *Russkaia armiia (1917–1920): Obmundirovanie. Znaki razlichiia. Nagrady i nagradnye znaki*, St Petersburg, 1991, p. 27.
76. 'Iz dnevnika generala V.G. Boldyreva', *Krasnyi arkhiv*, 1927, t. 4 (23), p. 257.
77. *Ezhenedel'nik morskogo sbornika*, 1917, no. 5, pp. 3–5; V.D. Dotsenko, *Russkii morskoi mundir 1696–1917*, St Petersburg, 1994, pp. 142–7; *Russkaia armiia (1917–1920)*, pp. 28–30.

removed their epaulettes and demanded the same from their officers, pointing out that in doing so they were acting in solidarity with the sailors.
Even before the Bolshevik insurrection the refusal by an officer to remove
his epaulettes was likely to provoke a lynching by the soldiers – and even
in some cases murder.[78] The Provisional Government's commissars actively
supported the campaign against epaulettes. V.B. Stankevich, for example,
stopped wearing his as early as July.[79] Others, such as Kerensky, dressed
in a fashion, without epaulettes, that soldiers took as support for their
own reforms in dress.

On the other hand, as late as the autumn of 1917 there were still
some supporters of the Bolsheviks who continued to wear their epaulettes.
It was not until the Decree on the Equal Rights of All Military Personnel,
passed by Sovnarkom on 16 December 1917, that symbols of rank were
finally abolished. The decree annulled all ranks and titles, privileges and
'insignia of distinction'.[80] From then on epaulettes were only used by –
and associated with – the various anti-Bolshevik forces. The term 'golden
epaulettes' became a form of abuse in Soviet circles, and anyone retaining
the old regalia was likely to be arrested. During the civil war the symbolic
struggle against the epaulettes could assume sadistic proportions: captured
White officers would be tortured by the Reds with mock epaulettes cut
into their shoulders. (The Whites cut red stars into the chests of the
captured Bolsheviks.) The rejection of all rank was a symbol of the revolution
in the armed services and it was only in 1943 that Stalin restored the
epaulette. So deep, however, was the egalitarian rejection of such symbols
that, even then, it met with 'silent' opposition in the ranks.

During the revolution portraits of the Tsar and the Imperial family
were defaced and destroyed indiscriminately. Cheap reproductions and
pictures of artistic value were equally at risk. The revolutionary crowd
scratched out the eyes of the royal visages, slashed the canvases and wrote
slanderous graffiti over them. Occasionally the military and civil leadership
attempted to prohibit the destruction or removal of these portraits. This
could lead to bitter struggles with the crowds which, in turn, became the
focus of a broader conflict over power.[81] In an attempt to avoid such
conflicts the government's officials sometimes took responsibility for the
removal of Imperial portraits. The Ministry of Education ordered that
pictures of the Tsar and his heir should be taken from all schools. Meanwhile,
there were calls from the provinces for currency and postage stamps to

78. Knox, *With the Russian Army*, vol. 2, p. 623; E. Ogloblev, 'Moi korpus', *Kadetskaia pereklichka*,
    1987, no. 43, p. 122. It is probable that German sailors, who tore the epaulettes from their
    officers in November 1918, were following the example of the Russian sailors.
79. 'Iz dnevnika generala V.G. Boldyreva', p. 267.
80. *Dekrety sovetskoi vlasti*, t. 1, pp. 242–3.
81. *Russkii invalid*, 11 March 1917, *Rabochaia gazeta*, 10 March 1917; Wildman, *The Old Army*, p. 225.

be replaced, since such depictions of the Tsar were causing 'doubt and hesitation' among citizens as to whether they could use the coins and stamps. Although large-scale changes of this sort were technically impossible, new denominations were printed without the image of the Imperial eagle, or with, among others, the inscription 'Liberty, Equality, Fraternity'.[82]

Iconoclasm was not limited to urban Russia. Even before the February Revolution peasants had been prosecuted for defacing portraits of the Tsar and the Imperial family. After the revolution this phenomenon became even more widespread. A German prisoner of war wrote home in April 1917: 'The revolution is not readily perceptible, only really in the fact that people are putting out the eyes on pictures of the Tsar, to whom only yesterday they were praying.'[83] Peasants, resentful of requisitions, mobilizations and the death of their kin at the Front, turned to voodoo spells and rituals, 'blinding' portraits to rob them and their real-life subjects of their power.

During the February Days city monuments became a focal point for the revolutionary crowd. They were the landmarks of the old regime's political space; and their destruction – or transformation with red flags and slogans – became a symbol of the revolution as a whole. Monuments and statues that had dominated the Tsar's city landscapes had a significant symbolic value for the revolutionaries. Both in the capital and the provinces they were scenes of ritualized demonstrations of the revolution's victory. In Tver the corpse of a governor who had been killed by the revolutionary crowd was placed at the monument to his predecessor, himself murdered by terrorists in 1906. The governor's coat, a general's, was turned inside out, so that its red lining was on the outside, and hung on the monument next to his body.[84]

The most detested monument to Tsarist tyranny was the prison, and its destruction was a potent symbol of the liberty enshrined in the revolution. The assault on the Tsarist prisons was of major symbolic significance: in the realm of 'eternal freedom' there was no place for jails and their removal was seen as a condition for the establishment of a 'new and better world'. This entailed not only a political revolution but a moral one. As one woman wrote to the Petrograd Soviet shortly after the February Days, it was to be the 'Christian mission' of the Russian Revolution to abolish all the jails, since there was no criminal who could not be reformed.[85] Such sentiments were widely shared. The political prisoners of the Shlisselburg

82. *Russkoe slovo*, 12 March 1917; 'Obzor polozheniia v Rossii za tri mesiatsa (Po dannym otdela snosheniia s provintsei Vremennogo komiteta gosudarstvennoi dumy)', *Krasnyi arkhiv*, 1926, t. 2 (15), p. 35; Malyshev et al., *Bumazhnye i denezhnye znaki Rossii i SSSR*, pp. 78–9.
83. RGIA, f. 1405, op. 521, d. 476, ll. 301, 306, 465, 466 and *passim*; OR RNB, f. 152, op. 3, d. 98, l. 41.
84. Metropolit Veniamin (Fedchenkov), *Na rubezhe dvukh vekov*, Moscow, 1994, p. 148.
85. RGA VMF, f. r–2063, op. 1, d. 7, l. 12.

Prison, for example, having been released in the February Days, demanded that their comrades in captivity, the common criminals, should also be set free – but only if they promised to give up drink and gambling. Indeed, such was the commitment to this high ideal – the closing of all prisons – that many socialists believed it was the essence of the whole revolution. When one 'believing socialist', a long-time member of the Jewish social democratic union, the Bund, found out that prisons still existed in revolutionary Russia, she declared: 'This is not my revolution.'[86]

Even in the prisons which remained in service after February the daily routine was revolutionized. Prison buildings were decorated with red flags. Prisoners were allowed to hold political meetings and even demonstrations outside the prison walls: surrounded by a convoy, they marched around the city carrying flags and banners to proclaim their support for the government. G.I. Kotovskii, the Bolshevik hero of the civil war, played a significant part in organizing the self-administration of the prison population in Odessa. He had turned down an offer of release after the February Revolution so as to agitate for the new regime among prisoners both inside the jail and, on day release, outside too.[87]

During the February Days the crowds tried to capture and destroy the prisons in all the major towns. Prison buildings were set on fire and destroyed. This was usually on the initiative of the crowd itself, but sometimes it was on the instructions of the new authorities. The revolutionary committee of Shlisselburg, for example, decided to destroy its prison blocks. In revolutionary songs, the 'Old World' is depicted as the 'world of coercion' and 'eternal bitterness', the reign of 'captivity'. It was an age symbolized above all by the prison with its 'fetters' and 'shackles of slavery'.

All prisoners in the capital's Kresty Prison were released by 27 February. On the same day crowds began to gather at the Peter and Paul Fortress, the 'Russian Bastille'. No prison was more symbolic of Tsarist oppression and tyranny, and the crowds were naturally convinced, as the sansculottes had been, that this dreaded fortress was still full of 'politicals', heroes of the people's struggle, languishing in its dark and dingy cells. That, after all, was the well-established myth of the revolutionaries' propaganda. They brought up lorries with heavy mounted guns ready to fire at its thick stone walls. The Fortress Commandant telephoned the Duma appealing for help, and Shulgin (for the Duma) and Skobelev (for the Soviet) were sent to negotiate with him. They returned to report that in fact the prison was completely empty – apart from nineteen mutinous soldiers of the Pavlovsky Regiment who had been imprisoned in it on the 26th – and proposed to calm the crowds by allowing them to send representatives to

86. 'Vospominaniia A.M. Maiskoi', private archives.
87. *Pravo*, 1917, no. 10; *Russkoe slovo*, 10 March 1917.

inspect its cells. But even this was not sufficient to convince the crowds that the fortress was 'for the revolution'. Some of the mutinous soldiers accused Shulgin of working for the counter-revolution. There was fighting between them and the fortress guards until, finally, the red flag was raised above this bastion of the old regime.[88] Its capture was a symbolic victory, even if strategically, in the battle for the city, it was not that important.

Changing Names

A significant aspect of the symbolic revolution lies in the changing of public and personal names. Although more commonly associated with the Soviet state, the dissolution of monarchist titles and names after February anticipated the onomastic revolutions of the Bolsheviks. The idea that revolutionary leaders should be immortalized in place or street names also originates in this period. As early as 3 March the city Duma of Ekaterinoslav ordered that the central town square should be called after the chairman of the State Duma, M.V. Rodzianko.[89]

At a session of the Petrograd Duma on 8 March it was suggested that places named after 'Nicholas' and 'Alexander' should 'be given a new name associated with the great days of freedom'. So Nikolai Street was to become 27 February Street, Palace Bridge 'Freedom Bridge', and so on. A month later the city authority issued a comprehensive list of name changes. Monarchist names were to be altered to reflect the events and spirit of the revolution. Mikhail Street became 'The Street of Fraternity'; Alexeevsky Street 'The Street of Renewal'; Palace Embankment 'The Embankment of Freedom'; and Palace Square 'The Square of 27 February'.[90]

Such renaming was not confined to the capital. In Kremenchug the City Duma and public committee ordered that Ekaterinsky (Catherine) Street was to be renamed the 'Avenue of the Revolution'. The status of this thoroughfare was accordingly increased – its connection with the revolution giving it a new importance and dignity. Alekseevsky Street was renamed 'Shevchenko Street', while Stolypin Street became 'Iollos Street' (named after a Jewish politician killed by the Black Hundreds in 1907). The central square in many cities, including Kaluga and Baku, was renamed 'Freedom Square'. Governors' residences were renamed 'palaces of freedom'.[91]

88. A.P. Balk, 'Poslednie piat' dnei tsarskogo Petrograda (23–8 fevral'ia 1917 g.)', Russkoe proshloe, 1991, vol. 1, p. 55; V.V. Shul'gin, Dni, Leningrad, 1926, pp. 162–7; Petrogradskii sovet rabochikh i soldatskikh deputatov v 1917 godu dokumenty i materialy, vol. 1, St Petersburg, 1993, pp. 34–5, 46.
89. Russkii invalid, 8 March 1917. It suggested that a 'monument of liberation' be erected in the centre of the square, its central element to be the figure of Rodzianko. In the Ukrainian town of Ekaterinoslav, the local authorities planned to commission a statue of Rodzianko in the town hall.
90. Izvestiia Petrogradskoi gorodskoi dumy, 1917, no. 3–4, pp. 156–7; no. 5–6, p. 221.
91. Russkoe slovo, 20 April 1917; Rabochaia gazeta, 14 March 1917.

Some cities also changed their names after February. On 13 April the Ministry of the Interior proposed that the city of Alekseevsk should return to its founding name of Surazhevsk. A change in name had in fact already been anticipated by the local City Duma. As well as changing the names of several streets with monarchist titles the first session of the city's Duma on 10 April agreed that Alekseevsk should be renamed Free City.[92] Other towns with Tsarist monikers were renamed in a more geographically or politically appropriate fashion. The new port of Romanov on the Murman, for example, became Murmansk at this time.

The process of renaming took place with particular intensity in the navy. This was due both to the radical nature of the sailors and to the high proportion of battleships given monarchist names. Many sailors found it awkward wearing ribbons around their caps with names that reminded them of the 'cursed past'. The renaming of certain ships after February was seen by the sailors as especially important, since after the 1905–6 naval mutinies the Tsarist government had stripped these vessels of their names. This onomastic counter-revolution had caused much resentment: restoring the old names was a question of redress. The battleship *Potemkin* had been renamed the *Panteleimon* after its mutiny in 1905; the *Ochakov* the *Kagul*; and the *Memory of Azov* the *Dvina*. Returning these old names to the ships was initially seen as a gesture of revolutionary defiance. Subsequently, however, sailors on the *Potemkin* refused to bear the name of Catherine the Great's favourite and, by the end of April, the battleship was re-christened *Freedom-Fighter*.

Socialist influences were occasionally expressed in the new names: the supply ship *Nicholas II* was renamed *Comrade*. More often, however, the new names reflected general symbols of emancipation:

Old Name	New Name
Tsarevich	Citizen
Paul I	Republic
Alexander II	Dawn of Freedom
Mikhail Fedorovich	The Freeman
Alexander III	Freedom
Empress Catherine	Free Russia
Nicholas II	Veche[93]
Grand Duke Nikolaevich	Revival[94]

92. RGIA, f. 1276, op. 14, d. 39, l. 2; *Amurskoe ekho*, 12, 30 April 1917.
93. The medieval city-republican assembly.
94. N.A. Kalanov, 'Nazvaniia korablei revoliutsii i grazhdanskoi voiny', *Sudostroenie*, 1987, no. 12, pp. 46–8; *Russkoe slovo*, 16 March, 21 April 1917; *Rabochaia gazeta*, 17 March 1917; Rossiiskii Gosudarstvennyi Arkhiv Voenno-Morskogo Flota, f. p–661, op. 1, d. 81, ll. 9, 31; d. 133, l. 210.

At one level, all this was a simple changing of names. But at another it was something deeper and more complex. For while it might appear that the initiative for this renaming came from the command, the authorities were acting under pressure from the sailors and their organizations. The onomastic revolution concealed a real one on board the ships.

Commercial vessels also changed their names. Once again, *Freedom* was by far the most popular choice. Some new names given by the shipping authorities were not as overtly ideological. The ferries of the company 'On the Volga', for example, which previously had sailed with Tsarist names, were tamely renamed *Wind* and *Peasant*.[95]

The public image of certain names and titles did not escape the business world. Cafés were renamed 'Freedom', 'Liberty' or 'House of Friends'. Shrewd cinema producers set up new firms with fashionable names such as 'Freedom' and 'Will'. In Petrograd a new cinema was opened called 'The Republic'. Even prostitutes, more ironically, greeted prospective clients on the streets by inviting them to 'share some fraternity'.[96] Others approached clients with the greeting, 'Proletarians of the world unite. Let's go, comrade!'

The onomastic revolution also intruded into the private sphere. The first to be changed were personal names thought to be an insult to the dignity of their owners: 'Lackey' (Kholuev), 'Idiot' (Durakov), 'Snuffler' (Niukhalov) and 'Scoundrel' (Negodiaev). People with the surname 'Tsar' (Tsarev) and 'Gendarme' (Zhandarmov) changed them for obvious reasons. The surname 'Romanov' was widely deemed to be 'improper' and even 'offensive' after February. It was changed more often than any other surname during 1917, with the exception of variants of 'Brothel' (Bardakovym, Badakam, Bardachenko). One citizen, a certain Ivan Romanov, solemnly petitioned the Temporary Committee of the Duma to change his name to Ivan Republican (Respublikanskii). We can assume that people with the surname of the Tsar felt extremely uncomfortable. 'The very surname "Romanov" is now a synonym for every kind of filth, obscenity and disorder,' wrote the Grand Duke Dimitry Pavlovich on 23 April.[97] Almost as frowned upon was the surname Rasputin. Not surprisingly, the name Nikolai – which had been the most common male name in the pre-revolutionary period – declined dramatically in popularity during 1917. Even the surname Nikolaev was likely to be deemed an association with the old regime.

95. *Russkoe slovo*, 21 March 1917; *Amurskoe ekho*, 28 April 1917; *S'ezdy, konferentsii i soveshchaniia v Tobol'skoi gubernii*, Tomsk, 1992, p. 67.
96. I. Marcosson, *The Rebirth of Russia*, London, 1917, pp. 114–15. Marcosson did not reveal the outcome of the request.
97. 'K istorii poslednikh dnei tsarskogo rezhima (1916–1917 gg.)', *Krasnyi arkhiv*, 1926, t. 1 (14), p. 229. On petitions from Romanovs to have their names changed see RGIA, f. 1412, op. 16, d. 531–40, 543, 544; f. 1343, op. 43, d. 359. See also A.M. Verner, 'What's in a Name? Of Dog-Killers, Jews and Rasputin', *Slavic Review*, 1994, vol. 53, no. 4, pp. 1046–70.

Surprisingly, petitions to change the surname Romanov were often rejected by the authorities. This decision was usually justified by the argument that there were 'insufficient grounds, given there are no family connections to the former Imperial household'.[98] Here official and popular perceptions obviously diverged. Many people with monarchist surnames changed them without petitioning the authorities – by forging or buying false documents. Eventually, the procedure was simplified by the issuing of the Soviet decree 'On the Rights of Citizens to Change Their Names', passed in March 1918.[99]

Surnames were also changed for ideological reasons. Non-Bolsheviks with the surname Lenin, or with names specifically associated with his party (e.g. 'Pravdin'), chose names more fitting to their own beliefs. Many changed to names associated with the revolution: 'Will', 'Resurrection', 'Citizen', 'Republic', 'Renewal', 'Blossom', 'Democrat' and 'Freedom'. Some even took the names of popular politicians, especially Lvov and Kerensky.[100] One exiled revolutionary even named his daughter 'Revolution'. Such 'revolutionary names' only became widespread, however, after October 1917. They became the rage after 1923, when the cult of Lenin really took off.

Forms of Address

The February Revolution changed the way in which people perceived the social order. Consequently it necessitated a change in the terms of personal address. The old deferential forms 'Your Honour', 'Your Excellency', etc. were abolished in the military by Order No. 1. Initially those of higher rank had to be addressed as 'sir' (*gospodin*), but later this also became taboo: it was widely seen as an expression of social inequality. Revolutionary tradition held that only enemies of the people were addressed as 'sir'. From 1917 the term was used in a wide variety of gently mocking ways: 'The sirs are all in Paris'; 'There have not been any sirs for several years.' It was also increasingly reserved for foreigners – they were addressed as 'sirs' to distinguish them from Soviet citizens, who were all 'comrades'.

The people of the new Russia were called 'citizens', and their politicians 'first citizens'. For a while the idea of equality was mixed with deference

98. RGIA, f. 1412, op. 16, d. 529, l. 19.
99. *Dekrety sovetskoi vlasti*, t. 1, pp. 520–1.
100. Verner, 'What's in a Name?', pp. 146–70. These renamings became the butt of all kinds of jokes. In a satirical journal, for example, news was printed of a certain Roman Romanovich Romanov who wanted to become Republikan Republikanovich Republikanov (*Trepach*, 1917, no. 2, p. 10).

in hybrid forms of personal address – such as 'sir-citizen' – but gradually the straightforward 'citizen' emerged victorious. It was a direct and conscious reference to the European revolutionary tradition. During 1917, however, the word 'comrade' began to supplant the term 'citizen': it sounded more revolutionary. 'Citizen', moreover, was not deemed sufficiently removed from the official vocabulary of pre-revolutionary Russia: monarchists, for example, referred to themselves as 'Russian citizens and loyal subjects of the sovereign-Emperor'.[101] Prince Meshcherskii called his reactionary journal *Citizen*. And the title 'hereditary citizen' firmly belonged to the Tsarist era.

As early as the February Days the word 'comrade' was used on the streets as a challenge to the authorities, and as a demonstration of support for the revolutionary tradition. Socialist members of the Provisional Government were referred to as 'comrade ministers'; the great people's hero of the spring as Comrade Kerensky. Even the Cossacks and police were addressed as 'comrade'. Witch-doctors in the countryside were said to be addressed as 'comrade spirits'.[102]

The term 'comrade' was a badge of belonging to an inner circle of believers, a truly revolutionary self-identity. 'Comrades' were the leading activists and citizens of the revolution. This anticipated the moral connotations of the title in the Soviet era, when 'comrade' was interpreted and certainly promoted as the term of address by one fully emancipated citizen to another citizen with equal rights. In 1917 this sense of the word was barely apparent, yet enough so for some to notice it. It was for this reason that the word 'comrade', with all its connotations of equality, grated on the ears of monarchists, and was used ironically and sometimes even with contempt by conservatives and liberals. In the lexicon of the Whites 'comrade' had roughly the same connotation as the term 'burzhooi' – a general term of abuse for the privileged – had for the Reds.

From February to October – and Beyond

Many of the new symbols of the February Revolution were adopted by the Bolsheviks. Indeed, most of the Bolsheviks' symbols were inherited from the political culture of the February Revolution. Even the classic Soviet icon of the hammer and sickle, which has always been regarded

---

101. 'Iz arkhiva Shcheglovitova', *Krasnyi arkhiv*, 1926, t. 2 (15), p. 110.
102. *Russkoe slovo*, 14 March 1917; *Revoliutsiia v derevne: Ocherki*, Moscow, 1924, p. 9. The universal use of the comradely greeting inevitably inspired witticisms: a goose, in one cartoon, hails his friend the pig with the words, 'Hello Comrade!' (*Trepach*, 1917, no. 2, p. 11). There is a Russian proverb: 'The goose is no comrade of the swine.'

as of communist descent, was in fact first used, along with the sword, on a military banner after the February Days. During the May Day celebration of 1917 it appeared on banners in its 'classical' form, designed by L.V. Rudnev, without the sword. The hammer and sickle were used to decorate the Marinsky Palace, the seat of the Provisional Government, presumably with its knowledge. A subsequent version of the emblem replaced the sword with a bayonet.[103] Clearly the hammer and sickle meant something to many different political groupings in society, Bolshevik or not.

There were several plans for a new state emblem in 1917. The SR, D.O. Khelaev, suggested the globe on a red banner, framed by a laurel wreath, with each leaf standing for a different ethnic part of the republic. This too anticipated the state coat of arms of the USSR.[104]

Efforts were also made to create a new national anthem during 1917. F.I. Chaliapin proposed one version, using words he had written and music borrowed in part from the military song, the 'Garibaldisty'. However, as an author of the *Russkaia muzikaln'maia gazeta* ('Russian Musical Newspaper') commented: 'Just as the national flag has been replaced by the red flag of the socialists, the "Marseillaise" has assumed for us the role of the national anthem.'[105] It was sung at Provisional Government meetings, at receptions of foreign delegations, and at the opening of the autumn theatre season. Preparations for the June offensive were accompanied by its sound, including Kerensky's famous propaganda tour of the Front.

As already stated, there were two different versions of the 'Marseillaise'. Orchestras performed the classical version but the 'Workers' Marseillaise' was most often sung by the people in the streets. Everybody identified with their own preferred version of the song. The conflict between the liberal and socialist interpretations of the revolution was echoed by a similar conflict between the call to citizens in the French 'Marseillaise' and the call to social struggle in the Russian workers' one. There was a military interpretation of the anthem, which Kerensky particularly favoured; sometimes he even led the singing or conducted the musicians at public performances.

The Provisional Government's attempt to use the 'Marseillaise' as patriotic propaganda could be counter-productive, however, in so far as the 'Workers' Marseillaise' extolled the virtues of the class struggle and the anti-imperialist cause.

The socialists' anthem, the 'Internationale', was heard, meanwhile, with growing frequency at mass rallies and meetings during 1917. On 14 March

103. Kornakov, '1917 god otrazhenii veksillologichekikh istochnikov (po materialam petrograda i deistvuyushchei armii)', kand. diss., Leningrad, 1989, p. 105; Kornakov, 'Simvolika', pp. 358–9.
104. Kornakov, 'Simvolika', p. 363.
105. *Russkaia musykal'naia gazeta*, 1917, no. 19–20, p. 9.

the Petrograd Soviet made a celebrated proclamation 'To the Peoples of All the World', after which the orchestra struck up the 'Internationale', followed by the 'Marseillaise'. This order was deliberate, the leaders of the Soviet stressing by it their adherence to the principles of internationalism. But when the Moscow Soviet of Soldiers' Deputies joined in the proclamation, its deputies limited themselves to the singing of the 'Marseillaise'. Apparently, they assumed that this song was perfectly suitable for a demonstration of internationalism.[106] The 'Internationale' was comparatively novel and unknown in the early days of 1917. On 23 March, during the burial of the victims of the February Revolution in Petrograd, the Kronstadt sailors' orchestra thought it appropriate to play the tune. They were the only band to do so, and were so unfamiliar with it that they had to resort to sheet music.[107] In later weeks, however, the socialist anthem was heard more often.

When Lenin returned to Petrograd in April he was greeted by the singing of both the 'Marseillaise' and the 'Internationale'. On his journey into Russia he had been met at the Finnish border by party activists who sang the 'Marseillaise'. On his arrival in Petrograd the revolutionary anthem was performed again by a military band at the Finland Station. Some district party organizations also arrived with their own orchestras. The Bolshevik V.I. Zalezhskii recalled that when Lenin had finished his speech bands played a 'revolutionary anthem', presumably the 'Marseillaise'. Later in the evening, however, Lenin suggested to his party comrades at the Kshesinskaia Mansion that they should sing together 'Varshavianka' and 'Tormented by Captivity', two of the revolutionary movement's oldest songs, and, according to E.D. Stasova, when someone began to sing the 'Marseillaise' Lenin frowned severely and said, 'Let's sing the "Internationale".' Evidently Lenin was at best lukewarm towards the 'Marseillaise' and much preferred the 'Internationale'.[108]

The reasons are not difficult to find. All the Social Democrats (not only the Bolsheviks) perceived the 'Marseillaise' as a 'bourgeois anthem' of the revolution. 'In our barbarian and backward country a bourgeois revolution is taking place,' the Menshevik V.L. Lvov-Rogachevskii wrote in 1917, 'but the era of bourgeois revolutions in Western Europe is long past. The "Marseillaise" was replaced long ago by the "Internationale", and socialism is knocking on the door of an obsolete bourgeois system.'[109]

106. Sukhanov, *Zapiski o revoliutsii*, p. 267; *Soldat-grazhdanin*, 19 March 1917.
107. E.D. Stasova, *Vospominaniia*, Moscow, 1969, p. 94.
108. *Pravda*, 5 April 1917; Sukhanov, *Zapiski o revoliutsii*, p. 285; *Vospominaniia uchastnikov revoliutsionnogo dvizheniia v Petrograde v marte–oktiabre 1917 g.*, Leningrad, 1987, p. 58; Stasova, *Vospominaniia*, pp. 134–5; Stasova, *Stranitsii zhizni i bor'by*, Moscow, 1957, p. 94; A. Bromhead, 'Russian Diaries, 1916–1917', Imperial War Museum (London), A. Bromhead Papers.
109. *Sotsializy o tekushchem momente: Matirialy velikoi revoliutsii 1917 g.*, Moscow, 1917, p. 2.

Other socialists, like Lenin, shared this distaste for the 'bourgeois' 'Marseillaise'. When the Izmailovsky Regiment arrived to defend the Tauride Palace in the July Days, they struck up a thunderous rendition of the 'Marseillaise' – the same song played by the Kronstadters when they came to demand all power to the soviets. Both sides, in other words, the defenders and the opponents of the Coalition, used the 'Marseillaise' as a symbol of their cause. As they heard the sound of the regiment approaching, the Soviet leaders embraced each other with tears of relief. Standing arm in arm they broke spontaneously into the stirring chorus of 'Aux armes, citoyens'. It was, as Martov angrily muttered, 'a classic scene from the start of a counter-revolution'.

Moreover, the 'Marseillaise' was the national anthem of an 'imperialist' power as far as the left-wing socialists were concerned. This distinguished them from 'social patriots', who recognized the sovereignty of national boundaries and concerns. This difference was enough to lead to clashes – as at a meeting in Paris to commemorate the Russian Revolution, where, as Ilya Ehrenburg recalled, 'some began to sing the "Marseillaise", and others the "Internationale". It all ended in fighting.'[110] For the French, the 'Internationale' was a song of rebellion and internationalism, whereas the 'Marseillaise' was a song of patriotism. It was not until the 1930s, during the period of the Popular Front, that the French communists even acknowledged the 'Marseillaise'.

In 1917 the songs coexisted in Russia. They were perceived as the partners of a united revolutionary political culture. Equally, a performance of the 'Marseillaise' on the Russian–German Front served as the signal for fraternization between soldiers of opposing sides.[111] The feelings of the German intelligence officers (who were directing the fraternization from the German side) when they heard the music coming from the Russian trenches can only be guessed at, but for the Russian soldiers it was a symbol of international brotherhood.

Soviet researchers always claimed that the conflict between the 'bourgeois' 'Marseillaise' and the 'proletarian' 'Internationale' was a symbolic reflection of the political struggle after February. There is some truth to this. Even before Lenin's arrival in April, the Bolsheviks in Petrograd had been considering the propaganda potential of the 'Internationale'. An article by M.S. Ol'minskii in *Pravda* on 10 March argued that the Bolsheviks should encourage the soldiers in all units of 'the Russian army to learn to sing the "Internationale" '. It was written in the manner of a military directive, and even mimicked the official style of military decrees. The

110. I.G. Ehrenburg, *Liudi, gody, zhizn*, Moscow, 1961, kn. 1–2, p. 333.
111. R. Khabas, 'Pervoe maia v Rossii v 1917 godu', *Proletarskaia revoliutsiia*, 1917, no. 5 (54), p. 38; *Istoriia latyshkikh strel'kov (1915–1920)*, Riga, 1972, p. 129.

Bolsheviks, however, were slow to learn the song themselves, let alone to teach it to anybody else. 'Few of us knew the words of the "Internationale",' recalled the Bolshevik N.I. Podvoiskii, at the time of a military conference in June 1917.[112] Yet it was the official party anthem and it was sung at the conclusion of the April Party Conference and Sixth Party Conference in August. Not that the Bolsheviks were the only ones to claim the song: it was also sung by the delegates to the Menshevik Party Conference and to the Third Congress of the Socialist Revolutionaries in 1917. The text of the 'Internationale' was published in song books by a wide variety of party and non-party publishers.[113] Indeed, throughout 1917 there was a good deal of symbol-sharing by all the major parties, particularly of the 'Marseillaise' and the red flag.

In contrast to the February Revolution, songs and music were rarely heard on the streets of Petrograd in the October Days. There are occasional references in the memoirs of Red Guards to the singing of 'Bravely Keep Together, Comrades' – a Red Guard favourite. This was the melody used in a multitude of Soviet films dedicated to the 'Great October Socialist Revolution'. It is possible, indeed even likely, that, in recalling (or inventing) columns of armed workers singing on their way to the Winter Palace, these Red Guard veterans were consciously attempting to present October as a festive occasion, like the February Revolution, and thus just as popular. This desire to romanticize the event is evident in all the Soviet arts of the period. October was depicted 'in the style of Eisenstein', and 'in the style of Mayakovsky': music was heard where there was none. During the Stalinist era 'Great October' was presented by memoirists as an ever more triumphant and majestic event. The effect was to raise to the status of factual history the triumphal and ceremonial version of events which had been drummed for so long into the public consciousness by Soviet propagandists. This version was imposed on official records too. Thus, according to one Soviet scholar, 'in the historic days of Great October columns of Red Guards, soldiers and sailors sang the "Internationale" as they marched to storm the Winter Palace.'[114] This, one may presume, is hardly likely to have been the case. Such a spectacle would not have gone unnoticed by the rest of Petrograd or indeed by the foreign correspondents in the Russian capital who were on the look-out for such colourful events to spice up their reports. Songs were definitely heard, however, at the Second Soviet Congress: after the proclamation of the Decree on Peace the delegates

112. M.S. Kedrov, 'Vserossiiskaia konferentsia voennykh organisatsii RSDRP (bol'shevikov)', in *Oktiabriu navstrechu: Vospominaniia uchastnikov revolintsionnogo dvizheniia v Petrograde v marte–oktiabre 1917 goda*, Leningrad, 1987, p. 58.
113. *Pravda*, 2 May 1917; *Rabochii i soldat*, 6 Aug. 1917; *Trud*, 6 June 1917; *Men'sheviki v 1917 godu*. t. 1: *Ot ianvaria do iul'skikh sobytii*, Moscow, 1994, p. 443.
114. A. Nutrikhin, 'Pesni russkikh rabochikh', *Pesni russkikh rabochikh* (XVII – nachalo XX veka), Moscow, 1962, p. 37.

began to sing the 'Internationale' and then – in memory of those who had fallen – the revolutionary burial hymn, 'You Fell Victim'.

On 3 November John Reed saw columns of Red Guards marching to confront the forces of Kerensky: 'Two thousand Red Guards were moving along Zagarodny Prospect with a military orchestra playing the "Marseillaise" (how well it suited the tone of these troops).'[115] Evidently, then, there were many Bolsheviks, or at least Red Guards, who, in contrast to Lenin, continued to sing the 'Marseillaise' and regard it as 'their' song.[116] Red Guards returning from the battle at the Tsarskoe Selo railway station were greeted by an orchestral rendition of the 'Marseillaise' followed by the 'Internationale'.[117]

Increasingly, it is true, the 'Internationale' began to supplant the 'Marseillaise' as the main revolutionary song. Ilya Ehrenburg wrote to Max Voloshin about the singing of the 'Internationale' during the battles for Moscow: 'The Patriarch went by and sprinkled holy water . . . a unit of soldiers moved towards him, yelling the "Internationale".'[118] During the burial of those killed in the fighting (on the Bolshevik side) in Red Square in Moscow, the military orchestra began to play the 'Internationale' and the song was quickly joined by the assembled crowds. Next the orchestra began to play 'You Fell Victim', and the crowd, taking their hats off as a mark of respect, joined the singing in unison.[119]

The October insurrection gave new meaning to the revolution's songs, and indeed the act of singing them. The Bolsheviks' political opponents, however, did not easily cede to them their songs and symbols, which they saw as part of a universal revolutionary tradition. These same songs were sung in protest – against the Bolsheviks – on the streets of Petrograd on 5 January 1918, the day of the opening of the Constituent Assembly. The singing of the 'Workers' Marseillaise' and 'Bravely Comrades Keep Together' was on this occasion a mark of solidarity with the parliament. According to the *Novaia zhizn'* correspondent, the crowd also sang 'Rise Up Working People' and 'We Will Build a Road to Freedom': 'The words sounded strange from demonstrators protesting against the policies of the Bolsheviks, who considered themselves to be the representatives of the worker and peasant masses.' That evening, before the third act at the Marinsky Theatre, the 'Marseillaise' was played on the demand of the audience, which rose to its feet and sang along to show support for the assembly. After the

115. J. Reed, *Ten Days that Shook the World*, London, 1961, p. 204.
116. In this connection, the fictional hero of one of G. Belikh's stories, 'House of the Happy Beggars', celebrated the coming of the Bolsheviks to power by loudly playing on his gramophone a record of the 'Marseillaise'. G. Belikh, *Dom veselykh nishchikh*, Leningrad, 1930, p. 195.
117. A.Ia. Grunt and V.I. Startsev, *Petrograd – Moskva, iiul' – noiabr' 1917*, Moscow, 1984, p. 255.
118. I. Ehrenburg, 'Savinkov, Voloshin v gody smuty', *Zvezda*, 1996, no. 2, p. 195.
119. Reed, *Ten Days*, pp. 216–17.

curtain was finally raised a member of the audience got up on the stage and made a speech against the Bolsheviks.[120]

As for the Constituent Assembly itself, it was moved by a different tune. After the opening of the first session there was a cry 'from the left': 'Comrades, the "Internationale"!' According to the SR, Mark Vishniak, the cry came from the Bolshevik I.I. Skvotsov-Stepanov. The situation was extremely ironic, for, as another SR delegate recalled, 'for many SRs – and for me too – this anthem was just the same beloved fighting song for our party as it was for the Bolsheviks. Forgetting where I was, I leapt up and began to sing with them . . . It was a magnificent scene, the Constituent Assembly in its entirety, without distinction of party or faction, sang as one the fighting anthem of the revolutionary socialists.' Perhaps N.V. Sviatitskii, who wrote this in his memoirs, had his memory jogged or his recollections censored by the Soviet editors who published them in 1928. Certainly, Vishniak remembers the scene differently, without any such enthusiasm. 'From time to time,' Vishniak recalled, 'Chernov turned towards the various factions and, with sweeping gestures, tried to inspire them and carry them along.' This 'conducting' of the factions was mentioned by other witnesses to the scene. As the *Novaia zhizn'* correspondent wrote: 'The Socialist Revolutionaries had Chernov conducting them, but the Bolsheviks had their own conductor.' F.F. Raskol'nikov, on the other hand, talked of the SR leader using the singing of the anthem as an opportunity to stage a protest against the Bolsheviks: 'at the words, "but if the thunder should strike a pack of hounds and hangmen . . .", he made a gesture towards the Bolsheviks'.[121]

The 'Internationale' and the 'Marseillaise' were also both performed at the Third Congress of Soviets shortly after the dispersal of the Constituent Assembly. In maintaining the 'Marseillaise' the Bolsheviks were appropriating the anthem of February as one of the symbols of their regime. Subsequently, however, the 'Internationale' became the exclusive anthem of the Bolsheviks. It accompanied all official ceremonies, congresses, meetings and parades by the revolutionary leaders. In June 1919, when Voroshilov arrived at the headquarters of Nestor Makhno (at that time still considered an ally of the Bolsheviks), Makhno's orchestra played the 'Internationale'. It was the song of the anarchists as well.[122]

120. *Novaia zhizn'*, 6 Jan. 1918; *Russkaia muzykal'naia gazeta*, 1918, no. 1–2, p. 29.
121. *Uchreditel'noe sobranie: stenograficheskii otchet*, Petrograd, 1918, p. 4; M.V. Vishniak, 'Sozyv i razgon uchreditel'nogo sobraniia', in D. Anin, *Revoliutsiia 1917 g. glazami ee rukovoditelei*, Rome, 1971, p. 458; N.V. Sviatitskii, '5–6 ianvaria 1918 goda: Iz vospominanii byvshego esera', *Novyi mir*, 1928, no. 2, p. 225; *Novaia zhizn'*, 6 Jan. 1918; F. Raskol'nikov, *O vremeni i o sebe: Vospominaniia, pis'ma, dokumenty*, Leningrad, 1989, pp. 338–9.
122. Iu. Siakov, 'Pod znamenem chernym gigantskoi bor'by', *Chas pik*, 24 Aug. 1991.

After October there were many different types of political meeting –
obligatory for workers in their factories, residents in their apartment blocks,
etc. – organized and orchestrated by the Bolsheviks. The 'Internationale'
was played at all of these. This Bolshevik appropriation of what had once
been a pan-socialist symbol could not but irritate the moderate socialists.
As the Menshevik E. Anan'in recalled, there were ways, however, to fight
back: 'At a signal, we all stood up and sang the "Internationale". And
at the chorus we made sure to sing: "this is *not* (and will *not* be) our last
decisive battle". This was all done from a sense of insufferable oppression,
just as it used to be under the Tsars, when we were all made to stand
up and sing "God Save the Tsar".' In the new political situation, then,
just as in the old, ritual obligation could be turned into symbolic protest.
The refusal to sing the 'Internationale' at meetings and gatherings became
a clear sign of anti-Bolshevik sentiment, as was evident in the workers'
refusal to sing the 'Internationale' on the eve of the Kronstadt uprising
in March 1921.[123] Some opponents of the Bolsheviks used the songs of
the underground to create their own anthems. In the Ukraine there was
a 'Bandit's "Internationale"' during the years of the civil war. And
Antonov's peasant rebels in Tambov province had their own anti-Bolshevik
version of the song.

The soldiers of the Izhevsky-Votkinskii Division, made up of workers
from the popular anti-Bolshevik uprising in 1918, sang a song based on the
tune of the 'Varshavianka'. Another of their songs used the melody of the
'Internationale' to accompany its words of protest against the Bolsheviks.[124]

For its short duration, or perhaps even less, the February Revolution commanded the support of diverse political and social forces. It was a mark
of the unifying power of the revolutionary symbols on which it was based.
These symbols had a quasi-religious status in the political culture of 1917.
They represented the sacred ideals of the revolution – liberty, fraternity
and social justice – which could be interpreted in many different ways but
which were, none the less, held in common as a moral ideal by nearly
everyone in 1917. This polyvalent nature of its symbols was the revolution's
principal advantage: by allowing diverse interests to project their own
goals and ideals on to them, it became a force of national unity.

The unifying symbols of 1917 were developed in the revolutionary
underground, whose subculture emerged as the official culture after

123. E. Anan'in,' Iz vospominanii revoliutsionera, 1905–1923', *Men'sheviki*, Benson, Vt., 1988,
     p. 251; 'Kronshtadt v marte 1921 g.', *Otechestvennye arkhivy*, 1996, no. 1, p. 53.
124. V. Bilii, 'Koroten'ki pisni ("chastushki") rokiv 1917–1925', *Etnografichnyi visnik*, Kiev, 1925, kn.
     1, p. 32; *Pamiatkniki otechestva*, 1995, no. 1–2, p. 177.

February. The Russian underground intelligentsia had, in turn, drawn upon the cultural traditions of the European revolutionary movement stretching back to 1789. French and Polish influences were very much in evidence – Poland being a laboratory and one of the main channels for the transfer of European culture to the Russian Empire – and for a while the 'Red Flag' continued to be sung by Russians in Polish.

Yet once this culture of the underground spilled out on to the streets in the February Days, it quickly came to dominate the whole of the country's political sphere. There may have been political pluralism after the February Revolution, but in cultural terms the symbolism of the underground enjoyed a complete monopoly. Any criticism of it was perceived in itself to be a 'counter-revolutionary' act. The revolution was embodied in its symbols.

They were not just commonplace but all-pervasive, dominating popular culture and permeating almost every aspect of people's daily lives. The 'Marseillaise' and the 'Internationale', to take just one aspect of this revolutionary culture, were played on every conceivable occasion: before and after concerts, films, plays, sporting events, political rallies, weddings, funerals, and so on. Restaurant orchestras were asked to perform them. Gramophone recordings were immensely popular, as were the sheet-music versions of the songs.[125]

Such was the domination of the revolution's symbols that even its most ardent right-wing opponents were obliged to acknowledge them. The 'clamorous din' and the 'howling' of the 'Marseillaise' 'grated on the nerves' of the monarchist Shul'gin – yet even he stood up when it was performed. Like many other monarchists, he was sucked into a grudging acceptance of the new revolutionary culture.[126] Such groups had little choice – for there was no real alternative culture of the Right. The liberals, for one, shunned all propaganda for the masses. It is telling, for example, that in 1917 the Kadets failed to publish a single collection of political songs, whereas virtually every socialist grouping, however small, had its own (and sometimes several) collections. The problem was, as Miliukov recalled, that the Kadets 'were reluctant to make a clean break with the political symbolism of the past', believing as they did that continuity was the basis of legitimacy.[127] Yet, as we have seen, the symbols of the past were violently rejected by the masses in the February Revolution. The Kadets were dressed up with nowhere to go.

Because of their almost universal acceptance, the symbols of the revolutionary underground became *de facto* state symbols during 1917. This,

125. *Grammofonnyi mir*, 1917, no. 6–7, pp. 6–7, 8–9, 14–15; no. 8, pp. 8–9.
126. V.V. Shul'gin, *Dni 1920: Zapiski*, Moscow, 1989, pp. 183, 190–1, 197, 210.
127. P.N. Miliukov, 'Pri svete dvukh revoliutsii', *Istoricheskii arkhiv*, 1993, no. 1, p. 171. See also Stites, *Revolutionary Dreams*, p. 82.

despite the fact, which Miliukov was at pains to point out, that there was no legal basis for this creeping invasion of the state, and indeed it contradicted the principles on which the Provisional Government had been established (to act as the neutral guardian of the state until its legal forms were decided by the Constituent Assembly). None the less, government ministers actively adopted – and thus legitimized – the symbolism of the revolutionary movement. The red flag, for example, was flown over the Winter Palace when it became the seat of government. From that point on, if not from February, the red flag became the national one. Equally, the 'Marseillaise', which was played as a greeting for all ministers of the government, as well as for foreign dignitaries, became in effect the national anthem.

The all-pervasiveness and general acceptance of these revolutionary symbols made them a powerful political tool. It was a tool that surely helped to maintain the fragile 'national compromise' of 1917. For without the unifying symbols of 'the revolution' (and indeed without the unifying fear of its enemies which we shall explore further in Chapter 6) it is hard to see the diverse parties of the Coalition burying their differences for as long as they did. In this sense, perhaps, the February Revolution's greatest strength – the appeal of its symbols – was at the same time its main weakness: for these symbols acted like a cloak to conceal the deeper social and political divisions, which, if confronted earlier, might have enabled the moderate socialists, if not the Coalition as a whole, to prevent the collapse of authority which allowed the Bolsheviks to seize power. And of course, in seizing power, the Bolsheviks inherited (or, if you like, usurped) these revolutionary symbols with their mass appeal – symbols such as the red flag which had previously been shared by all the Left, but which from this point on would be used to legitimize the Bolshevik regime as the sole heir and defender of 'the revolution'.

3

The Cult of the Leader

The February Revolution was presented at the time as a 'democratic' revolution. Its leaders based their mandate on the 'will of the people', which would be expressed in the elections to the Constituent Assembly, and in the meantime set themselves the task of instituting democratic rights and government. There were attempts to democratize the theatre, the Church and the schools – in fact every institution of the country from the army to the zoos. The word 'democracy' assumed the status of a magic charm: in 1917 people believed it would heal all the wounds of society. Such was the cult of 'democracy' that it became 'politically correct' to do everything – to dress and speak and think – in a 'democratic way'. Everybody called themselves a 'democrat' – from the army general to the peasant soldier – and some took this to literal extremes. There was a peasant called Durakov ('Idiot') who changed his surname to Demokratov.[1]

The popular rejection of the monarchy was widely perceived as the definition of this 'democratic revolution'. The end of the monarchy was marked by scenes of rejoicing throughout the Russian Empire. The February Revolution was, in its essence, a revolution against monarchy. The new democracy to which it gave birth defined itself by the negation of all things Tsarist. In the rhetoric of its leaders the Tsar was equated with the dark oppression of old Russia, while his removal was associated with enlightenment and progress. The symbols and emblems of the revolution – printed in the press and the pamphlet literature – were the images of a broken chain, of the radiant sun appearing from behind the clouds, and of a toppled throne and crown.[2]

Politically, the monarchy was destroyed by the February Revolution. All its main institutions of power were destroyed overnight. The army

---

1. See O. Figes, A People's Tragedy: The Russian Revolution 1891–1924, London, 1996, p. 358.
2. P.K. Kornakov, 'Simvolika i ritualy revoliutsii 1917g.', in Anatomiia revoliutsii (1917 god v. Rossii: Massy, partiia, vlast'), St. Petersburg, 1994, p. 361.

commanders soon threw in their lot with the Provisional Government. The Church was reformed from within by its own democratic revolution. The provincial apparatus collapsed in most places like a house of cards, and it was only very rarely that armed force was needed to remove it. The police were soon replaced by the civil militias. Even the Okhrana was dissolved. No one really tried to revive the monarchy. It is telling, for example, that none of the White leaders in the civil war embraced monarchism as a cause, despite the efforts of the many monarchists in their ranks. They all realized that politically it would be suicide for them to do so. For as Trotsky put it with his usual bluntness, 'the country had so radically vomited up the monarchy that it could not ever crawl down the people's throat again'.[3]

But if the monarchy was dead politically, it was still alive in a broader sense. The Russian people, or at least the peasants, conceived of politics in monarchical terms. This 'monarchical psychology' did not make them monarchists politically. But it did mean that they were receptive to authoritarian or patriarchal leaders, whose power was projected in either kingly or quasi-religious forms. Here were the roots of the cults of Kerensky, Kornilov and Lenin, all of which were attempts to fill the missing space of the deposed Tsar, or perhaps the vacuum left by the myth of the Tsar as the people's saviour and liberator.

George Buchanan, the British Ambassador, noted this monarchical mentality during the first days of the February Revolution, when one soldier said to him: 'Yes, we need a republic, but at its head there should be a good Tsar.' Buchanan, as usual, saw this as a confirmation of the Russians' political backwardness. 'Russia is not mature enough for purely democratic forms of government,' he concluded.[4] The American Frank Golder similarly noted such misunderstandings in his diary on 7 March: 'Stories are being told of soldiers who say they wish a republic like England, or a republic with a Tsar. One soldier said he wanted to elect a President and when asked, "Whom would you elect?", he replied, "The Tsar".'[5]

It may well be that Buchanan and Golder were writing about the same soldiers. Foreigners in Petrograd formed a close community and often exchanged stories such as these. But we also find this attitude in other documents. Military censors, for example, often found it voiced in insults and slanders against the Imperial family: 'We need an elected tsar'; 'The sovereign should be elected by the top people, like a village elder is elected'; and so on. Messengers sent into the villages to report the news of the

3.   L.D. Trotsky, *The History of the Russian Revolution*, trans. M. Eastman, London, 1977, p. 193.
4.   Sir George Buchanan, *My Mission to Russia and Other Diplomatic Memoirs*, London, 1923, vol. 2, pp. 86, 114.
5.   *War, Revolution and Peace in Russia: The Passages of Frank Golder, 1914–1927*, Stanford, 1992, p. 46.

February Revolution also noted calls for a 'people's tsar'. One paraphrased what the peasants said: 'The Tsar's rule has ended and now the people have complete freedom . . . Soon a tsar will be elected.' Soldiers' letters voiced the same confusion. 'We want a democratic republic and a tsar-batiushka for three years'; 'It would be good if we had a republic with a sensible tsar.'[6] The peasants, it appears, found it difficult to distinguish between the person of the monarch (*gosudar*') and the abstract institutions of the state (*gosudarstvo*). Their conception of the democratic order was similarly couched in personalized terms. It was for this reason that many peasant soldiers refused to swear an oath of loyalty to the Provisional Government: the mention of 'the state' (*gosudarstvo*) in the text of the oath was seen by them as a counter-revolutionary attempt to restore the monarch (*gosudar*'). 'We don't have a state,' one group of soldiers claimed, 'but a republic.'[7]

A clear illustration of this confusion – between the anti-monarchist politics and the monarchical mentality of the peasant soldiers – is given by a certain Menshevik, a deputy of the Moscow Workers' Soviet, in his diary during March. He describes how he went to agitate at a regimental meeting near Vladimir:

> A platform stood in the middle of the field. Two or three soldiers were on it, and a crowd of thousands stood around. It was black with people. I talked, of course, about the war and about peace, about the land – 'land to the people' – and about the advantages of a republic over a monarchy. But when I had finished and the endless 'hurrahs' and applause were over, a loud voice cried out: 'We want to elect you as our Tsar', whereupon the other soldiers burst into applause. I refused the Romanov crown and went away with a heavy feeling of how easy it would be for any adventurer or demagogue to become the master of this simple and naive people.[8]

In this testimony the contrast between the 'enlightened Westerner', who speaks the 'correct' political language, and the 'dark' soldier-peasants, who do not understand it, is extremely suggestive. The 'democratic intelligentsia' spoke a different language from 'the democracy', and the fact that they employed the same words ('democracy', 'republic', 'Tsar' and 'socialism') merely created the illusion of mutual understanding.[9]

6. RGVIA, f.2003, op. 1, d. 1494, l. 14; OR RNB, f. 152, op. 1, d. 98, l.34.
7. D.P. Os'kin, *Zapiski praporshchika*, Moscow, 1931, pp. 110–11.
8. St Antony's College (Oxford), Russian and East European Centre, G. Katkov Papers. 'Moskovskii sovet rabochikh deputatov (1917–1922)', p. 10.
9. The historian N.I. Kareev tells us in his memoirs how he got into a conversation with the blacksmith of the village, where he spent the summer of 1917. 'I want our republic to be socialist,' the blacksmith declared. It turned out, however, that by this he meant that he wanted to retain his rights of property, and that he did not want the village to be ruled by a president

Likewise, although the peasant soldiers spoke in the language of monarchy, this by no means signified that they were monarchists. To be sure, many of them conceived of politics in terms of an authoritarian or patriarchal ideal, as we shall explore further in Chapter 5. Yet this could be reconciled with various political ideologies: monarchist, democratic, anarchist and socialist. The concept of a 'democratic republic' (which could be taken to mean generally 'the new life' or a 'glorious future') could coexist with the concept of the 'good Tsar' in the popular consciousness, at least in the first weeks of the revolution when all such terms were ill-defined. Leaders who expressed or were thought to stand for the people's democratic and socialist ideals could be seen by them as kings.

The Cult of the Freedom Fighter

The political culture of the revolutionary underground, which emerged as the defining influence on the February Revolution, encouraged the cult of the revolutionary leader. The cult of the fallen revolutionary hero was essential to that underground, as each successive generation of recruits looked to them as model 'fighters for the people's cause'. As in pre-revolutionary France,[10] there was a huge illegal literature of hagiographies, histories and legends, broadsides and prints, celebrating the exploits of Pugachev and Razin, the Decembrists, Nechaev, the SR terrorists and other martyrs of the revolutionary underground in Tsarist Russia. The 'freedom fighter' (*borets za svobodu*) figured in almost all revolutionary songs and poems of the underground. He or she was a symbol of 'the cause' – an embodiment of the courage and self-sacrifice demanded of its leaders – from which people derived inspiration and support.

The Menshevik leader Tsereteli recalled the almost religious veneration of the revolution's leaders by the common people during the spring of 1917. Peasant soldiers looked upon the leaders of the Soviet as Christ-like figures who had liberated them. 'They related towards us,' he wrote in his memoirs, 'as if we were saints, since in their eyes we and our comrades in Petrograd had created the miracle of the revolution.'[11] Kerensky, in particular, was worshipped like a saint. The Mogilev Peasant Soviet, for example, sent its greetings to him on 20 May, calling him the 'apostle of the revolution and the liberator of the peasantry'.[12] The cult of Lenin

(N.I. Kareev, *Prozhitoe i perezhitoe*, Leningrad, 1990, p. 268).

10. On the French tradition see especially Rolf Reichardt, 'Prints: Images of the Bastille', in Robert Darnton and Daniel Roche (eds), *Revolution in Print: The Press in France 1775–1800*, Berkeley, 1989, esp. pp. 230–7.
11. I.G. Tsereteli, *Vospominaniia o fevral'skoi revoliutsii*, Paris, 1963, kn. 1, pp. 20, 27.
12. GARF, f. 1779, op. 1, d. 293, l. 293; *Russkoe slovo*, 21 May 1917.

too, although better known for the extremes it reached in later years, had already assumed similar proportions in some quarters of his party during 1917.

In part this religious veneration was created by the propaganda of 1917 – especially the cult of the 'freedom fighter' advanced by the revolutionary festivals in the first weeks after February. Veterans of the revolutionary cause, many of them recently released from prison or returned from exile, were hailed as heroes at these festivals. The longer they had 'sat' (in jails) the higher their prestige. Prisons and places of political exile became sites of pilgrimage. The bones of well-known revolutionary martyrs were even reburied in special commemorative ceremonies.

The leaders of the Soviet parties reinforced their own positions through the promotion of this cult. There was thus, to some extent, a hierarchy of freedom fighters, with each party promoting its own pantheon of revolutionary heroes. Hence the phrase 'true fighters for freedom' (*istinnye bortsy za svobodu*) was used by parties to distinguish their leaders from those of rival parties and organizations. Some parties published pamphlets to celebrate the lives of their fallen fighters in poems, songs and short biographies.[13] Others put out postcards with pictures of their leaders, past and present, arranged like icons on an iconostasis.

The quasi-religious status of this cult was explicit. The freedom fighters were portrayed as martyrs of the people's cause, revolutionary saints, in the propaganda of the socialists. The newspaper *Krasnoyarskii rabochii*, for example, ran an article on 10 March to mark the festival of the revolution in the town, in which it described the 'fallen fighters' of the revolutionary movement as 'people's saints'.[14] The burial of the victims of the February Revolution on 23 March similarly took on a religious character, although priests were specifically excluded from the procession through Petrograd and from the funeral on the Champ de Mars. *Izvestiia* declared a solemn civic prayer for the 'martyrs of the Great Revolution' and pledged to guard their common grave 'like a sacred object'.[15] And sure enough, from that point on the Champ de Mars became a site of pilgrimage. May Day and other commemorative marches in the revolutionary calendar were routed to end up on the hallowed ground. Later on, the Bolsheviks transformed the Champ de Mars into a sacred site of the October Revolution. Newly married couples went there (and still go there) after their wedding ceremony.

13. See e.g. *Pesni terrora*, Petrograd, 1917.
14. *Krasnoyarskii rabochii*, 10 March 1917.
15. *Izvestiia*, 23 March 1917.

The Cult of Alexander Kerensky

Kerensky was the central figure of the February Revolution. He embodied it. A simple listing of his offices – Minister of Justice (from March to April), Minister of War and the Navy (May to August), Prime Minister (from 8 July) and Commander-in-Chief (from 30 August) – does not convey his real authority in the country at large, or the power he enjoyed from the outset in the first revolutionary cabinet.

Kerensky was the real force in the Provisional Government and, in the absence of G.E. Lvov, frequently determined the cabinet's decisions. Miliukov's departure from the government in April strengthened Kerensky's domination of it, since he was the only effective counterweight. But even before then Kerensky was referred to as the 'only . . . man in the Cabinet who had any power' (R.H. Bruce Lockhart), 'the most influential member of the government' (George Buchanan), 'the real Prime Minister' (V.M. Zenzinov), 'the most influential minister' (Z.N. Gippius) and 'the strongest man in the Council of Ministers' (Arthur Ransome).[16] In a conversation with the French socialist Albert Thomas, Kerensky himself hinted that his position within the cabinet was 'special', and that without him everything 'would collapse'.[17] This notion of the Minister of Justice's particular influence was widely shared by the public at large – innumerable petitions containing demands quite unrelated to his official competence were addressed to Kerensky personally. It was a continuation of the old tradition of sending petitions directly 'to the Tsar'.

Some of his contemporaries ascribed Kerensky's influence, and even his entry into the Provisional Government, to the Masonic solidarity of certain members of the cabinet. Lvov, Nekrasov, Tereshchenko and Konovalov belonged to the same Masonic circles as Kerensky. The influence of the 'Supreme Council of the Peoples of Russia' has received a great deal of attention from certain historians.[18] After his election to the Duma in 1912, Kerensky was invited to join the Lodge of the 'Great East', founded in that year. This lodge was exceptional – for the presence of women and the absence of ritual within it. It was less a mystical union than an élite

---

16. Cambridge University Library, Harding Papers, letter from Sir George Buchanan to Lord Hardinge, 2 April 1917, vol. 31, p. 27; Z.N. Gippius, *Siniaia kniga*, Belgrade, 1929, p. 116; R. Abraham, *Alexander Kerensky: The First Love of the Revolution*, New York, 1887, p. 157.

17. P.N. Miliukov, *Vospominaniia (1859–1917)*, New York, 1955, vol. 2, p. 272. Abraham, *Alexander Kerensky*, p. 117.

18. N. Smith, 'Political Freemasonry in Russia: A Discussion of Sources', *Russian Review*, 1985, vol. 44, no. 2; B.F. Livchak, 'O politicheskoi roli masonov vo vtoroi russkoi revoliutsii', in *Mezhvuzovskii sbornik nauchnykh trudov*, Sverdlovsk, 1977, vyp. 56; B.T. Norton, 'Russian Political Masonry and the February Revolution of 1917', *International Review of Social History*, 1983, vol. 28; V.I. Startsev, 'Rossiiskie masony xx veka', *Voprosy istorii*, 1989, no. 6; B.I. Nikolaevskii, *Russkie masony i revoliutsiia*, Moscow 1990; D.A. Andreev, 'Evoliutsiia politicheskoi doktriny russkogo masonstva, 1906–1917 gg.', *Vestnik MGU*, ser. 8, *Istoriia*, 1993, no. 4; L.D. Kandaurov, 'O velikom vostoke narodov rossii', *Vestnik MGU*, ser. 8, *Istoriia*, 1994, no. 3.

political club, whose aim was to unite all the parties for the overthrow of the autocracy. Kerensky played a large role in this lodge. One scholar has even described it as 'Kerensky's organization'.[19]

However, the reasons for Kerensky's broad public influence had very little do with his Masonic links. There was a widespread notion at the time that he was 'the right person in the right place'. This expression was used, quite independently, by people of such diverse political persuasions as Nicholas II, Zinaida Gippius and V.V. Shul'gin.[20] But what did they mean?

Kerensky was certainly well placed to take advantage of the political situation in the February Days: he was both a member of the Temporary Committee of the Duma and a deputy chairman of the Executive Committee of the Petrograd Soviet. According to I.V. Gessen, the decision of the Duma leaders to bring Kerensky into the Provisional Government was influenced by the fact that he already had a prominent role in the Soviet.[21] Likewise, according to G.L. Sobolev, the organizers of the Petrograd Soviet advanced Kerensky's name for a government post in the hope that his authority would strengthen the position of the Soviet.[22] Kerensky's influence was also important in the formation of the Duma Committee – his name was placed second in the official list of members of the committee, after that of M.V. Rodzianko, the chairman. For many contemporaries it was Rodzianko and Kerensky who personified the Temporary Committee of the Duma – just as it was Lvov and Kerensky who personified the Provisional Government. As D.V. Filosofov wrote in the spring of 1917: 'There are two ministers in our government whose very names are symbols of the liberated Russia. I am talking of the guardian of the law, Prince Lvov, and of the prophet and hero of the Russian Revolution, Kerensky.'[23]

At the time when the power structures of revolutionary Russia were being created, Kerensky already enjoyed considerable authority. He was known as a defence lawyer at political trials, as a member of the commission which investigated the events surrounding the Lena massacre of 1912, and as one of the most outspoken members of the Duma. Kerensky was famous enough for his face to be instantly recognized in public – something that could not be said of most revolutionary leaders in 1917. His picture appeared often in newspapers and journals. And the ban on the publication of his speeches during the last years of the old regime simply increased

19. Smith, 'Political Freemasonry', p. 158.
20. Gippius, *Siniaia kniga*, p. 140; 'Dnevnik Nikolaia Romanova', *Krasnyi arkhiv*, t. 2 (21), 1927, p. 91, entry from 8 July 1917.
21. I.V. Gessen, 'V dvukh vekakh', *Arkhiv russkoi revoliutsii*, Berlin, 1937, t. 22, p. 366.
22. G.L. Sobolev, *Aleksandr Fedorovich Kerenskii*, in G.L. Sobolev (ed.), *Aleksandr Kerenskii: Liubov i nenavise revoliutsii*, Cheboksary, 1993, p. 19.
23. D. Filosofov, 'Novyi Stroi', *Sovremennaia illiustratsiia*, 1917, no. 3, p. 18.

his appeal, especially among the radical intelligentsia of the capital. Boris Sokolov called him 'the most popular man in the city'.[24] Many of the rank-and-file activists of the revolutionary underground who marched towards the Tauride Palace in the February Days did so because they wished to see Kerensky and wanted to receive instructions from him.

Kerensky was well known in the semi-legal and illegal circles of the radical intelligentsia. Sukhanov wrote that he acted like a 'professional revolutionary'. During the war years he had been in the forefront of attempts to revive the SR organizations – and many radicals in the capital presumed that these would be the 'centre of events' in the coming crisis.[25] This link with the revolutionary underground was an important reason for his emergence as the central figure of the February Days. Kerensky received essential information from his contacts on the street – and this in turn increased his standing in the eyes of his colleagues in the Duma, even though he possibly exaggerated the extent of his contacts with the crowds.

But however much his past activities and connections helped, Kerensky's reputation as 'the leader of the revolution' was above all a result of his decisive actions on 27 February 1917. Witness his call to disobey the Tsar's decree on the dissolution of the Duma, his speeches to the soldiers in revolt, his order for the arrest of the Tsarist ministers, and his personal involvement in the organization of the movement on the streets. These bold actions – unmatched by any of the other leaders in the Tauride Palace – made him the central figure of the revolution as far as the people of the city were concerned. 'He was the only person who gave himself completely, with enthusiasm and complete trust, to the spontaneous movement of the masses,' recalled Stankevich. 'Only he could honestly and truthfully talk with the soldiers as "one of them".' Sukhanov wrote in a similar vein about Kerensky's unique role – referring to him as 'the indispensable Kerensky of the last days of Tsarism, the ubiquitous Kerensky of the February-March days'. No wonder conservatives such as V.V. Shul'gin regarded Kerensky as a revolutionary 'dictator'. Perhaps Kerensky saw himself as such.[26]

Kerensky's wife conveys the feverish tempo of her husband's actions during the February Days: 'For the first few days he lived without leaving the Duma, where the work went on all day and night. He and the other deputies snatched a few hours' sleep only when they were completely exhausted, sleeping on the sofas and in the armchairs of their offices.'[27]

24. B. Sokoloff, *The White Nights: Pages from a Russian Doctor's Notebook*, London, 1956, pp. 7–8.
25. N.N. Sukhanov, *Zapiski o revoliutsii*, Moscow, 1991, t. 1, kn. 1, pp. 63, 69.
26. V.B. Stankevich, *Vospominaniia (1914–1919)*, Berlin, 1920, p. 75; Sukhanov, *Zapiski*, kn. 1, p. 63; V.V. Shul'gin, *Dni*, Leningrad, 1926, pp. 106, 133–4, 140–2.
27. House of Lords Records Office, Historical Collection, no. 206, The Stow Hill Papers, DS 2/2, Box 8, O.L. Kerenskaia, 'Obryvki vospominanii', p. 4.

But Kerensky's rise to virtual 'dictator' was not only the result of his constant presence in the institutions of power. The political life of the country between February and October was shaped by a coalition of all the so-called 'living forces of the nation' – the Soviets as well as the various committees led by the moderate socialists and the 'bourgeois' liberals. It was Kerensky's role – and his principal achievement – to bring about this national compromise.

Although he was formally a member of the SR Party, Kerensky was by no means partisan. Indeed his political position was exactly in between the two camps of the Duma and the Soviet. He straddled the socialist and liberal camps – and 'personified', as Skobelev put it, 'the coalition of all the living forces of the nation'. Tsereteli noted that Kerensky tried to play the role of a 'national' figure, and that his ideal was 'non-party and supra-party power'.[28] Indeed, Kerensky saw himself as the embodiment of the 'all-national character of the Revolution'. His political fate, his very existence as a politician, depended on the preservation of the Coalition which he symbolized and, more than anybody, brought about.

Yet precisely because he straddled both, neither camp considered Kerensky entirely 'theirs'. Kerensky was not a 'party man'. He was a one-off, a negotiator and collaborator between the parties. This was the sort of supra-party figure the situation called for in the February Days and the weeks that followed, when it was a question of uniting all the 'living forces' of the revolution in a national compromise. But as the parties of the Left and Right grew further apart, Kerensky's 'vacillation' angered both. The Right accused him of weakness and hesitation – failing to take the necessary measures for the nation's salvation – while the Left dubbed him a 'Russian Bonaparte'. Both sides reproached him for 'sitting on two stools'.

But Kerensky's political role does not in itself explain the 'Kerensky phenomenon'. His influence in the power structures was primarily the result of his enormous popularity within the country. To cite Buchanan: 'From the very beginning Kerensky was the central figure in the revolutionary drama, and alone among his colleagues enjoyed evident support on the part of the masses.'[29] Not one of the revolutionaries of 1917 enjoyed that sort of honour. Kerensky was the charismatic leader of revolutionary Russia: to challenge the 'people's tribune' was, in the early days, simply dangerous.

How can Kerensky's 'dazzling' influence be explained? The origins of it are surely to be found in the complete collapse of the country's political institutions in the February Revolution. For it led to a situation in which

28. Tsereteli, *Vospominaniia*, kn. 1, pp. 123–4; kn. 2, pp. 35, 388.
29. Buchanan, *My Mission to Russia*, vol. 2, p. 215.

the charisma of the revolutionary leader could become a new source of authority and power. This peculiar quality of the mass political consciousness is the basis of the 'Kerensky phenomenon'.

Many years later Kerensky himself wrote about the February Revolution: 'That was the historical moment which gave birth to "my Russia", an ideal Russia which took the place of that Russia which had been defiled and polluted by Rasputin and the universally hated monarchy.' There were few revolutionaries who could have said that. Who else could have claimed democratic Russia as 'theirs'? F.A. Stepun, a supporter and colleague of Kerensky, called him 'the only . . . true-born son of the Revolution' among the members of the government. This not entirely dispassionate characterization can be extended: outside the ranks of the cabinet there were very few leading political figures who could have identified themselves so completely with 'the Revolution'. For the liberals the February Revolution was too radical; for the socialists it was too 'bourgeois'. Kerensky alone identified with it. As such his position expressed the emotions of the public at that time – the euphoric and excited mood of the first weeks after February. He was 'sincere' and caught the public mood.

The cult of Kerensky was a product of the political culture created by the February Revolution. He was precisely the sort of politician who was likely to appeal to the millions of ordinary Russians who were newcomers to political life – the soldiers above all. Tsereteli (like other envious rivals of Kerensky) described his admirers as 'the masses of soldiers . . . [who were] not well-informed about anything'.[30]

Kerensky reflected the non-partisan politics of the vast majority of Russia's newly enfranchised citizens. He was not a party man. In this sense Sukhanov had some reason for calling him an 'undemocratic democrat', although by that, of course, Sukhanov meant a demagogue. Kerensky's own particular political convictions were underpinned neither by participation in mass democratic organizations, nor by a knowledge of Western democratic models. He scornfully admitted the latter point himself in various speeches of 1917. In the SR Party Kerensky was seen by many of the veteran party leaders either as a novice or as an outsider. A rare and important exception was E.K. Breshko-Breshkovskaia, the 'grandmother of the Russian Revolution', who openly supported Kerensky (and received an apartment at the Ministry of Justice and then in the Winter Palace after he became the Prime Minister). Her support added to his prestige. None the less, at party congresses he did not gain enough votes to be elected to the Central Committee – and, as a result, Breshko-Breshkovskaia refused to join it. This did not, however, prevent the SRs from widely using Kerensky's name – the 'people's tribune' – in their own

30. Tsereteli, *Vospominaniia*, kn. 1, pp. 121–2.

political campaigns; and this in itself contributed to the cult. Indeed the British agent R.B. Lockhart put down the party's success in the Moscow city Duma elections in June to 'the magical influence of the name of Kerensky'.[31]

Kerensky did not have fixed views on labour or agrarian questions, issues which acquired crucial importance as politics developed on party lines. At a later stage his lack of strong connections with political parties or with tried and tested political colleagues would have serious consequences for him. However, in the initial phase of the revolution, not to be strongly identified with any party was a kind of political trump card. 'Strength lies in unity' was one of the most popular slogans of the spring. To be 'partisan' was seen as a threat to that unity. The politicized masses were irritated by inter-party arguments and polemics. Kerensky's style, in short, corresponded to the conciliatory spirit of fraternity and national unity – the spirit of *sobornost'* – that marked out that first euphoric spring. In the words of Tatiana Gippius: 'Thank God that *sobornost'* triumphs over *partiinost'*.'[32]

Kerensky's style also corresponded to the early festive spirit of the revolution. At a time such as this when politics became in part a form of theatre, the pathos of accomplished orators was a factor of political significance. Kerensky, in this sense, made a real contribution to the Soviet and the government. He was a great orator – not so much in the parliamentary context, which demanded eloquence and intellectual balance, but in the sense that could appeal to the crowds. His speeches were fiery and emotional. They were not concerned with detailed policies but with moral principles and spiritual values. They often sounded more like the preachings of a priest than the prescripts of a politician. In his youth Kerensky had wanted to become an actor (he had even trained as an opera singer). His speeches were full of dramatic pathos, theatrical gestures, and even fainting fits (these were genuine but Kerensky somehow managed to time them to coincide with the climax of his speech). All this tugged on the heart-strings of his audience. Sukhanov called him an 'impressionist-politician' who could catch instinctively the mood of an audience, reflect it brilliantly and thereby amplify that mood.[33] Trotsky, in a long-forgotten article of August 1917, enviously explained the success of Kerensky's speeches by the effect they created in his listeners: 'they made each one of them believe that he himself was speaking from the tribune'.[34] High praise indeed

31. PRO, Foreign Office, 371, 3000, no. 229108, p. 4.
32. Figes, A People's Tragedy, p. 352.
33. Sukhanov, Zapiski, kn. 1, p. 70.
34. L. Trotskii, 'Itogi i perspektivy', Proletarii, 15 Aug. 1917.

from such a brilliant orator. Chernov echoed this idea of Kerensky merging with his audience:

> Revolutionary epochs are epochs of mass hysteria, of psychological epidemics, and the leaders of the crowd have to play on this psychology. They have to be able to whip the people up with the force of their oratorical passion. Leaders such as these are often born actors: consciously or not they find their way to the people's hearts by the theatricality of their words and gestures. There was a lot of this acting ability in Kerensky – it helped him to give the deepest expression to the spiritual feelings of his audience.[35]

At 'concert-meetings' (at which speeches by politicians would be inter-spersed with performances by actors) Kerensky was the undoubted 'star'. People went 'to see Kerensky' above all – and his performances were fre-quently described as creating a 'frenzy of enthusiasm' or 'mass hysteria' among the audience.

The Bolsheviks of course took a more caustic view, comparing him on his propaganda trips to a prima donna and playing on the theme of the femininity which would be so vital to Kerensky's downfall (on which more below): 'There is a huge car adorned with red roses, and sitting in it, wallowing in the soft petals, Kerensky lies on a pillow. What is this? The entry of a ballerina or the official tour of a minister?' Yet even this cruel cartoon sketch communicates the atmosphere of triumph surrounding the appearances of Kerensky.[36] Many politicians tried to copy Kerensky's style – including the Bolshevik commissar Dmitrii Furmanov, as he himself acknowledged in his diary on 29 May 1917.

The revolution had an immediate effect on Kerensky's public image. The 'people's minister' refashioned his dress style to present a more democratic appearance – and this contributed to his cult. In press reports he appeared as the 'Minister Democrat', the 'Minister Socialist' or 'Comrade Minister'. Kerensky made a point of shaking hands with porters, doormen and messengers in government buildings, so that it was said that 'he greets everyone in the same democratic manner'. He won the hearts of provincial delegates who made the pilgrimage to Petrograd to see him, by talking to them all in the same 'familiar and friendly way'.

According to Miliukov, Kerensky once declared that the masses would not recognize power 'in a suit'. In some post-revolutionary photographs Kerensky appeared in a 'bourgeois' suit and tie, but he quickly 'democratized' his appearance by dressing in a black tunic, which to Lockhart looked

---

35. V. Chernov, *Rozhdenie revoliutsionnoi Rossii (fevral'skaia revoliutsia)*, Paris, 1934, p. 332.
36. *Kievlianin*, 3 July 1917.

like 'skiing kit over a black Russian workman's blouse'. Even at this early stage there was a noticeable 'militarization' of Kerensky's appearance, which Stepun regarded as a 'tribute to the revolutionary epoch and his role within it'.[37] After he had been made War and Navy Minister, Kerensky wore a semi-military costume: at the Front he appeared in a field shirt and puttees; but otherwise he wore a finely tailored field jacket, officer's breeches and knee-high leather boots. Kerensky could thus be considered to have started the fashion for semi-military dress adopted by the early Soviet *nomenklatura*. In the 1920s such jackets became known as *vozhdevki* ('leaders' suits'), and then as *Stalinki* ('Stalin suits'). In Communist China, where Mao was to adopt the military tunic, they were known as the 'Lenin suit'.

Kerensky took great care over his personal appearance, and it was a huge source of pride for him. It was all part of his vanity – and of his awareness of the importance of public image to the revolutionary minister. Even at the height of the fighting during the October Days, when he appeared before the Cossacks during the battle for Gatchina against the Red Guards, Kerensky made sure to wear his favourite tunic, as he still recalled in his memoirs fifty years later, 'the one to which the people and the troops had grown so accustomed', and to 'salute, as I always did, slightly casually and with a slight smile'. During his famous tours of the Front, Kerensky even wore his right arm in a sling (some people joked that he had worn it out by too much hand-shaking). Perhaps it was an attempt to echo the image of Napoleon. In any case, it was a *coup de théâtre*. Initially the pose was enthusiastically welcomed by his adoring public – and Kerensky was often photographed in the 'Napoleonic pose' – but later on it became a source of caricature.

It has been observed many times that one cannot fully grasp the effect of Kerensky's speeches on the basis of their textual content alone. However, they do give an impression of Kerensky's style as a politician. Both his famous ('rebellious slaves') speech at the Conference of Delegates from the Front, and his strange speech at the closure of the Moscow State Conference were a kind of public confession, which his detractors described as 'hysterical ravings'. According to Mel'gunov, many at the latter conference thought Kerensky had lost his mind, and A.I. Shingarev commented that 'Kerensky was either playing Hamlet, or he had lapsed into the psychopathic hysteria of Fedor Ivanovich' (Tsar Fedor I). Kerensky saw himself as a 'moral politician', for whom not only pragmatic success, but also sincerity and fidelity to a certain ethical position were important. This could be seen particularly clearly in his attitude to the death penalty and to the use of force in politics. He knew that many of his political

37. F. Stepun, *Byvshee i nesbyvsheesia*, Moscow/St Petersburg, 1995, p. 332.

friends and supporters would judge and assess him as a 'moral politician', a person with 'clean hands'.

This is not surprising: the Petersburg Religious-Philosophical Society, whose meetings Kerensky had occasionally attended, considered political problems through a religious-ethical prism. Like many other intellectuals, Kerensky had a syncretic (moral-religious-political) consciousness. It was from this point of view that the people from that circle initially assessed him. According to Berdiaev, when Andrei Belyi met Kerensky during the spring of 1917, the poet used the expression 'the birth of the new man' – a phrase used by many representatives of the Russian 'silver age'.[38] Even Kerensky's opponents considered sincerity his main virtue.

This does not mean that in his speeches and his actions Kerensky was always sincere and above politicking. As early as March and April 1917, he gave contradictory interpretations of the Soviet and its political role to different audiences. He was a master of political intrigue. However, the image, appearance and reputation of a 'moral' politician were very important to Kerensky. In the political culture of 1917 his 'confessional speeches' were absolutely natural. Their 'passionate sincerity' corresponded to the mood of the moment.

The mass political consciousness of the first months of the revolution was also a syncretic moral-religious-political consciousness. This was the basis of the Kerensky cult. Soldiers at the Front admitted that they read Kerensky's speeches 'not without a trembling of the soul', and that they considered them to be the 'most sincere speeches coming from the soul of the sincerest man'. At the other end of the social spectrum the geographer Shokal'skii believed that Kerensky was 'completely sincere . . . unlike the demagogues Chernov and Skobelev'. As E.H. Wilcox, the Petrograd correspondent of the *Daily Telegraph*, put it in the spring of 1917:

> He became the personification of everything that was good and noble in Russia. He was no longer the leader of a political party, but the prophet of a new faith, the highest priest of a new doctrine, which were to embrace all Russia, all mankind . . . Kerensky may have been by nature little more than a mediocrity, but he had been fired by the revolutionary enthusiasm which surrounded him and inspired by a fervent and profound belief in the religion of freedom. Russia had a new and great message of hope for the world, and he was to be its bearer. Under the sense of his high mission, his physical and mental powers were purified and enhanced.[39]

Wilcox himself was, of course, in part under the spell of the 'Kerensky

38. N.A. Berdiaev, *Samopoznanie*, Leningrad, 1991, pp. 192, 223.
39. Pitcher, *Witnesses of the Russian Revolution*, London, 1994, p. 236.

phenomenon'. But his words convey the sense in which Kerensky had come to symbolize, as its high priest, the cult of the February Revolution. Even official publications of the Church glorified Kerensky.[40]

The 'master of men's minds', the creative and artistic politician – these were the other images of Kerensky in 1917. He was even called 'the poet of the revolution'.[41] Acts such as throwing flowers (a gesture copied from the theatre) were in keeping with this artistic pose – as were his bows and kisses to the audience at political meetings. On one occasion he even took up the conductor's baton of the Volynskii regimental orchestra. All this was consistent with the theatrical style of political life in 1917. But such behaviour can also be explained in terms of national cultural-political traditions. For the Russian intelligentsia, art, and particularly literature, were surrogates for politics and ideology: the aestheticization of politics was a corollary of the politicization of aesthetics. It is not surprising that some of Kerensky's supporters referred to themselves as his 'admirers' and 'worshippers', as if he was some sort of performing artist.

A striking feature of Kerensky's speeches was his notion that he had been 'chosen'. 'Kerensky believed that he was summoned to be "the soul" of the revolution, "the uncrowned king" of the hearts and minds of Russia,' observed Chernov, 'a man whom the people would worship and to whom they will say: "Lead us! Show us the way!"' Tsereteli similarly noted Kerensky's conviction 'that he was a providential figure, destined to save Russia'.[42] Miliukov wrote that Kerensky 'identified the Revolution with his own person'.[43] This malicious assessment contains an element of truth. Kerensky did regard himself as a unique and irreplaceable political leader, as the personification of 'Russian democracy'. He often claimed that he had been called to power 'by the will of the people', that 'the will of the Russian people summoned me to stand at the head of the Russian state'.[44] He frequently identified his own person with the revolution. 'I will not allow the people to distrust me,' Kerensky declared preposterously at a meeting of the soldiers section of the Petrograd Soviet at the end of March. 'I will not allow the entire Russian Revolution to be insulted by such an insult against me.' (The response of the soldiers satisfied Kerensky: 'The army believes in you, Alexander Fedorovich, as the leader of Russian democracy.' And Kerensky was carried in triumph from the hall on the shoulders of the delegates.[45]) Kerensky often claimed that he was the only

40. See e.g. *Vserossiiskii tserkovno-obshchestvennyi vestnik*, 19 July 1917; *Svobodnaia tserkov'*, 28 July 1917.
41. A. Turov, 'Poet revoliutsii (Kerenskii)', *Svobodnaia Rossiia*, 12 June 1917.
42. Chernov, *Rozhdenie revoliutsionnoi Rossii*, p. 334; Tsereteli, *Vospominaniia*, t. 2, p. 348.
43. P.N. Miliukov, *Rossiia na perelome*, Paris, 1927, vol. 1, p. 104.
44. A.F. *Kerenskii ob armii i voine*, Odessa, 1917, pp. 12, 20; A.F. Kerenskii, *Prikazy i rechi pervogo russkogo voennogo i morskogo ministra-sotsialista A.F. Kerenskogo*, n. p., 1917, p. 5.
45. *Petrogradskii sovet rabochikh i soldatskikh deputatov v 1917 godu: Protokoly*, t. 1, pp. 588, 590.

alternative to chaos and dictatorship. He demanded not only trust but faith. In his speeches there were two political subjects: Kerensky himself, the revolutionary leader, and the revolutionary people. Those closest to him regarded him in the same way. 'All of Russia,' recalled his wife, O.L. Kerenskaia, 'immediately recognized its leader in Kerensky . . . They knew, loved and believed in him.'[46]

On the other hand there were more objective politicians who equally recognized Kerensky's unique role. I.V. Gessen wrote that 'the revolution revolved around Kerensky', and the famous banker Putilov declared in 1917 that Kerensky was 'the only strong personality the revolution has produced'.[47]

Public acclaim, moreover, reinforced his sense of destiny. The press called Kerensky 'the knight of the revolution', 'the lion heart', 'the first love of the revolution', 'the people's tribune', 'the genius of Russian freedom', 'the sun of Russia's freedom', 'the people's leader', 'the leader of freedom', 'the saviour of the fatherland', 'the hero-minister', 'the prophet and hero of the revolution', 'the Prometheus of the Russian Revolution', 'the good genius of free Russia', 'the leader of the Russian Revolution', and 'the pride and joy of the revolution'. (This last phrase was later used by Trotsky to describe the Kronstadt sailors.) By June 1917 'Long live the people's leader Kerensky!' had become almost an official greeting. It was used by Kerensky's future opponent L.G. Kornilov to greet him on a visit to the Front.[48]

Special badges and medals of Kerensky – modelled on those to commemorate the Imperial family – were produced for mass circulation, along with postcards of the 'people's minister'. One of the badges was particularly telling: on one side there was 'a depiction of A.F. Kerensky bedecked with flowers, looking to the right'; and on the reverse the slogan was inscribed: 'the glorious, wise, true and beloved leader of the people – 1917'.[49] Similar badges were later made of Lenin. The same factory produced all these badges – of Nicholas, Kerensky and Lenin.

It should be borne in mind that many of the most prominent representatives of the intelligentsia took part in this cult. Kerensky had connections in many of the clans of the radical intelligentsia through friendship as well as personal and professional relationships. Consequently, he was 'their' man in the world of politics. Kerensky had the authority of the intelligentsia on his side, and his cult was, in this sense, a manifestation

46. Kerenskaia, 'Obryvki vospominanii', Box 8, p. 4.
47. Gessen, 'V dvukh vekakh', pp. 366–7; *Svobodnaia Rossiia*, 12 June 1917.
48. Abraham, *Alexander Kerensky*, p. 218.
49. O.V. Kharitonov and V.V. Groshkov (eds), *Russkaia armiia, 1917–1920: Obmundirovanie, znaki razlichiia. Nagrady i nagradnye znaki*, St Petersburg, 1991, pp. 47–8; V.D. Kritsov, *Avers no. 2: Sovetskie znachki i zhetony*, Moscow, 1996, pp. 172–3.

of their strong caste solidarity. It was no accident that in 1917 he was elected to such organizations as the Free Economic Society and the Teachers' Union, bastions of the intelligentsia. He was regarded as an 'intellectual-politician', as both Dybenko and M.M. Zoshchenko noted. Subsequently caricatures of Kerensky played a certain role in inflaming anti-intellectual attitudes in Soviet Russia.[50]

The poets Marina Tsvetaeva, P.A. Olenin-Volgar' and A.S. Roslavlev all wrote poems dedicated to Kerensky during 1917. Tsvetaeva felt moved to compare Kerensky with Napoleon:

And someone, falling on the map,
Does not sleep in his dreams.
There came a Bonaparte
In my country.[51]

Repin painted Kerensky's portrait. Vladimir I. Nemirovich-Danchenko, K.S. Stanislavskii and the collective of the Moscow Arts Theatre addressed Kerensky thus: 'you personify the ideal of the free citizen, which the human soul has cherished throughout the ages, and which the poets and the artists of the world have passed on from generation to generation'. The writer Vasilii I. Nemirovich-Danchenko described the impression made upon him by a speech by Kerensky: 'When you listen to him, you feel as if all your nerves are stretching out towards him and joining with his in one knot.' Academician S.A. Vengerov wrote: 'I am always irritated when they call Kerensky the Russian Danton. He is Kerensky, and that is enough to make him immortal.' A.I. Kuprin called Kerensky 'the people's heart': 'In every age and among all nations in severely testing times, there has been an inscrutable and direct spiritual receiver, a divine resonator, a mysterious mouthpiece for the people's will, which I call the living, beating heart of the people.'[52]

One cannot help noticing that these are not purely political views of Kerensky – they are combined with ethical and aesthetic judgements. Some of these judgements reflect an assessment of the immediate political situation, but many of the writers were being perfectly sincere. According to Gippius, even in the autumn of 1917 certain members of the Petrograd intelligentsia regarded Kerensky as 'sacred' and would not tolerate any criticism of him. Of course, many intellectuals had other views, but Kerensky was still very popular in that milieu.

The Kerensky cult became the most important factor in Russian political

50. P.E. Dybenko, *Miatezhniki (Iz vospominanii o revoliutsii)*, Moscow, 1923, p. 62; M. Zoshchenko, 'Besslavnyi konets', *Literaturnyi sovremennik*, 1938, no. 1, pp. 223–63.
51. M. Tsvetaeva, *Stikhotvorenia i poemy*, New York, 1982, vol. 2, p. 63.
52. *Russkoe Slovo*, 30 May 1917; *Svobodnaia Rossiia*, 12 June 1917.

life. Lockhart wrote that 'for four months [he] was worshipped as a god'. Once he had become War Minister, despite his completely non-military past, he enjoyed enormous influence in the army. 'Kerensky is the idol of the army,' wrote a journalist in June 1917, at the climax of his cult and just before the offensive at the Front. 'His name resounds from the Riga positions to the Danube. The soldiers' resolutions, appeals and addresses constantly refer to his authority – Comrade Kerensky says this. . . . , Comrade Kerensky says that . . . , Our dear Kerensky orders. . . . – That is all the soldiers need to know.'[53] (The similarity between this passage and later reports of Soviet leaders' visits is striking.) During Kerensky's tour of the Front he was hailed as a hero everywhere. Soldiers carried him shoulder-high, pelted him with flowers and threw themselves at his feet. An English nurse watched in amazement as they 'kissed him, his uniform, his car, and the ground on which he walked. Many of them were on their knees praying; others were weeping.'[54] This kind of religious adulation had not been seen in Russia since the days when peasants believed in the 'Father-Tsar'.

The resolutions of military committees referred to Kerensky as 'the people's minister', 'the irreplaceable leader of the revolutionary forces', 'a tireless fighter for an idea', 'beloved leader', 'the true leader of Russian democracy', 'the symbol of democracy' and 'our supreme leader'. Of course, the positions of army organizations did not always coincide with the attitudes of the rank-and-file. However, these sentiments are echoed in letters from ordinary soldiers: 'I live in the trenches, but I forget all my troubles and am happy that at the head of our people's revolutionary army there is such a glorious and beloved leader as Minister Kerensky.' His speeches were regarded as 'the most sincere, coming from the soul of the most sincere person'.[55]

So, it seems, in a matter of a few weeks after the most radical anti-monarchist revolution in history, there emerged a cult of the revolutionary leader which went far beyond the adulation of the Tsars. What is more, all this happened without any external compulsion – the cult of Kerensky developed quite spontaneously – and within a climate of democracy.

'The Kerensky phenomenon' was created by three main factors: the 'people's minister' himself, the propagandists of his cult, and the political culture of his audience. The creators of the cult adopted a variety of models. The image of Kerensky as leader was influenced by the tradition of the leader of the liberation movement, the image of the artist as the master of men's minds, the militarist tradition of the war leader, and the

53. A.G. Golikov, 'Fenomen Kerenskogo', *Otechestvennaia istoriia*, 1992, no. 5, p. 68; V. Iur'ev, 'Vozhd' armii' *Novaia Zhizn'*, Ekaterinodar, 28 June 1917; Abraham, *Alexander Kerensky*, p. 200.
54. F. Farmborough, *Nurse at the Russian Front*, London, 1977, pp. 269–70.
55. GARF, f. 1778, op. 1, d. 83, l. 95; d. 85, l. 7; d. 90, l. 50; f. 1779, op. 1, d. 293, l. 60.

ancient Russian tradition of the saintly prince. Indeed this syncretic ideal of the politician-artist and military leader was shared by other leader cults (e.g. those of Hitler and Churchill). The February Revolution, moreover, created a situation in which the law ceased to be the source of power. The state, meanwhile, lost its monopoly on the use of force, especially after the Provisional Government declared a break from the Tsarist traditions of coercion. In such circumstances the personal authority of the revolutionary leader – his public image – acquired real importance in the exercise of power. Without law or coercion, power rested on the third of Max Weber's trilogy – authority. This was especially the case in 1917, when Russia's political culture remained firmly rooted in monarchical traditions. The institutions, the psychology, even the language of political democracy had yet to be rooted in Russia's virgin political soil. Most of the common people still conceived of politics in monarchical terms – and they looked towards a charismatic leader to represent, uphold and defend their revolutionary ideals. Many of the peasants, according to observers, believed Kerensky was the 'new Tsar'.

The Fall of Kerensky

The cult of the leader had its disadvantages: Kerensky would personally take the blame for the mistakes of his government. In the climate of 1917, when euphoria could quickly turn to anger, it did not take much for the public to transform its idols into demons; and this was the case with Kerensky.

His opponents on both the Left and the Right increasingly directed their criticisms against Kerensky in person, once he had become War Minister. The authority of the 'people's minister' was undermined by the failure of the June offensive, which became known as the 'Kerensky offensive'. He came to personify the military catastrophe and the political chaos which followed on from it.

More than anyone, Kerensky was reponsible for launching the offensive. Brusilov, the Commander-in-Chief, had serious concerns about the morale of the troops, and as the time of the offensive approached he warned Kerensky of his growing doubts. But the War Minister ignored all his warnings. He was convinced of the need for an offensive – not just to fulfil the government's commitments to the Allies and strengthen its campaign for a general peace, but to rally 'the democracy' behind it for the defence of the nation's liberties – and there was no room for last-minute doubts.[56] Brusilov was not the only one to be concerned. Many people

56. See Figes, *A People's Tragedy*, pp. 414–18.

at the time regarded the offensive as adventurist, as something forced upon the government by the Allies. Kerensky himself refuted these ideas in several interviews. He thus took personal responsibility for the launching of the offensive. Indeed, he staked his reputation on its success.

Why did Kerensky gamble in this way? It appears that he had no real idea of the poor state of the front-line troops' morale. The adulation which he had received on his tours of the Front had convinced Kerensky that the soldiers were willing and eager to fight. Fifty years later, in his memoirs, he still insisted that a 'healthy mood of patriotism at the Front had become a definite force'. But this was far from the truth. Kerensky's visits did not always bring him into contact with a representative cross-section of the army. To be sure, he could have a powerful effect at soldiers' meetings. His speeches conjured up the sweet illusion of a victorious end to the war with one more heroic heave, and a weary soldier might well be tempted to believe in this, even if deep down he knew it to be false, simply because he wanted to. But outside these meetings, among the vast majority of the rank-and-file, the mood was much more negative. Kerensky was frequently heckled by such troops during his trips to the Front, yet he never seemed to register the warning this conveyed. On one occasion near Riga, a soldier was pushed forward by his mates to question the Minister. 'You tell us we must fight the Germans so that the peasants can have the land. But what's the use of us peasants getting land if I am killed and get no land?' Kerensky had no answer – and there was none – but ordered the officer in command of this unit to send the soldier home: 'Let his fellow-villagers know that we don't need cowards in the Russian Army.' The soldier could not believe his luck, and at once fainted; while the officer scratched his head in disbelief. How many more men would have been sent home on this basis? It was clear that Kerensky saw the soldier as an exception, of whom he could make an example. He did not seem to realize that there were millions of others just like him. Even stranger is the fact that, half a century later, Kerensky still related the episode as a propaganda victory for himself.[57] In this sense he was and always remained the victim of his own cult and propaganda: the constant adulation he received gave him a false confidence in his own impressions and policies.

After the collapse of the offensive and the July crisis Kerensky took over as Prime Minister from Prince Lvov. Hailed as the 'strong man' to reunite the country and halt the drift towards civil war, he was the only major politician who had a base of popular support, yet who was also broadly acceptable to the military leaders and the bourgeoisie. Kerensky

57. A.F. Kerensky, *The Kerensky Memoirs: Russia and History's Turning Point*, London, 1965, pp. 274, 282.

was, in short, the ideal figure to bring the Coalition back together: as a member of both the Soviet and the Duma circles he made a human bridge between the socialist and the liberal camps. This placed him in a unique position – and the fate of the whole revolution now seemed to depend on him. The powers of the new Prime Minister were significantly increased – he moved his offices to the Winter Palace, moved himself into the Imperial Suite and was perceived as a 'national president'[58] – while his obligations to the Soviet were drastically reduced, giving him complete freedom of initiative.[59] Kerensky personally picked the cabinet of the new Coalition, whose formation he had overseen, and which he now called the 'Government of Salvation of the Revolution'.

However, his popularity began to melt away. It was not just a question of his losing support – more a question of the complete transformation of his political identity. He went from being an idol of the public to 'an ordinary politician'. This deflation of the Kerensky cult was emphasized by the fact that it took place at a time when public attitudes towards politics were changing from the idealism and euphoria of the spring to the disillusionment and cynicism of the autumn and the winter of 1917. Kerensky had been 'the first love of the revolution' – a symbol of the general public hope and belief in politicians. So the public's 'falling out of love' with him was bound to play a part in this general disillusionment with politics.

The collapse of Kerensky's authority was manifested in growing criticism of his policies, and in a broadening of the opposition to his government. As enthusiasm for the idea of a coalition waned, there was a corresponding increase in personal attacks on Kerensky from both Left and Right. Perhaps the most striking evidence of the transformation of his image was the circulation of malicious gossip and rumours similar to those that had helped to bring about the downfall of the Romanovs (see Chapter 1).

In right-wing circles Kerensky's alleged Jewish (and more rarely German) origins were frequently discussed. Judaeophobia and xenophobia were also to be found among certain sections of the Bolshevized masses. Kerensky himself recalled that as he fled the Winter Palace on 25 October 1917 he saw, written on the wall, 'Down with the Jew Kerensky, Long Live Trotsky!'[60] The graffiti was doubly ironic. Kerensky was no Jew, and there were no Jews in the Provisional Government – although it was often said that it was a 'Jewish government' (no doubt because it had given equal civil and religious rights to Jews). On the other hand, Leon Trotsky (a.k.a. Bronstein) was perhaps the best-known Jew that Russia ever had. But

58. Gippius, Siniaia kniga, p. 175.
59. See Figes, A People's Tragedy, pp. 437–8.
60. M. Ferro, October 1917: A Social History of the Russian Revolution, London, 1980, p. 285.

whoever wrote these words – a factory worker or Red Guard, a soldier from the city's garrison, or perhaps a sailor from the Kronstadt naval base – was not so much concerned with Kerensky's ethnic origins as with what he stood for as a general 'enemy' (see Chapter 6). The terms 'Jew', 'German' and 'burzhooi' had become confused and even interchangeable in the plebeian language of the streets. Kerensky had become a metaphoric 'Jew' – a symbol of the fears and prejudices which had won the Bolsheviks their militant support. He had become the embodiment of all the enemies and evils – the democrats, the educated, the bourgeois, the foreign, the weak and the feminine – which the street lumped together and associated with 'the Jews'.[61] Indeed the anti-Semitism of the Right – as a plebeian protest against all perceived foreigners and social enemies – was not that different. 'The Bolsheviks have gained the upper hand,' the Black Hundred newspaper *Groza* (Thunder) reported on 29 October.[62]

Rumours of Kerensky's moral decadence were even more widespread. The transfer of his offices to the Winter Palace, his use of the Tsar's personal apartments (including, according to rumours, the bed of Alexander III), his 'Bonapartist style', and, not least, his break-up with his wife provided fertile soil for this sort of gossip. 'Power has gone to Kerensky's head,' wrote the political analyst of the British War Office, 'he has left his wife, taken up with a ballerina and sleeps in the Tsar's bed.'[63] The press was full of rumours of his involvement with the actress E.I. Time. Friends and acquaintances would ring Kerensky's wife to express their deepest sympathy. 'I could not understand why they were being so solicitous,' she later recalled, 'but then it turned out that there was some story in the left-wing press that Kerensky had left his wife and had run off with some actress. Poor Time had to spend the whole day answering questions and messages of congratulation from her friends, and at the evening performance she had to come on stage holding her husband's hand and explain that she was married, that she was happy with her husband and that she had no intention of marrying Kerensky.'[64] (In fact Kerensky was having an affair and living in the Winter Palace with the doctor Elena Biriukova, his wife's first cousin.) It was even said that one of the Tsar's daughters had become his lover.

There were constant rumours of his drunkenness, of his addiction to morphine and cocaine, and of his thefts of state property from the Winter Palace. It was even claimed that he used the Tsarina's bed linen. This

61. See further O. Figes, 'Down with the Jew Kerensky: Judaeophobia, Xenophobia and Popular Anti-Semitism in the 1917 Revolution', *The Jewish Quarterly*, July 1998.
62. See *Groza*, 29 Oct. 1917 and below p. 174.
63. PRO, War Office, 158/964, p. 6.
64. Kerenskaia, 'Obryvki vospominanii', Box 8, p. 13.

last rumour was supposed to show the effeminate nature of Kerensky. It was also true of the sobriquet 'the new Alexandra Fedorovna', supposedly coined by the poet Khlebnikov. During the final weeks of his government the joke circulated round the country: 'Q: What is the difference between Russia today and at the end of last year? A: Then we had Alexandra Fedorovna [the Empress], but now we have Alexander Fedorovich [Kerensky].' There was much that was rather feminine in Kerensky's physique, his high-pitched voice and gestures (Zinaida Gippius called him her 'girlish revolutionary'), and this no doubt made him appear weak to many of the workers, in particular, compared with the muscular masculinity of the Bolsheviks and the Whites, with their macho style and militant rhetoric. It was often rumoured that Kerensky liked to dress in women's clothes; and the story spread that on 25 October he had fled the Winter Palace in the outfit of a nurse.[65] Later it was repeated by both the Bolsheviks and the Whites – and became a part of the revolution's myth.

Kerensky's manners and appearance, which had earlier been taken as an expression of his democratic nature and military courage, now became an object of ridicule. His fainting fits and high-pitched voice were stressed, as he became a symbol of physical sickliness and impotence. People called him a 'little Bonaparte', the 'chief chatterbox'; even his old friend Dmitrii Filosofov said that he resembled a 'chauffeur in a rich household'.[66] It was from these comic images that the Bolsheviks and right-wingers developed their satires of Kerensky – epitomized by the filmic images of him in Eisenstein's *October* – that have since become the basis of his presentation in the history books as a vain and slightly hysterical buffoon.

The Kornilov Affair dealt the final blow to the Kerensky cult. If Kerensky had hoped to bolster his own diminishing authority by rallying the forces of the revolution against Kornilov's alleged 'counter-revolutionary plot', then he achieved precisely the reverse. For the affair accelerated the social and political polarization that had been eroding Kerensky's base – as a 'national leader' straddling Left and Right – since the failure of the offensive.[67] On the one hand, Kerensky had fatally spoiled his relations with the Right, which by and large remained faithful to Kornilov and condemned Kerensky for betraying his cause. Kornilov became a sort of political martyr for all those who blamed Kerensky's regime for the growing chaos in the country at large. In this respect, the whole Kornilov Affair had its greatest political impact after it was over. The word 'Kornilovite' began to enter the political vocabulary to describe an out-and-out opponent of the discredited '*Kerenshchina*' (Kerensky rule). On the other hand, Kerensky's

65. The rumour was used by several generations of Soviet propagandists and memoirists. See e.g. P.E. Dybenko, *Revoliutsionnye baltiitsy*, Moscow, 1959, pp. 50–3.
66. Gippius, *Siniaia kniga*, p. 174; OR RNB, f. 814, op. 1, d. 3, l. 13.
67. For an account of the affair see Figes, *A People's Tragedy*, pp. 438–55.

standing on the Left had equally been weakened. The mass of the soldiers and workers that had rallied to the defence of the Provisional Government during the Kornilov crisis nevertheless suspected that Kerensky had himself been somehow involved in the Kornilov movement. Many saw the whole affair as a personal feud between the two would-be Napoleons (and in this they were not far wrong). But others believed that Kerensky had been in league with Kornilov, or else had tried to implement his own 'counter-revolutionary' plans through him. This conviction was strengthened by Kerensky's failure to pursue a more democratic course once the crisis was over. For one thing, there was no real inquiry into the Kornilov Affair, and this merely fuelled the popular suspicion that Kerensky had something to hide. His continued support for a coalition with the Kadets (who had clearly been associated with the Kornilov movement) and his appointment of Alexeev (who was widely suspected of having sympathized with it) were seen as added reasons to suspect Kerensky's intentions. The phantom nature of this 'counter-revolution' only made it seem more powerful, a hidden force behind the government, not unlike the shadow of treason that hung over the Tsarist regime in 1916. It was to be a powerful symbol enabling the Bolsheviks to mobilize their forces in October against the threat of the 'Kornilovite' Kerensky.

Kerensky's victory over Kornilov was thus also his own political defeat. 'The prestige of Kerensky and the Provisional Government was completely destroyed by the Kornilov Affair,' recalled Kerensky's wife; 'he was left almost without supporters.'[68] Even Zinaida Gippius, Kerensky's staunchest patron in the spring, turned against him. In the unpublished version of her 'diary' she accused him of adultery and drug abuse and described him in the harshest terms. He was 'puffed up', 'hysterical' and a 'lunatic'. He was 'an old woman', a 'petty tyrant' and a 'chatterbox'. By the end she was using the language of the Right, condemning Kerensky as 'a slave of the Bolsheviks' and admitting on the eve of the October coup that while 'nobody wants the Bolsheviks, nobody is prepared to fight for Kerensky either'.[69]

The Western Allies, who had always been supporters of Kerensky, also turned against him after Kornilov. The British Foreign Office was clearly taken in by the rumours about Kerensky's private life. It was under the absurd impression that his secretary, David Soskice, was a German agent and a crypto-Bolshevik, and that Kerensky himself was about to conclude a separate peace with Germany. One Foreign Office report claimed that the 'syphilitic' Prime Minister was conspiring with the Germans to disrupt

68. Kerenskaia, 'Obryvki vospominanii', Box 8, p. 8.
69. Gippius, *Siniaia kniga*, pp. 99, 112, 113, 118, 137, 139, 153, 161, 175, 202, 228; OR RNB, f. 481, op. 1, d. 3, ll. 161–2, 202.

the Russian war campaign, and that he had been financed by Berlin since before the war. It was even stated that Kerensky had married a ballerina of German origins who had been 'selected for him' by the German government. Buchanan, the British Ambassador in Petrograd, blamed Kerensky's 'policies of hesitation' for the Russian crisis. Colonel Knox, the British military attaché, spoke even more harshly at a conference of the Allied military missions in Petrograd on 20 October: 'I am not interested in Kerensky's sort of government. It is too weak. The Cossacks are called for. The people need the whip.' An analyst from the War Ministry noted: 'In the end he has to go, and the sooner the better – for RUSSIA.' Nabokov, the Provisional Government's representative in London, thought that by October the British had decided to wash their hands of Kerensky – believing him to be 'on his way out', once Kornilov's reforms had been jettisoned.[70] He was almost certainly correct. The British appeared to favour the Kornilov solution – a military dictatorship – to the crisis of authority. Once that had been ruled out they seemed to share the view of Kornilov's supporters that a Bolshevik coup was preferable to the continuation of Kerensky's government. The Bolsheviks, they presumed, could not last in power, and once they were swept aside the socialist experiment would be discredited, leaving the way clear for a military dictatorship to restore order in the country and stiffen its resolve for the continuation of the war.

There were obvious parallels between Kerensky, the fallen idol, and Nicholas, the fallen Tsar. In 1918 Viktor Chernov looked back at the politics of 1917 and characterized them as the 'personalization of ideas' and the 'fetishization of the individual': 'The Russian public acted like a crowd of idol-worshippers: when their idols failed to meet their expectations they ceased to worship them, threw them to the ground and kicked them in the dirt.'[71] Indeed, the attitude of many common people towards Kerensky was shaped by comparison with the Tsar. One soldier wrote to Kerensky from the Front: 'It will be worse for you than for Nicholas, for the Tsar was an enemy; nothing good can come from an enemy. But from you, a friend of the people, there should have been some good.'[72] Like Nicholas, Kerensky became the personification of the people's discontents, an object of their anger, and he became a focus for their destructive violence in October 1917. The term Kerenshchina became a synonym for the crisis of the autumn of 1917, although different groups used it in different ways. For the Right it signified political weakness and chaos, for the Left the

70. PRO, Foreign Office, 371, 3016, N 205925: 542–5; N 210021: 582; N 208373: 577–8; 3017 N 209501: 10–11; N 208214: 567–70; N 210844: 572–3; Nabokov, Ispytaniia diplomata, Stockholm, 1921, pp. 97, 99–100, 102, 139–40.
71. V.M. Chernov, 'Stranitsy iz politicheskogo dnevnika', Mysl', 1918, no. 1, pp. 249–51.
72. Revoliutsionnoe dvizhenie v Rossii v iiule 1917 goda: Iul'skii krizis (Dokumenty i materialy), Moscow, 1959, p. 410.

rule of the bourgeoisie, which, on the streets, Kerensky symbolized. When, in the autumn of 1917, Kerensky's wife asked a group of soldiers what they wanted, the reply she received was 'To kill Kerensky.'[73] He had become, like Nicholas before him, the embodiment of everything the soldiers thought was wrong with the social order; and hence, as with Nicholas, his physical destruction, or at least the physical removal of his power, was seen by them as an important part of the solution. That is surely why the Bolsheviks focused their propaganda campaign on 'the traitor Kerensky' during the October Days; and why the stormers of the Winter Palace became so enraged – and ransacked the Palace – after they discovered that Kerensky was not there.

The Cults of Kornilov and Lenin

The cult of Kerensky encouraged the rise of rival leader cults in 1917 – notably those of Kornilov and Lenin. It is not an exaggeration to say that the growing divide between Left and Right was expressed politically in the competition between these two cults. As Miliukov was to put it in his history of the Russian Revolution, 'either Kornilov or Lenin'.[74] The extent to which the conflict betweeen Left and Right was perceived by ordinary people in terms of the struggle between these two can be gauged by an incident which took place in the October Days. On 29 October a policeman (*militsioner*) apprehended a Red Guardsman on Znamenskaia Square after he had scuffled with a group of citizens who had condemned Lenin. 'Your spy Lenin,' the policeman told the Red Guardsman, 'has no authority for us citizens.' Whereupon the Bolshevik replied, hurling himself with his rifle at the officer, 'I'll show you, you Kornilovite, the mighty fist of our spy Lenin.'[75]

   The cult of Kornilov was of special significance. It was already largely formed by 1917. Kornilov had achieved the status of a national saviour in right-wing circles by the time he was appointed as Commander of the Petrograd Military District in March 1917. Small and agile, with a closely shaven head and Mongol moustache, Kornilov came from a family of Siberian Cossacks. His father was a smallholder and a soldier, who had risen to become a lower-ranking officer. His mother was Kirghiz. This comparatively 'democratic' background – and his lack of any links with the Romanov court – set Kornilov apart from the rest of Russia's generals.

73. Kerenskaia, 'Obryvki vospominanii', Box 8, pp. 27–8.
74. P.N. Miliukov, *The Russian Revolution*, ed. and trans. G.M. Hamburg, 3 vol., Gulf Breeze, 1984, vol. 2, p. 39.
75. TsGASP, f. 131, op. 4, d. 31, l. 32.

In the democratic atmosphere of 1917 it was the ideal background for a national military hero.

Kornilov's early army career had been spent in central Asia. He had mastered the Turkic languages of the region and later, in 1917, built up his own bodyguard of Tekke Turkomans, dressed in scarlet robes, who called him their 'Great Boyar'. Kornilov's appointment was hardly merited by his military record. By 1914, at the age of forty-four, he had risen no higher than divisional commander in the 8th Army. Brusilov, his Army Commander, considered him just a brave and dashing soldier, well loved by his men, yet inclined to disobey orders. He thought that Kornilov had cultivated his own 'cult of bravery'; and this cult was certainly behind his meteoric rise to fame. In 1915 Kornilov had been wounded and taken prisoner by the Austrians after his refusal to obey Brusilov's command to withdraw his division. The following year he had escaped from prison and, disguised as an Austrian soldier, had made his way back to Russia by foot, where, instead of being court-martialled, he received a hero's welcome.[76]

Kornilov now began to attract powerful political backers such as the new War Minister, Guchkov. They secured his appointment as Commander of the Petrograd Military District in March. Even at this stage he had a circle of supporters – right-wing journalists, bankers, industrialists and military officers – who saw him as a potential 'strong man' with the capacity to restore order. During the April crisis Kornilov wanted to bring his troops on to the street. The Soviet had opposed this and taken control of the garrison, forcing Kornilov to resign. Right-wing groups were scandalized by the Soviet's interference in army matters, and looked to Kornilov as a champion of their cause. The Officers' Union and the Union of Cossacks campaigned for the abolition of the soldiers' committees and the restoration of military discipline. These groups came together through the Republican Centre, a clandestine organization of bourgeois patriots, officers and war veterans formed in the spring.[77]

Kornilov was the servant and the figurehead rather than the master of these right-wing interests. A typical soldier, he was a man of very few words, and of even fewer ideas. 'The heart of a lion, the brains of a sheep' was one verdict on him. During his time in prison he had read about the life of Napoleon, and he seemed to believe that he was destined to play

76. E.A. Vertsinskii, *God revoliutsii: vospominaniia ofitsera general'nogo shtaba za 1917–18 gg.*, Tallinn, 1929, p. 18; A.P. Bogaevskii, *Vospominaniia 1918 goda*, New York, 1963, p. 39; G. Katkov, *The Kornilov Affair: Kerensky and the Break-up of the Russian Army*, London, 1980, pp. 39–41; Brusilov, *A Soldier's Notebook 1914–18*, London, 1930, pp. 100–2, 321; L.-H. Grondijs, *La Guerre en Russie et en Sibérie*, Paris, 1922, p. 264.
77. J.D. White, 'The Kornilov Affair: A Study in Counter-Revolution', *Soviet Studies*, 1968, vol. 20, pp. 187–9; Katkov, *Kornilov*, pp. 138–9.

a similar role in saving Russia.[78] All that was needed, in his view, to stem the tide of anarchy was a military dictator like Bonaparte.

However, while Kornilov was no politician, he was not averse to using revolutionary symbols or rhetoric, and in this sense could be described as a 'political general'. He played on his democratic roots ('I, General Kornilov, the son of a Cossack peasant . . . ' began his most famous pronouncement, in answer to Kerensky's charges of treason).[79] Before the crisis that led to his dismissal he had the image of a 'democratic' general – it was on this basis that he was posted to the 8th Army to replace Kaledin (considered 'counter-revolutionary') as late as May – and had cultivated good relations with the Soviet.[80] During the February Days Kornilov had worn a red ribbon on his uniform. It was he who had told the Empress of her arrest on 8 March – and there are reasons to suppose that he performed this task deliberately to increase his prestige among the revolutionary soldiers. Many monarchists refused to forgive him for this act, considering him a political intriguer and unprincipled careerist of the revolutionary mode.[81] Kornilov was no monarchist. He denounced the old regime in his speeches, blaming it for the military defeats of 1914–16. In May 1917 he was made Commander of the 8th Army. He ordered a special regiment of volunteers to be formed within it, the 'Kornilovites'. They adopted black and red as their regimental colours, adding to the arms of their uniforms an emblem of their own design – a skull, crossed sabres, a grenade and the name 'Kornilovites'. The regimental song was anti-monarchist:

> We don't want the past,
> The Tsar is not our idol . . .

The language of the revolution manifested itself in the formation of the cult of Kornilov. His supporters hailed him as 'the first people's Commander-in-Chief', the 'people's general', and so on. He was a 'true son of the people', the 'beloved leader of the democratic army' and 'the true defender of the revolution'.[82] Savinkov described the general as 'a true democrat and unwavering republican'. Democracy was politically correct – and obligatory for all politicians – in 1917. This in itself was a

78. E.I. Martynov, *Kornilov: Popytka voennogo perevorota*, Leningrad, 1927, pp. 16–20.
79. R.G. Browder and A.F. Kerensky (eds), *The Russian Provisional Government 1917: Documents* (3 vols), vol. 3, Stanford, 1961, p. 1573.
80. A. Wildman, *The End of the Russian Imperial Army: The Road to Soviet Power*, Princeton, 1980, pp. 78–9.
81. G.Z. Ioffe, *Semnadtsatyi god: Lenin, Kerenskii, Kornilov*, Moscow, 1995, p. 43.
82. See e.g. V.D. Pletnev, *Pervyi narodnyi glavnokomanduiushchii general-leitenant Lavr' Georgievich Kornilov*, Petrograd, 1917, pp. 1, 2 and *passim*; N. Tuzemtsev (N.T. Dobrovol'skii), *General Lavr' Georgievich Kornilov*, Rostov on Don, 1918, pp. 1, 2 and *passim*.

sign of the extent to which all the revolution's political forces – from the Reds to the Whites – were obliged to identify themselves as 'democrats' and anti-monarchists.[83] The establishment of the pro-Kornilov publishing house Democratic Russia – sponsored by the British and the French to pump out anti-German propaganda – was a further illustration of the ways in which the Right was forced to resituate itself on 'democratic' ground.[84]

The cult of Kornilov was also a cult of the national leader and saviour. Its symbolic height was Kornilov's triumphal entry into Moscow for the State Conference on 13 August. Well-dressed ladies pelted him with flowers at the Aleksandrovsky railway station. The millionairess Morozova fell on her knees before him, while the Kadet, Rodichev, called on him to 'Save Russia' and receive the thanks of the whole people as their leader (*vozhd*). Kornilov was carried from the station on the shoulders of officers and cheered in the street outside by a crowd of patriots. Seated in an open car, at the head of a motorcade that any twentieth-century dictator would have envied, he then made a pilgrimage to the sacred Iversky shrine, where the Tsars had usually prayed on their visits to Moscow. On the following day he entered the conference to a standing ovation from the Right. His speech was a poor one – words were not Kornilov's strength – but it did not seem to matter: it was what he stood for, not what he said, that made him the patriots' great white hope.[85]

Pamphlets published by Kornilov's entourage to promote his cult quoted letters from 'ordinary people' calling on the general to 'come and save Russia'. 'Russia everywhere is suffering a great deal,' claimed one of these pamphlets, 'and everywhere the people are appealing to Kornilov as their leader and saviour. They are expecting great things from their hero.' Indeed in the military archives there are many letters to 'our beloved supreme leader', and so on, calling for the 'salvation of Russia'. 'All of thinking Russia [*mysliashchaia Rossiia*] is looking to You [*sic*],' pronounced the resolution of a conference of public activists on 9 August. Other resolutions declared that 'only Kornilov' could save the country.[86] Such was the cult of Kornilov among certain sections of the military that one group of officers from the Kornilov Regiment, not satisfied with the special emblems on

83. On this, in connection with Kornilov, see N.A. Berdiaev, 'O svobode i dostoinstve slova', *Narodopravstvo*, 1917, no. 11, p. 6.

84. See B.I. Kolonitskii, ' "Demokraticheskaia Rossiia", inostrannye missii i okruzhenie L. G. Kornilova', in *Rossia v 1917 gody: novye podkhody i vzgliady: Sbornik nauchnyh trudov*, St Petersburg, 1994, vyp. 2, pp. 28–31.

85. V. Vladimirova, *Kontrrevoliutsiia v 1917 g. (Kornilovshchina)*, Moscow, 1924, p. 84; F. Stepun, *Byvshee i nesbyvsheesia*, New York, 1956, vol. 2, pp. 162–3; Browder and Kerensky (eds), *Russian Provisional Government*, vol. 3, pp. 1510–15.

86. Pletnev, *Pervyi narodnyi glavnkomandyiushchii general-leitenant L.G. Kornilov*, p. 46; RGVIA, f. 2003, op. 1, d. 1784, ll. 125–99.

their uniforms, decorated their arms with tattoos of their idol.[87] There could be no more suitable expression of the military machismo for which Kornilov stood.

The later history of the cult of Kornilov is well known and remarkable. After his imprisonment in Bykhov he became a magnet for the anti-Bolshevik forces, especially the officers. The anti-'Kornilovite' propaganda of the left-wing parties merely served to increase his cult status among such right-wing elements. After October he fled to the Don where he emerged as the charismatic leader of the Whites, despite the opposition of the solid (but uninspiring) Alexeev, who himself could not deny the immense popularity of Kornilov among the younger officers and the effect this could have in drawing more to the White movement. The arrival of a group of officers and soldiers from the Kornilov Regiment was also extremely important in securing Kornilov's ascendancy. Throughout the civil war there continued to be a great deal of rivalry between men from the Kornilov and Alexeev regiments. But the symbol of Kornilov held the movement together as a whole, even after his death. He was killed by Red forces near Ekaterinodar in April 1918 and buried by his troops in a secret place. But the Reds found the corpse, paraded it through crowds in the town, and quartered it with sabres before burning it in the town square. Later, however, the place where he was killed became sacred in White mythology.

The cult of Lenin gained fresh impetus in the Bolshevik subculture of 1917 – a period neglected in most studies of the Lenin cult.[88] Even earlier, in the revolutionary underground, Lenin had enjoyed the status of supreme leader and teacher of his party. Bolshevism was defined by a personal pledge of loyalty to him; and Menshevism, though to a lesser extent, by opposition to him. The veteran Social Democrat Nikolai Valentinov, on his arrival in Geneva in 1904, was shocked by the 'atmosphere of worship which people calling themselves Bolsheviks had created' there around the figure of Lenin. Lenin's violent attacks on his opponents and his generally authoritarian leadership style reinforced this culture of obedience. The Bolsheviks were known as 'Leninists' by other Social Democrats – and indeed the police used this term as well.[89]

However, during 1917 not all Bolsheviks were happy with this label. Indeed, at party conferences held before Lenin's return to Russia in 1917 his name was barely mentioned. There was, moreover, a strong movement among the provincial delegates (who had worked together with the Mensheviks in the revolutionary underground and who now shared power

87. *Revoliutsionnaia bor'ba v gomel'skoi gubernii: Istoricheskie materialy*, Gomel', 1921, vyp. 1, pp. 55, 58–9.
88. See e.g. Nina Tumarkin, *Lenin Lives! The Lenin Cult in Soviet Russia*, Cambridge, Mass., 1983.
89. RGIA, f. 1405, op. 530, d. 1159, l. 5.

with them in the Soviets) for the reunification of the Social Democratic Party. Many of the Bolsheviks who turned out to greet Lenin at the Finland Station on the night of 3 April could never have seen him before. Some who took part in the demonstrations in Petrograd organized by the party on 20-21 April (and then again on 18 June) stated, in response to hostile cries that they were Leninists: 'We are not Leninists.'[90] The fact that *Pravda* reported this suggests that some leading activists as well were equally unhappy with the title 'Leninist'.[91]

The concern of these Bolsheviks to distance themselves from Lenin's position was in part a reaction to the tendency of the anti-Bolsheviks to label all of them as 'Leninists'. 'Leninism' became a general term for 'Bolshevism', 'militance' and 'maximalism' in the liberal discourse of 1917. Thus, for example, right-wing supporters of the war dubbed the moderate socialists and other advocates of a democratic peace 'semi-Leninists' and 'quarter-Leninists'. The phrase 'Mr Lenins' (*gospoda Leniny*) was used in right-wing circles to ridicule those moderate socialists who failed to denounce him emphatically enough.[92]

However, the consciously non-Leninist Bolsheviks were no more than a minority, even in 1917, and most party members idolized their leader. Lenin's success in winning over the rank-and-file to the April Theses cannot be explained without taking into account his towering domination of the party. No other political party had ever been so closely tied to the personality of a single man. Lenin was the first modern party leader to achieve the status of a god: Mussolini, Hitler and Mao Tse-tung were all his successors in this sense. Being a Bolshevik had come to imply an oath of allegiance to Lenin as both the 'leader' and the 'teacher' of the party. It was this, above all, that distinguished the Bolsheviks from the Mensheviks (who had no clear leader of their own). None of the other leading Bolsheviks could compare with Lenin.

Lenin's domination of the party had more to do with the political culture of the party than with his own charisma. Lenin's oratory was rather grey. It lacked the brilliant eloquence, the pathos, the humour, the vivid metaphors, the colour or the drama of a speech by Trotsky or Zinoviev. Lenin, moreover, had the handicap of not being able to pronounce his r's. Yet his speeches had an iron logic, and Lenin had the knack of finding easy slogans, which he crammed into the heads of his listeners by endless repetition. He spoke with his thumbs thrust under his armpits, rocking back and forth on his heels, as if in preparation to launch himself, like a human rocket, into the listening crowd (this is how he was portrayed

90. 'Aprel'skie dni 1917 goda v Petrograde', *Krasnyi arkhiv*, 1929, t. 2 (33), pp. 33, 56.
91. *Pravda*, 28 May, 20 June 1917.
92. *Rech'*, 20 May 1917.

in the hagiographic portraits painted during the Soviet era). Gorky, who heard Lenin for the first time in 1907, thought he 'spoke badly' to start with; 'but after a minute I, like everybody else, was absorbed in his speech. It was the first time I had heard complicated political questions treated so simply. There was no striving after beautiful phrases. He presented every word clearly, and revealed his exact thought with great ease.' Potresov, who had known and worked with Lenin since 1894, explained his appeal by a curious 'hypnotic power':

> Only Lenin was followed unquestioningly as the indisputable leader, as it was only Lenin who was that rare phenomenon, particularly in Russia – a man of iron will and indomitable energy, capable of instilling fanatical faith in the movement and the cause, and possessed of equal faith in himself. Once upon a time I, too, was impressed by this will-power of Lenin's, which seemed to make him into a 'chosen leader'.[93]

Slogans proclaiming 'Long Live Comrade Lenin!' appeared on the streets of Petrograd as early as the April crisis. Posters with the same slogan appeared shortly after.[94] Factory and local party resolutions expressed solidarity with 'our leader Lenin' from approximately this time too. The party's publishers pumped out Lenin's works in pamphlet form. In the provinces they published little else, unlike the party's publishers in Petrograd and Moscow, which also printed pamphlets by Zinoviev and Kamenev – and later, of course, Trotsky. For the provincial Bolsheviks, it was Lenin who personified the Bolsheviks.

The cult of Lenin was not simply engineered by the party's leaders and publishers, however. It was also generated from below. Olga Kerensky recalls the excitement with which the Bolsheviks in Petrograd greeted the return of Lenin: 'There was the most frenzied jubilation that Lenin was arriving – here was the real leader of democracy, the saviour and liberator of the Russian people, and when he and his companions arrived they were greeted by excited workers, clamouring for Lenin, as if they were waiting for the Messiah.'[95] A group of soldiers from the Front wrote to *Pravda* in early May: 'We send warmest greetings to the leader of democracy, the defender of our interests, comrade Lenin.' Others greeted him as 'our saviour', or as 'holy' (*sviatyi*) Lenin.[96] Thus long before the mass propaganda of his cult, following the attempt on Lenin's life on 30 August 1918, the basis of it was already to be found in the political culture of the Bolshevik Party.

93. L. Fischer, *The Life of Lenin*, London, 1965, pp. 57–8; G. Aronson, *Rossiia v epokhu revoliutsii*, New York, 1966, pp. 47–52; N. Valentinov, *Encounters with Lenin*, London, 1968, p. 42.
94. 'Aprel'skie dni 1917 goda v Petrograde', pp. 56, 73.
95. Kerenskaia, 'Obryvki vospominanii', Box no. 8, p. 11.
96. *Pravda*, 11, 19 May 1917; M. Vishniak, *Dan' proshlomu*, New York, 1954, p. 322.

The overthrow of the monarchy and the spread of anti-monarchist attitudes after February 1917 left a legacy of authoritarian and patriarchal mentalities that remained at the heart of Russia's revolutionary political culture. The monarchical psychology reappeared in a different form – the cult of the leader, the 'peasant king', whose 'master's hand', as the peasants put it, would defend the revolution and its gains (see Chapter 5). As in the myth of the 'benevolent Tsar' there was a quasi-religious faith in the moral qualities and divine power of the people's chosen leader and national saviour: all the country's problems could be solved by giving him more power. This was in part a natural reaction to the breakdown of the state as an instrument of power and reform in 1917. Yet it was also rooted in traditional Russian political concepts: in the confusion between the person of the monarch (*gosudar'*) and the abstract institutions of the state (*gosudarstvo*); and in the linkage in the peasant mind between truth and justice (*pravda*) and government (*pravitel'stvo*). Power was conceived in personal and religious terms – the 'Tsar-Deliverer' – and this was the popular conception of the revolution and its leaders too.

4

Languages of Citizenship, Languages of Class: Workers and the Social Order

To understand the attitudes and actions of the workers during 1917 we must first know how they thought about the social order and their own position in the world. Did they see themselves as the members of a class? And what, in any case, did they understand by 'class'? Did they view it in the same terms as their leaders? Or did they attach a different set of values to the words their leaders used to represent the interests of 'the working class', the 'proletariat', the 'labouring people' and all the other social categories that dominated political discourse during 1917?

Western historians of the labour movement in 1917 have long been aware of the need to address these questions of self-identity. As Leo Haimson wrote in 1988, representations of the social order played a crucial part 'in the shaping of political and social attitudes and patterns of collective behaviour, especially during those periods of acute political and social crisis when individuals and groups had to establish – indeed to decide – who they were in order to determine how they should feel, think, and ultimately act.'[1]

As Haimson has emphasized, there was a great deal of ambivalence and fluidity in the way that people, whom one might rush to call 'workers', actually regarded their own identity and relationship to society. Older notions of social status derived from the system of estates (*sosloviia*) were intermingled with the newer conceptions of social class which developed in the urban industrial environment.[2] Workers could identify themselves in many different ways – by their native region (which usually meant the countryside); by their *artel* or collective working group; by their trade or profession, their workshop or their status (*stazh*) within the factory; by their gender ('brothers', 'working women'); by their ethnic origins; by

1. L.H. Haimson, 'The Problem of Social Identities in Early Twentieth-Century Russia', *Slavic Review*, 1988, vol. 47, p. 4.
2. See G. Freeze, 'The Soslovie (Estate) Paradigm and Russian Social History', *American Historical Review*, 1986, vol. 91, pp. 11–36.

their 'class' (the 'working class') or some other general category (the 'labour-ing people', the 'proletariat', etc). Indeed, there were times when a worker might decide not to call himself a 'worker' at all, but instead a 'citizen', or when he even thought of himself as a professional. By the same token, there were times when other social groups might identify themselves as 'working class'.[3] For example, in 1917 (when there was some kudos in being 'working class'), it was common for officials (e.g. industrial ad-ministrators, railway clerks and service personnel) to identify themselves as 'intellectual workers' (*rabochie intelligentnogo shtata*). Or for soldiers to call themselves the 'vanguard of the international working class' (*avangard mirovogo rabochego klassa*). Or for the intelligentsia to identify themselves as a 'proletariat of intellectual labour' (*proletariat umstvennogo truda*). In 1917 a meeting of schoolteachers in Petrograd resolved to send a delegate to the Soviet of Workers' Deputies, arguing, in the words of the motion's proposer, that 'a teacher, after all, is a member of the proletariat'.[4]

How are we to explain this ambivalence? Russian labour history has been dominated by the Marxist/social history paradigm. Traditionally, this tended to see the question of social identity as a product of the social environment, the relations of production in particular. It also tended to assume that there would be a linear development towards 'class consciousness' as the workers were exposed to the urban industrial en-vironment. This was the basis of the Soviet school of labour history which Marxist historians in the West subscribed to by and large. Factory com-mittees, Red Guards, trade unions, city soviets, the size of the factories, the levels of the workers' skills and literacy, the number of years they had lived in the city, strikes and demonstrations – all of these were scrutinized mainly for the light which they might shed on the development of a consciousness of class, in hostile opposition to other classes, among their members. Underlying this project was the assumption that the 1917 Revolution – the culminating point of this labour history – was a 'workers' revolution' in the towns, a 'class struggle' in which the workers organized and became conscious of themselves as a 'working class' in hostile opposition to the 'bourgeoisie'.

The problem was, however, that the more historians discovered about labour the more it became clear that it neither saw itself nor acted as a 'class' – at least not in the straightforward manner insisted on by Marx and his followers in the Soviet Union. There were too many other self-identities which could not be simply subsumed under 'class'. Workers could be loyal to their factory or their workshop, to their craft or trade,

3. See the comments by Haimson in *Reformy ili revoliutsiia? Rossia, 1861–1917: materialy mezhdunarod-nogo kollokviuma istorikov*, St Petersburg, 1992, p. 318.
4. N.N. Smirnov, *Na perelome: Rossiiskoe uchitel'stvo nakanune i v dni revoliutsii 1917 goda*, St Petersburg, 1994, p. 105.

in a way that weakened any broader solidarity.[5] Some could remain loyal to their village, even after years of living in the city. Others could adopt an urban pride, yet at times of stress, such as 1917, rebel against the city in acts of vandalism that 'conscious' workers and socialists condemned as a form of 'peasant' rioting. All these conflicts of identity complicated the attitudes and collective actions of 'the workers' in 1917 – to the extent that one can barely say there was a 'workers' movement' in that year at all, at least not without so many reservations and qualifications that the term itself becomes almost meaningless.

If the old labour history does not provide the answers, the new cultural history, with its focus upon language, may yet help us understand how workers saw their 'class' and the reformed social order in 1917. Labour historians of nineteenth-century Western Europe, such as Gareth Stedman Jones and Patrick Joyce (on England) or William H. Sewell (on France), looked again at class as a cultural construction. They showed persuasively that class was not a fixed or pre-existing social entity but, as E.P. Thompson had once said, was made culturally. It was constructed, in particular, through the development of a political language or discourse of class which identified and expressed collective interests in the course of social and political struggles. Class and class consciousness were both identities that could not exist until they had been constructed through language. Labour history thus made its 'linguistic turn'. Its focus switched from the workplace to the word.

Stedman Jones, Joyce and Sewell explored the rhetoric of their respective labour movements, emphasizing that their languages of class expressed an older moral vision of 'the people' which attracted and united labouring people by giving them a claim to the rights of citizens. All three stressed that these languages of class were based on the rhetoric of human rights. Stedman Jones, in his study of the Chartist movement, found that its leaders spoke the language of political exclusion and democratic rights which stemmed from the radical political tradition. It united the Chartist followers in their common sense of injustice and oppression after the restructuring of the British state in the 1830s which had tipped the balance in favour of the middle classes and against the poor. Joyce also found that the workers' understanding of the social order in nineteenth-century Britain was expressed in a moral vision of the people which sought to resolve social inequalities by giving all men – but only men – equal political rights as citizens. Finally, Sewell's work on the language of French labour

5.   S.A. Smith, 'Craft Consciousness, Class Consciousness: Petrograd in 1917', *History Workshop Journal*, 1981, vol. 11, pp. 33–56; C. Ward, 'Languages of Trade or a Language of Class? Work Culture in Russian Cotton Mills in the 1920s', in L.H. Siegelbaum and R.G. Suny (eds), *Making Workers Soviet: Power, Class, and Identity*, Cornell, 1994, pp. 194–219; W.B. Husband, *Revolution in the Factory: The Birth of the Soviet Textile Industry, 1917–1920*, New York and Oxford, 1990, pp. 11–12 and *passim*; D.P. Koenker, 'Collective Action and Collective Violence in the Russian Labor Movement', *Slavic Review*, 1982, vol. 41, p. 447.

stressed how far it was couched in the rhetoric of 1789, and in an older corporate language which expressed the idea of fraternity and equality rather than of conflict between the workers and the bourgeoisie.[6] The important contribution of the new cultural history was to look at labour movements not as the expressions of a pre-existing class but as movements that used language to *create* a class by articulating a collective interest and identity attached to a broader vision of society.

The approach is not without its difficulties. Its focus on rhetoric and language privileges the leaders of the labour movement, who shaped and developed and left the written records of this language, at the expense of the labour rank-and-file.[7] It should not be assumed that the latter conceived of the social order in the same way as their leaders, or indeed that different types of workers used languages of class in the same way. But trying to find out, through the language which they used, how ordinary workers thought about the social order and their place in it is, if not impossible, at least extremely hard. At best it can only be achieved by citing individual examples, such as workers' letters and resolutions, whose inferences could be contradicted by as many counter-examples. There is also the more fundamental problem – a recurring theme throughout this book (especially in this and the following chapter) – that the language workers used was itself ambivalent, that its terms and idioms could mean different things to different people and could be appropriated and deployed by them to many different ends. Indeed, such dissonances within the discourse of the revolution are bound themselves to play an important part in any social movement or conflict during it.

This chapter explores the ambiguities of the language used by the workers and other urban groups, its idioms of class and expressions of morality and social justice, in an effort to define the elements that made up their political culture and ideals in 1917.

Constructions of Social Identity

When we try to understand the languages of class used by Russian workers in 1917 we are faced at once by a paradox. Judging by the events of that year, Russia had the most revolutionary workers in the world; yet their militancy did not appear to derive from a consciously developed sense of 'class' as defined by Marx. Most urban workers had not read their Marx,

6. G. Stedman Jones, *Languages of Class: Studies in English Working Class History, 1832–1982*, Cambridge, 1983; P. Joyce, *Visions of the People: Industrial England and the Question of Class, 1848–1914*, Cambridge, 1991; W.H. Sewell, Jr., *Work and Revolution in France: The Language of Labour from the Old Regime to 1848*, Cambridge, 1980.

7. M.W. Steinberg, 'Culturally Speaking: Finding a Commons between Post-Structuralism and the Thompsonian Perspective', *Social History*, 1996, vol. 21, no. 2, pp. 199–200.

even in the most vulgar pamphlet forms, and had little understanding of class structure and exploitation in the capitalist economy. As a comparatively new industrial formation, moreover, the Russian workers had a relatively embryonic 'working-class culture' compared, for example, with the well-developed notions of the working class in Britain or Germany, where corporate forms of class identity (trade unions and so on) had become sedimented in distinctive cultural patterns over a longer period of time.

What the Russian workers did have, however, was a strong sense of themselves as 'the labouring people' (*trudiashchikhsia narod*) united by a common sense of injustice and exclusion from society. This in itself was a rudimentary form of class consciousness, according to the more traditional definitions of class which see it as comprising, on the one hand, a sense of corporate identity and, on the other, a hostility towards other more privileged groups in society. This dichotomous view of society – its division between 'us' and 'them', the *nizy* and the *verkhy*, the *narod* and *obshchestvo* – had deep roots in Russian culture. It did not by itself amount to a class consciousness but it did provide a basic cultural context within which a discourse of class could be developed by the socialist intelligentsia and understood by the urban lower classes, albeit in many different ways, but in ways that had meaning for their daily lives. Indeed, this basic class division of society into 'us' and 'them' was not only the main social discourse of the revolution in 1917 (one can see it, for example, in the split between the 'demokratiia' and the 'burzhooi' – on which see Chapter 6) but persisted for decades after that, despite the efforts of the Soviet regime to encourage a more developed consciousness of class.[8]

Within this basic language of class, however, there were many rival idioms – Populist and Marxist, political and social, inclusive and exclusive – which workers understood and used in various ways. These idioms, moreover, often overlapped and intersected, depending on the circumstances in which they were used. Such complexities and ambiguities reflected the position of the Russian workers, divided as they were between the rival cultures of the village and the town.

It is reasonable to suppose that many of the workers' ideas of class and social justice were influenced by the traditions of the peasantry. But it is hard to establish the links. Some historians have argued, for example, that the collective customs of the peasant commune (*obshchina*) influenced the organization of the workers' *artels* and factory committees.[9] This is

8.   See e.g. S. Davies, '"Us against Them": Social Identity in Soviet Russia, 1934–41', *Russian Review*, 1997, vol. 56, no. 1, pp. 70–89.
9.   See e.g. N.V. Mikhailov, 'Samoorganizatsiia trudovykh kollektivov i psikhologiia rossiiskikh rabochikh v nachale xxv.', in *Rabochie i intelligentsia Rossii v epokhu reform i revoliutsii 1861–fevral' 1917 g.*, St Petersburg, 1997, pp. 149–65. See also the telling reservations of Reginald Zelnik on pp. 202–3.

possible: unlike the trade unions, which relied on individual membership, the early factory committees relied on the enrolment of whole workers' collectives, which may indeed have sprung from the customs of the *obshchina*. But institutions similar to the factory committees appeared in other countries during the First World War (the Rate in Germany or the shop steward committees in Britain or the factory committees in Italy and France) and none of these had the peasant communal tradition. So it is hard to argue that in Russia the influence derived from the peasantry.

None the less, there are some general connections that can be made between the peasants' and the workers' constructions of social identity and justice. The populist idiom of class – as a 'family of toilers' (*sem'ia trudiashchikhsia*) or simply as the 'labouring people' (*trudiashchikhsia narod or trudovoi narod*) – probably owed something to the peasant milieu and was certainly echoed by peasants. These ideas were central, after all, to the ideology of the *obshchina* which was taken up by the Populists. It was a moral, even religious, conception of the collective good that lay at the heart of the peasant commune. This peasant conception of social justice – that surplus wealth was immoral, that property was theft and that manual labour was the only source of value – could intersect, however, with moral and/or Marxist idioms of class that had no association with the peasantry. Workers' resolutions in 1917 often echoed all three, for example, when they described the factory owners or the 'burzhoois' as 'selfish people' or 'greedy parasites', who 'robbed the honest toilers', 'lived off the backs of the labouring people', or 'grew fat on the people's blood'.[10] Moreover, peasants who had become 'conscious' workers often developed their own distinctive idiom of class that set them apart from the 'grey' or 'peasant' workers by repackaging these populist ideas in slightly more sophisticated Marxist forms. Thus, the idea of 'the people' (*narod*) or 'the toilers' (*trudiashchiesia*) would be counterposed by these 'conscious' workers to the 'bourgeoisie' – synthesizing populist and Marxist idioms. Or the term 'burzhooi' – which came straight from the Marxist idiom – was appropriated by many of the workers and reinflected in their own populist terms: the 'burzhooi' was constructed in this way as a general enemy of the people or *narod*, a parasite who lived off the toilers' sweat and blood (see Chapter 6).

Yet while echoing these peasant idioms, the workers in their language just as, if not more, often sought to set themselves apart from other groups in a more exclusive idiom of the working class. It was not a question of polarity. The identity and the language of 'the worker' was an open filter through which groups could pass in both directions. But in the main its

10. See e.g. *Proletarii* (Kharkov), 3 June 1917.

purpose and effect was to establish a new social hierarchy of the lower orders in the towns. There was a general correlation between a worker's position within that hierarchy, the sort of language and symbols he or she might use to identify themselves, and the political movement that was likely to appeal to them. Some male workers, for example, might be more attracted to the party idiom of 'brotherhood', or the 'toiling collective', particularly if such ideas reflected the ways in which their lives were already organized (e.g. through artels or *zemliachestva*).

The gendered basis of brotherhood was important for many different forms of workers' self-identity. It could serve to distinguish workers from the peasantry: male workers set themselves apart from female workers either on the grounds of their role and status in the factory (women workers did less heavy work with machinery, were lower paid and on the whole less skilled) or on the grounds that women tended more often to return to the village for seasonal employment and retained more elements of the old village culture (attachment to the Church and rural superstitions, folk songs and expressions, peasant ways of dress), all of which could be deemed marks of lower status by the type of factory labourer yearning to escape the peasant way of life and acquire the *kultur'nost*, the urban manners and attitudes, central to their new self-identity as 'conscious' workers. The masculine identity of the factory worker was crucial to the image and development of the revolutionary movement. Women rarely appeared in emblems or symbols of the socialist movement (even during 1917 when women's liberation was a prominent issue); and when they did it was in the form of a peasant woman, or stylized national figure, but never as a female industrial worker. On the other hand, the male worker invariably appeared – either as the brother of the male peasant and/or the soldier (with whom he is pictured shaking hands), or else as the liberator of the world, breaking chains and crowns.[11]

Among the male and more conscious workers too there were many different forms of self-identity – defined by age and experience, skill and trade, ethnicity and place of residence, cultural interests and associations – which defined their place in the social order and influenced the ways in which they might relate to various idioms of class and political ideologies. Some workers, such as the printers, for example, might define themselves (and increasingly did in the final years before the First World War) as a 'workers' intelligentsia' or indeed as professionals – both identities that lent themselves to the ideology, the rhetoric and the tactics of the Mensheviks. On the other hand, at this time many young metal-workers, even the most skilled, were inclined to identify themselves with 'the united

11. P.K. Kornakov, 'Znamena fevral'skoi revoliutsii', in *Geral'dika: materialy i issledovaniia*, Leningrad, 1983, pp. 12–26, 126, 129.

working class' – an identity that accorded with the language and the ideology of Bolshevism.[12]

The degree to which the workers identified themselves with an exclusive working class can be gauged from the language of their slogans and their songs. Marxist and populist idioms of class were often intermingled in these songs, which equally combined the idea of the class or social struggle with the idea of a moral or political battle between all the forces of the revolution and the dark forces of the old regime:

Song	Self-identification	Image of the enemy
'Workers' Marseillaise'	The working people (*rabochii narod*) The hungry people (*liud golodnyi*)	Tsar-vampire (*Tsar-vampir*) Rich men-kulaks (*bogach-kulaki*) The rich (*bogatye*)
'The Internationale'	The whole world of the hungry and of slaves (*ves' mir golodnykh i rabov*)	Parasites Gang of hounds and hangmen (*svora psov i palachei*)
'Varshavianka'	The working people (*rabochii narod*) Brothers	Dark forces (*temnye sily*) Tyrants Tsar-plutocrats Parasites of the labouring mass (*parazity trudiashchikhsia mass*)
'Bravely Comrades Keep Together'	Comrades Children of the labouring family (*deti sem'i trudovoi*) Workers (*rabochie*)	The powers (*vlasti*) Tsar

Many factory songs expressed the Populists' view of human liberation in a way that cut across the classes and identified the workers with 'the common people':

The people's freedom has been won,
Great is the year of seventeen.
Long live free Russia!
Long live the free people!

12. See the comments by Haimson in *Reformy ili revoliutsiia?*, pp. 333–4.

In the time of our great misfortune
Blood was spilled all year.
But whoever has been kissed by freedom,
Shall never be a slave . . .
(Workers song in the Putilov Factory, 1917)[13]

Slogans and songs such as these served to link the workers with the broader political movement and to include other groups in the workers' protest culture when they marched with banners singing in the streets.

On the other hand, a 'workers' chauvinism' was equally pronounced in 1917 (and that term was used by people both before and during the revolution). The workers saw themselves as the 'vanguard': in their view, it was they who had 'made the revolution' through their strikes and demonstrations, even though the soldiers of the garrison made precisely the same claim. This activist language of the workers, in relation to the revolution, contrasted strongly with the passive language of the peasantry, which in their petitions and messages of greeting to the new authorities tended to accept the revolution as a gift or miracle (see Chapter 5).

The workers' belief in their leading role was reinforced by socialist (especially Marxist) propaganda, which stressed the special mission of the 'working class' or the 'working people' as an agency of human liberation from capitalism and as pioneers of the new socialist society. It was the workers – and only the workers – who had nothing to lose but their chains. From this self-conscious vanguard status many workers derived a sense of pride in their own identity and a sense of superiority. They saw themselves as above the peasantry, the grey mass of unskilled labourers, and sometimes even displayed hostility towards the socialist intelligentsia, especially if they felt they were being patronized by them.[14] This hostility was often most marked among the 'workers' intelligentsia', who adopted many of the attitudes and manners of their teachers while resenting their paternal tutorship, real or imagined.[15] The revolutionary struggle in action provided the workers with an opportunity to assert their leadership over them, and this is reflected in many songs and slogans which emphasized the workers' leading role. Indeed, the workers were more energetic and better organized than any other class in 1917: they were responsible for the soviets, the factory committees, the trade unions, the workers' clubs and cooperatives, the workers' militia and Red Guards, newspapers, cultural and educational institutions. Even Proletkult (at least partly a workers' initiative) was

13. *Russkii sovetskii fol'klor. Antologiia*, Leningrad, 1967, p. 41.
14. See e.g. *A Radical Worker in Tsarist Russia: The Autobiography of Semen Ivanovich Kanatchikov*, ed. R. E. Zelnik, Stanford, 1986, pp. 105–8.
15. See B. Kolonitskii, '"Rabochaia intelligentsiia" v trudakh L.M. Kleinborta', in *Intelligentsiia i rossiiskoe obshchestvo v nachale xx veka*, St Petersburg, 1996, pp. 114–38.

established during 1917. Of course the intelligentsia had played a major organizing role in all of these, but that did not prevent many workers from seeing them as 'theirs' – and, at the very least, they all depended heavily on other workers joining them, giving up their time to them, paying subscriptions, and so on.

Their example inspired others to organize on the model of the workers – there were soviets of officers, Cossacks, students, and so on – and this acted as if to confirm the workers' vanguard role. Such was the domination of the workers and their class discourse in 1917 that many social groups on the margins of wage labour (and who in other political conditions might have stressed their separate identity) strove to identify themselves with them. Members of the 'labouring intelligentsia', professionals and even government officials applied to join the soviets of Workers' Deputies or identified themselves as 'workers', and the SR Party programme, for many years, identified the peasantry as members of a 'united working class'.[16]

This workers' pride did not just include the image of themselves as the leaders of the revolutionary nation; it extended to the idea that, as leaders of the first revolution in the world, they were the vanguard of an international proletarian movement. Working-class and Russian chauvinism were sometimes combined in this identity. But perhaps more common was the cosmopolitan idea of the worker as a member of the international working class. It was common for workers to adopt the identity of a European, as opposed to a Russian, worker, especially in Menshevik circles. It linked them with the working class and the social democratic movement of Western Europe and set them apart from the relatively 'backward' Russian workers. As one worker expressed it in his memoirs: 'Orthodoxy, Tsarism, Great Russian chauvinism, the Russian tunic, long beards and the Russian peasant haircut – I began to hate them all.'[17]

The notion of Russia as 'the freest country in the world', the vanguard of the international socialist movement, was heavily promoted by the Soviet leaders during 1917, and at times was even advanced to incorporate the idea of the revolution's export throughout the world.[18] This revolutionary messianism – symbolized by depictions of the globe on banners and red flags in 1917[19] – no doubt contributed to the sense of an international mission, giving workers confidence to see themselves as the vanguard of the workers of the world. It was an image which the socialists encouraged, none more so than the Bolsheviks.

16. A. Nishchenskii, *Polnyi sbornik programm vsekh politicheskikh partii v Rossii*, Lumiaki, 1917, p. 16.
17. A. Shapovalov, *Put' molodogo rabochego*, Moscow, 1923, p. 66.
18. RGIA, f. 806, op. 5, d. 10313, l. 131; M.IA. Fenomenov, *Russkii patriotizm i bratstvo narodov*, Moscow, 1917, pp. 5, 24.
19. Kornakov, 'Znamena', pp. 12–26.

Class and Human Rights

The discourse of class was ambivalent. It could be inclusive, uniting the whole of the 'labouring people' in a common sense of injustice and exclusion from society; or it could be more class exclusive, separating off a 'working class' and expressing pride in its distinctive identity. The idea of social justice was equally expressed in a multitude of different idioms. One was the pursuit of economic justice – increasing wages, the eight-hour day, better working conditions, and so on – which by definition was exclusive to particular groups of workers or the working class in general. On the other hand was the pursuit of moral and political ideals – respect for the dignity of all workers, the granting of basic rights, and so on – which could be perceived as universal human rights. These two idioms were intermingled in a language of class that combined the sense of political exclusion felt not just by workers but by all the lower classes with a common sense of exploitation within the workplace and society as a whole. Most workers appear to have had little problem situating their own discourse of class and human rights between the two, without seeing any tension between them. For, as Victoria Bonnell has suggested, they seem to have subscribed to a dualistic conception of rights, demanding both the rights of citizens and the right of the workers to control their own labouring environment.[20]

The discourse of human rights and citizenship could often be a vehicle for the idea of class. The workers' assertion of their human dignity was itself a statement of their sense of class. By declaring themselves to be 'citizens', and demanding equal rights in society on this basis, workers were asserting their class power. Indeed, the ideal of the individual could be an important means of developing a class identity among many workers, for the heightened sense of self-worth which came with this ideal often had the effect of stimulating them 'to feel more intensely their class oppression'.[21] Class and human rights were related idioms of the same class language – related through such ideas as *bespravie*, a general lack of rights that described the workers' position both as citizens and as 'wage slaves'. 'We have no rights, we are slaves,' declared the 'Bloody Sunday' petition of the Petrograd workers on 9 January 1905.[22] One of the main reasons why the discourse of class was so powerful in 1917 was that it

20. V.E. Bonnell, *Roots of Rebellion: Workers' Politics and Organizations in St Petersburg and Moscow, 1900–1914*, Berkeley, 1983, p. 190. See also the illuminating essay echoing this point by S.A. Smith, 'Workers and Civil Rights in Tsarist Russia, 1899–1917', in O. Crisp and L. Edmondson (eds), *Civil Rights in Imperial Russia*, Oxford, 1989, pp. 145–69.
21. M.D. Steinberg, 'Worker Authors and the Cult of the Person', in S. Frank and M. Steinberg (eds), *Cultures in Flux: Lower-Class Values, Practices, and Resistance in Late Imperial Russia*, Princeton, 1994, p. 170.
22. Smith, 'Workers and Civil Rights', pp. 151, 155–6.

had so many idioms. It could articulate diverse ideals and grievances, which enabled it to bring together many different groups (worker and non-worker) around the general feelings of exclusion and oppression that had traditionally united the common people against privileged society.

Human dignity had always been a major issue for the workers. They would not be slaves, as their peasant ancestors had been under serfdom, and they set great store on the attributes of citizenship which they might acquire through hard effort in the city. The values of *kultur'nost'* – literacy, secular rationalism, urban ways and manners – became central to the discourse of the labour movement. Becoming 'conscious' as a worker entailed a process of assimilation into urban society – joining clubs and associations, receiving new ideas, and above all developing the sense of dignity and individual worth that was shared by 'citizens'.[23]

The demand for 'polite address', and more generally for respectful treatment 'as human beings', was central to this discourse. Workers wanted to be addressed with the polite 'you' (*vyi*) instead of the familiar one (*tyi*), which they associated with serfdom. They wanted an end to the foul language, the arbitrary beatings and fines, the insulting behaviour of the foreman or the guard at the factory gate, the degrading body searches for stolen goods, and the sexual harassment of female workers. These were what they saw as the worst aspects of the Tsarist factory regime. The demand for respectful treatment played a growing role in the labour movement. It was contained in one-fifth of all strike resolutions and was still there as an issue, even if not stated, in most of the rest between 1907 and 1914.[24] Workers' complaints to the Factory Inspectorate about 'bad treatment' (*durnoe obrashchenie*) rose from 2,136 in 1901 to 21,873 in 1913, a statistic which underlines that workers were becoming increasingly aware of their own dignity 'as human beings' and of their *bespravie* both within the workplace and in society at large.[25]

This assertion of their dignity and worth was reflected in the workers' dress and body language. Readers of Kanatchikov's winning memoirs will recall how the acquisition of a fashionable suit, or the wearing of a hat with a velvet band, or even just a stylish haircut could become a mark

---

23. This aspect of the labour movement has been stressed by many historians. See e.g. R.E. Zelnik, '"Russian Bebels": An Introduction to the Memoirs of Semen Kanatchikov and Matvei Fischer', *Russian Review*, 1976, vol. 3–4; Bonnell, *Roots of Rebellion*, esp. pp. 43–72, 170–1, 183–4 and *passim*; T. McDaniel, *Autocracy, Capitalism, and Revolution in Russia*, Berkeley, 1988, esp. pp. 169–74; M.D. Steinberg, *Moral Communities: The Culture of Class Relations in the Russian Printing Industry, 1867–1907*, Berkeley, 1993. It was also stressed (as 'revolutionary morals') by Soviet historians – e.g. V.F. Shishkin, *Tak skladyvalas' revoliutsionnaia moral': Istoricheskii ocherk*, Moscow, 1967.
24. R.B. McKean, *St Petersburg between the Revolutions: Workers and Revolutionaries, June 1907–February 1917*, New Haven, 1990, pp. 258–9. See also D.P. Koenker and W.G. Rosenberg, *Strikes and Revolution in Russia, 1917*, Princeton, 1989, pp. 172–4.
25. Smith, 'Workers and Civil Rights', p. 151.

of the worker's self-esteem.[26] The swagger of the dandy worker in his Sunday best was seen by him as a mark of his *kulturnost'*. All this set the 'conscious' worker apart from the 'semi-peasant' ones, who all dressed in the same tunics and had their hair cut around a bowl. But it set him in conflict with his employers, who were often known to prohibit workers from wearing hats or from turning up for work in their best clothes – simply as a way of keeping them in their proper place.

At the heart of these demands and practices was an ethical vision of society centred on the belief in the equal human worth and rights of everyone, regardless of their class or *soslovie*. This was essentially a discourse of citizenship – within which the idea of class was concealed and contained. It was a dominant influence on the labour movement during and after the 1905 Revolution. Workers demanded the rights of man. They wanted equality with, and inclusion in, the rest of society. Many objected to being called a 'worker' – the title *rabochii* was seen as denigrating, connected as it was to the word for a slave (*rab*) – and preferred to be called by general occupational terms such as 'masterovoi', 'metallist', 'pechatnik', etc.[27]

This discourse remained powerful in the early months of the February Revolution. Workers' resolutions continued to speak of universal human rights and of the liberation of the people. They identified the workers, not so much as an exclusive 'class', but as a part of the 'labouring people'. The inclusive class language of the Populists was still much more common than the exclusive class language of the Bolsheviks. It best expressed the political spirit of 'democracy' – the idea of the revolution as the 'victory of all the people' (*vsenarodnaia*) against the oppressors of the old regime – manifested in the euphoric hopes of the spring and the Menshevik commitment to the 'revolutionary democracy', a broad bloc of the 'progressive forces' (including the liberal bourgeoisie) that had united to bring down the monarchy. This was a time when even the factory committees – later to be bastions of Bolshevism – seemed to have the potential to develop as organs of conciliation and cooperation between labour and management.[28] It was a time best expressed by the new inclusive slogan of democracy: 'Strength in Unity!'

At this early stage of the revolution many workers' resolutions spoke the language of human rights. The respect and dignity of the workers featured prominently in strike demands, especially (for obvious reasons) among clerical and service workers.[29] Other strike demands could also be

---

26. *A Radical Worker in Tsarist Russia*, ed. Zelnik.
27. U.A. Shuster, *Peterburgskie rabochie v 1905–1907 gg.*, pp. 33–8.
28. For this interpretation of the factory committees see V. Cherniaev, 'Rabochii kontrol' i al'ternativy ego razvitiia v 1917 g.', in *Rabochie i rossiiskoe obshchestvo. Vtoraia polovina xix v. – nachalo xx v.*, St Petersburg, 1994, pp. 164–77.
29. Koenker and Rosenberg, *Strikes*, pp. 164, 172–4.

constructed (and were no doubt often perceived) as a demand for human rights. The campaign for the eight-hour day was frequently presented as a basic issue of dignity. In one of their leaflets the Moscow Bolsheviks portrayed it (in the language of the international labour movement) as a basic pre-condition of the workers' new life as 'citizens': 'Eight hours of labour, eight hours of sleep, eight hours of rest and freedom. These eight hours are needed by the worker to become a conscious citizen. In these eight free hours he forges the weapons of the revolution. And so the eight-hour working day is the first defence and the first demand of the revolution.'[30] Claiming the status of 'citizens' – equal with the rest of society – was a preoccupation of many strikers during the spring of 1917. Indeed, it may be one reason why so many strikers at this time, especially the clerical and service workers, dressed in 'bourgeois' suits and ties, and the ladies in hats and dresses, to go out on strikes and demonstrations. The striking waiters and waitresses of Petrograd marched in their best clothes with banners bearing the demands: 'We insist on respect for waiters as human beings! Down with tips: waiters are citizens!'[31]

Some workers also demanded the status of 'professionals'. The right to control their own working hours – to work from nine to five and not do overtime if they did not want to – would put them on a par with other groups in society. This professional self-identity was obviously most developed among the highly skilled and literate working groups: printers, pharmaceutical assistants, factory clerks and foremen, etc. The printers, for example, referred to themselves as anything but 'workers', a title they associated with unskilled manual labour and the degradation of semi-slavery. They described themselves by their individual trades ('typesetters', 'printers', 'binders', and so on) or more generally as 'literary blacksmiths', 'masters' or 'free masters' of the 'graphic arts'. The typesetters, who inhabited the exclusive world of a printers' aristocracy, even addressed each other as 'colleague', a term normally used by the liberal professions.[32]

This professional self-identity was not necessarily limited to the highly skilled. Many types of worker could effectively demand the status and working conditions of professionals in their strike factory resolutions. The female textile workers of the Kenig Factory demanded, among other things, the following conditions in their dispute with the management at the Petrograd Chamber of Conciliation in June 1917: clean working conditions;

---

30. *Revoliutsionnoe dvizhenie v Rossii v aprele 1917 g. Dokumenty*, Moscow, 1958, p. 95. It was widely believed in socialist circles that the eight-hour day had been first proclaimed in Australia in 1857. See Vasil'ev, *Vos'michasovoi Chasovei rabochii den' i ego znachenie*, Helsingfors, 1917. Australia and New Zealand had the status of a Utopia in the Russian socialist underground.
31. Koenker and Rosenberg, *Strikes*, p. 231.
32. D.P. Koenker, 'Rabochii klass v 1917 g.: sotsial'naia i politicheskaia samoidentifikatsiia', in *Anatomiia revoliutsii. 1917 god v Rossii: massy, partii, vlast'*, St Petersburg, 1994, pp. 207–8; Smith, 'Craft Consciousness', p. 48.

places to sit down and drink a glass of water; places to smoke; the employment of assistants to clean the machines; special uniforms for different types of work; gloves for dirty work; soap to wash their hands; a cupboard for workers to hang their clothes; a medical assistant to be constantly on duty; free doctors' services and medicines; four weeks' paid holiday for experienced workers; maternity leave for all workers; pension schemes for the longest-serving 'employees'; and polite address from employers at all times.[33]

The construction of workers' demands as human rights was most clearly illustrated in their rhetoric of the 'living wage'. Such was their belief in the moral justice of this cause that many groups of workers were prepared to suffer economic loss in the campaign for it. It is remarkable that so many workers supported the lowering of wage differentials in order to secure a 'living wage' for female and teenage workers during the spring of 1917. It went against the whole tradition of the labour movement – as an exclusive class movement – where the domination of the most skilled workers tended to demand the preservation of these differentials. Some 'aristocrats' of the Russian labour movement did make a last stand for their retention – sometimes even breaking from their factory committee or trade union in order to establish their own exclusive craft organization which negotiated with the employers separately for higher rates of pay.[34] But the general trend of the labour movement in the spring was to close the gap between the highest and the lowest rates of pay, although of course inflationary conditions were moving wages in that way in any case. The initiative came from below. It was only later, in the summer months, that this tariff campaign was taken over by the factory committees and trade unions. From the first weeks of the revolution workers on the shop floor had been calling for equal rates of pay. They supported a minimum wage and relatively higher wage rises for women and other low-paid workers than for those on better rates of pay.

How should one interpret this shop-floor egalitarianism? To some extent, it may have been a tactical manoeuvre by the labour leaders to secure the support of the less skilled workers – who had traditionally been the most difficult to organize in unions and other collectives (not least because of their hostility towards the skilled élites) – and thus ensure solidarity for long-term strikes. The fact that the Anarchists supported wage levelling perhaps added political pressure, but it seems more likely that moral arguments simply won the day. The campaign for the minimum wage was couched in terms of human decency: it was a question of a 'living wage'

33. G. Linko, 'Rabochee dvizhenie na fabrike Kenig v 1917 g.', *Krasnyi arkhiv*, 58, 1933, pp. 136–40.
34. *Petrogradskii sovet rabochikh i soldatskikh deputatov v 1917 godu. Dokumenty i materialy*, St Petersburg, 1993, pp. 424, 428, 449–50; Smith, 'Craft Consciousness', p. 49.

(*golodnaia plata*). Many workers saw this as a moral cause – the half-starved female or ragged teenage worker was a symbol of their struggle for human rights – for which some were prepared to make extraordinary sacrifices. At the Metal Works in Petrograd, for example, after negotiations between the factory committee and management over a minimum wage became deadlocked in the early days of March, a member of the committee proposed that skilled workers should supplement the wages of the unskilled out of their own pay packets until the issue was resolved: 'If the administration will not meet us halfway and lend a hand to the hungry and ragged unskilled worker, then we ourselves must decide who we are. Are we exploiters, like the bourgeoisie, or are we just a bit more aware and capable of helping the unskilled worker? Aren't we, the skilled workers (*masterovye*), capable of lending a hand to our starving, ragged comrades?'[35]

The interesting thing about this resolution is its use of moral exhortation to shame the employers into concessions. This may have been a deliberate tactical ploy, and it helps us to explain why so many workers accepted the idea of wage levelling: it allowed them to make an overwhelming moral case for a cause that was of major economic benefit to the average working family in so far as the household income was dependent on the women's wage.

It was not unusual for the workers to pursue their own class interests by shaming their bosses with moral arguments. They had done so before the revolution.[36] Indeed, it may be that this subversive use of the moral language deployed by state and Church was found in labour movements of other countries too. But it does appear that it was a prominent feature of the Russian labour movement in 1917, and it may reflect the increased sense of power which many workers derived from the knowledge or belief that they had made the revolution and were thus entitled to pass moral judgement on how their factories (and the country) should be ruled.

The workers' ethical ideal of society could contain a challenge to the existing order if they tried to hold their employers morally accountable to that ideal. The good behaviour of the factory workers became a powerful argument for equally good conduct by their employers: if the workers arrived promptly for work, were always neat and tidy and did not get drunk, they could expect to be given the respect they deserved as 'citizens'. Such expectations were reinforced by the conciliation boards, which preached the language of mutual respect and cooperation between labour and management.[37] Through the factory committees and the 'courts of

35. TsGASP, f. 1000, op. 73, d. 16, l. 17.
36. See M.D. Steinberg, 'Vanguard Workers and the Morality of Class', in Siegelbaum and Suny (eds), *Making Workers Soviet*.
37. H. Hogan, 'Conciliation Boards in Revolutionary Petrograd: Aspects of the Crisis of Labor–Management Relations in 1917', *Russian History*, 1982, vol. 9, no. 1; W.G. Rosenberg, 'Social Mediation

honour' (*sudi chesti*), workers would set themselves the task of earning the rights of citizens by sober and responsible behaviour at work. Drunkenness was frequently condemned as 'conduct unworthy of a citizen'.[38] This moral benchmark of the citizen was equally applied to employers. They were expected to behave in a civil manner towards their workers and were not to treat them as a master treats his slaves. This was the basis of a new moral vision of society. As a committee of the Nevka spinning-mill workers in Petrograd resolved on 20 March: 'We say to all the workers and administration of the factory alike that with the overthrow of the old regime the old factory order should go too. All the old rudeness, cheating and tricks between the administration and the workers should pass into legend. We, the representatives of the workers' committee of the factory, call on all the workers to do their utmost to re-educate themselves in the new life.'[39]

A notable aspect of this moral discourse was its tendency to use legalistic terms. It was as if the workers were trying to enforce their own moral order in the factories by appropriating the language of the courts. Many factory committees resolved to create a new 'constitution' in the workplace after the February Revolution. They tore up the old rule books, drove out informers and police agents, and in a few instances even improvised a sort of factory 'trial', where a crowd of workers, acting as judge and jury, forced their foremen and employers to 'repent' their sins under the old regime. The normal procedure was for the 'accused' to be made to stand on a table in the middle of the factory while the workers shouted the 'charges' at him and the 'testimony of witnesses' was heard. If the defendant convinced the crowd that he was basically a good person whose conduct had been forced upon him by the higher authorities, he would be released. But if not, he risked being expelled from the factory, a humiliating punishment which often involved being 'carted out' in a wheelbarrow and dumped in the nearest river or canal.[40] The new conciliation boards, which nearly always took the workers' side in disputes with employers, similarly adopted the adversarial language of the courts.[41]

The creation of this quasi-legal system enabled the workers to legitimize their restructuring of the moral order in the factory by giving it the same 'official' form and language as the new democratic government. This same impulse lay behind the fashion for committees in 1917: it was not just a

and State Construction(s) in Revolutionary Russia', *Social History*, 1994, vol. 19, no. 2.

38. TsGASP, f. 131, op. 1, d. 16, 1. 5; S.A. Smith, *Red Petrograd: Revolution in the Factories, 1917–18*, Cambridge, 1983, p. 94.
39. *Revoliutsionnoe dvizhenie*, pp. 69–70.
40. TsGASP, f. 9391, op. 1, d. 8, l. 14; V. Perazich, *Tekstili Leningrada v 1917 g. Iz materialov dlia istorii klassovoi bor'by tekstilei Leningrada*, Leningrad, 1927, pp. 20–1.
41. Hogan, 'Conciliation', p. 53.

"Самодержавие."

1   'Autocracy'. The postcard plays on the double meaning of the word 'derzhit'' – the verb 'to hold' but equally the root of the word 'autocracy' (samoderzhavie). Rasputin's 'hold' on the Empress makes him the true ruler of Russia. Many pornographic postcards of this type were produced in the wake of the February Revolution. They were in wide circulation during 1917.

ДЕМОНСТРАЦИЯ НА ЗНАМЕНСКОЙ ПЛОЩАДІ

2 'Demonstration on Znamenskaia Square.' This postcard of the February Days in Petrograd was widely circulated during 1917. The equestrian statue of Alexander III (the 'Hippopotamus') made the square symbolically significant in the crowd's struggle against the police.

3 Crowds outside the Tauride Palace during the February Days. Note the mixing of soldiers and citizens which suggests the scene is on or after 27 February. The banner reads: 'Long live the all-national socialist republic!'

4–5 Iconoclasm. Above: the removal of the Romanov insignia from a pharmacy. Below: a crowd on the Nevsy Prospekt in Petrograd stands around a bonfire with torn-down Tsarist emblems during the February Days. The display for the camera was an important part of the

6–7 Iconoclasm. Above: a group of Moscow workers playing with the stone head of Alexander II in front of a movie camera. Below: the police archives in Petrograd destroyed by fire in the February Days. The photograph was made into a postcard and circulated widely during 1917.

8   Iconoclasm. Romanov symbols too large to destroy were covered up. Here workers place red cloth covers over Tsarist emblems on the iron fence of the Winter Palace in Petrograd. March 1917.

9   Sergeant Timofei Kirpichnikov (fifth from the right), leader of the mutiny of the Volynsky Regiment in the February Revolution and (for a short while) the people's hero, with members of the British delegation in the spring of 1917. Note the red rosettes in their button holes.

10   The Revolution created an explosion of the printed word. A soldier activist distributes a party newspaper.

11   A political meeting in the army during the spring of 1917.

12   This postcard shows the mass political demonstration on 18 June in Petrograd. Thousands of similar postcard were sent to activists in the provinces to inform them of events in the capital. The main banner reads: "Peace to all the world. All power to the people. All land to the people.'

13–14   Funeral rites. Above: the burial of the victims of the February Revolution on the Champ de Mars in Petrograd on 23 March 1917. The event served as the basis for a national rallying behind the symbols of the Revolution. The slogans of the spring are featured on the banners: 'Strength in Organization', 'Victory to the People', and so on. Note the figure of Mother Russia pointing to the light of liberty (right); and the peasant (barely visible on the left) shaking hands with a soldier. Below: by contrast, the funeral of the seven Cossacks killed in Petrograd during the July Days lacked symbols to unite the Right.

15–18 The Kerensky cult. Kerensky's image was gradually militarized during the course of 1917 as he took on the role of, first, War Minister and then virtual dictator of the country during the war crisis of the summer. Above: as the people's Minister of Justice with senior officers during the spring. Below: as War Minister in a military-style tunic with ministerial hat, cane and trousers. Overleaf above: the War Minister in full military dress (a fashion emulated by Lenin and Stalin) on an inspection of the Northern Front. Note that Kerensky shakes hands with his left hand. His right hand, tucked into his breast, Napoleonic style, was mysteriously 'wounded' – a mark of sympathy for the millions of soldiers injured at the Front. (Some said he had wounded it from so much shaking hands.) Overleaf below: the veteran Marxist G.V. Plekhanov and delegates to the first All-Russian Soviet Congress group around a portrait of the people's hero Kerensky.

19   The cult of Kornilov. The General is greeted as a hero by the right-wing members of the Officers' Union on his arrival in Moscow for the State Conference on 12 August.

20   Waiters and waitresses of Petrograd on strike. The main banner reads: 'We insist on respect for waiters as human beings.' The three other banners call for an end to the degrading practice of tipping service staff. This emphasis on respect for workers as citizens was a prominent feature of many strikes and demonstrations. Note in this context that the strikers are well dressed – they could be mistaken for bourgeois citizens – since this was a demonstration of their dignity.

21   1 May celebration in the active army. The banner reads: 'Long live the international holiday of the proletariat!!' The term 'proletariat' was still confined largely to Marxist circles in 1917. It is questionable whether many of these peasant soldiers understood or identified with it.

22   A village meeting in 1917. The peasants stop to take a pinch of snuff and pose for the camera.

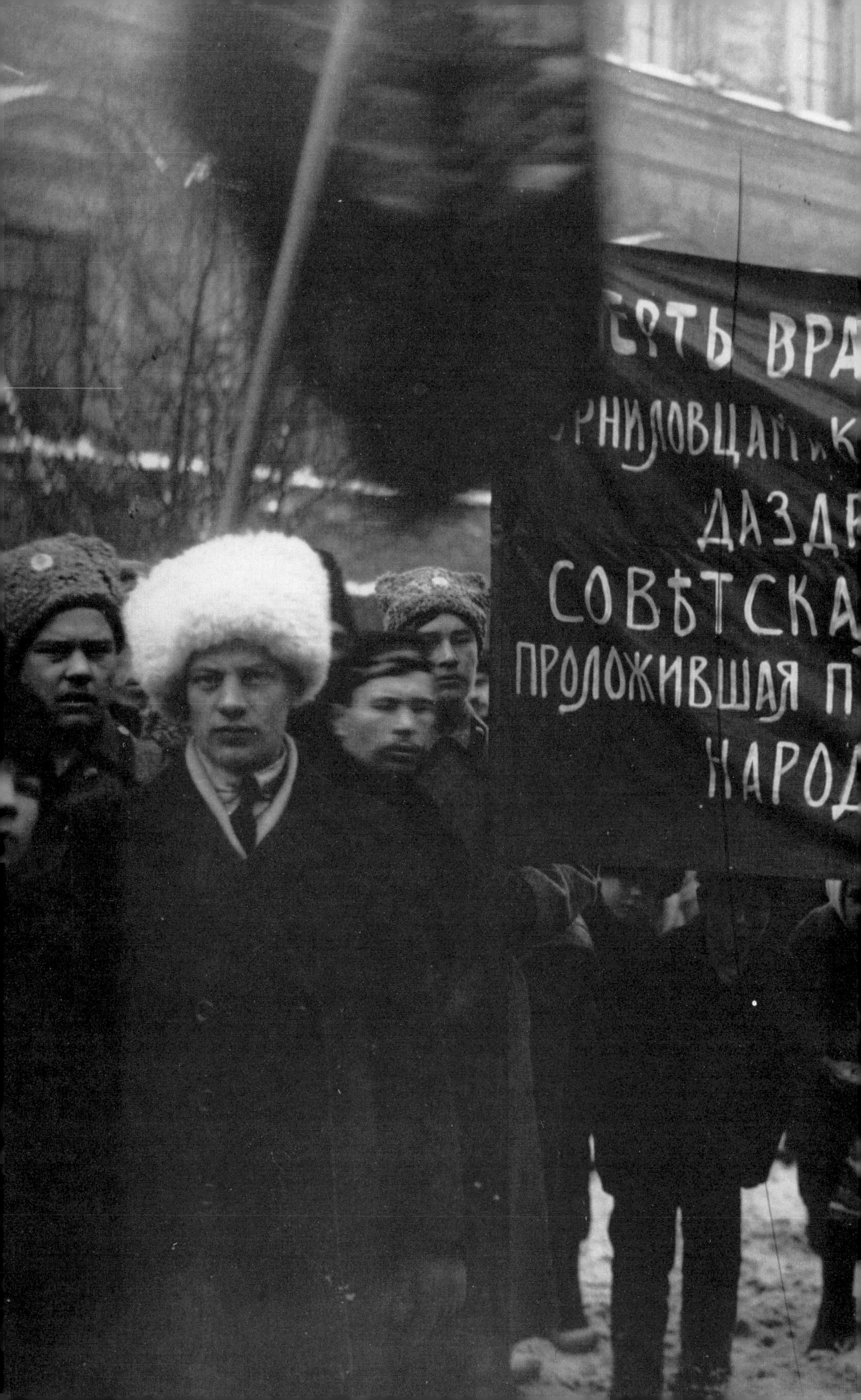
ЕРТЬ ВРА
РНИЛОВЦАМ И К
ДАЗДР
СОВѢТСКА
ПРОЛОЖИВШАЯ П
НАРОД

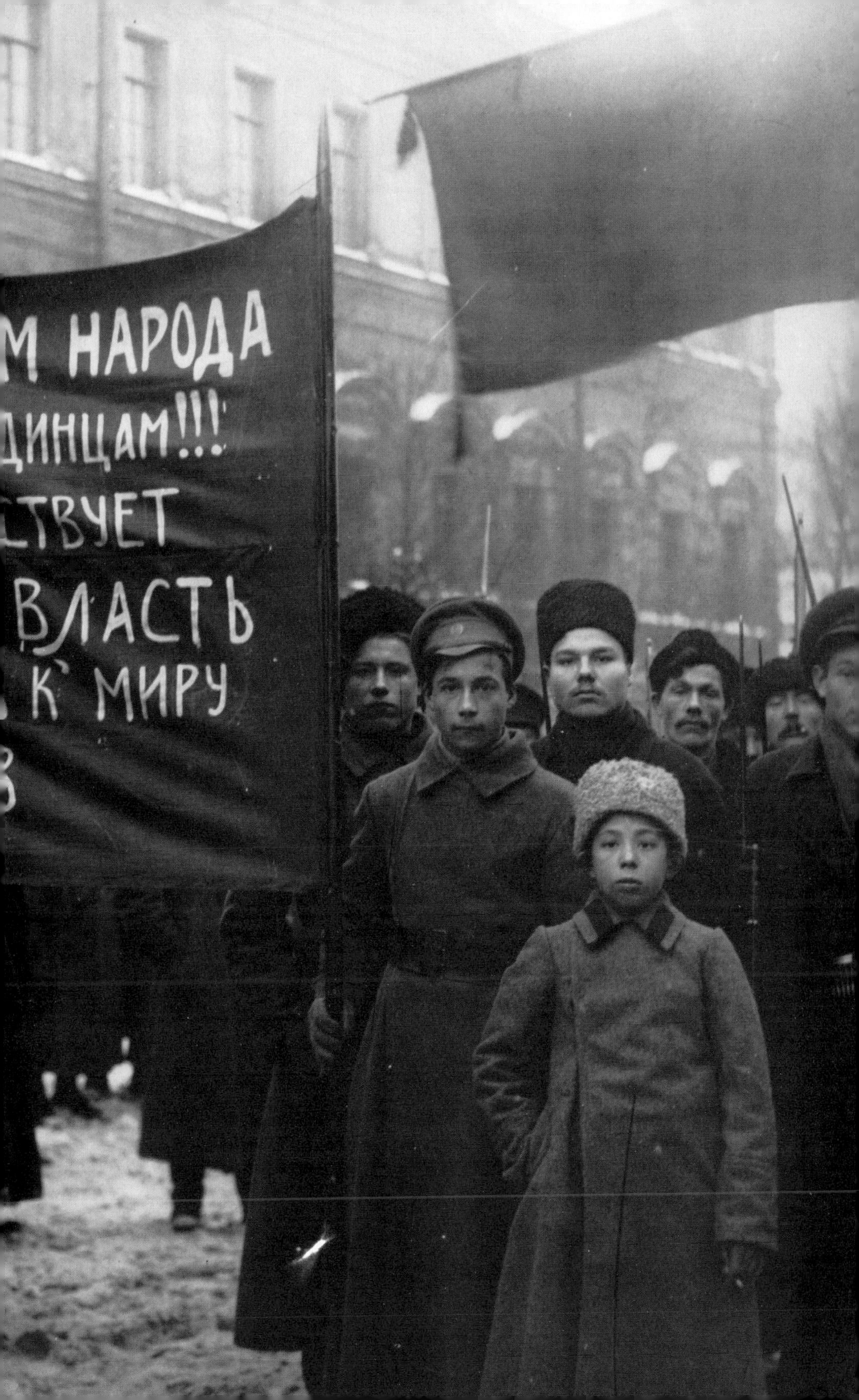

м НАРОДА
ДИНЦАМ!!!
ЕТВУЕТ
ВЛАСТЬ
К' МИРУ

23   Previous page: the culture of killing. The banner reads: 'Death to the enemies of the people, the Kornilovites and Kaledinites. Long live Soviet Power paving the way to the peace of all peoples.' Terror and utopia were intimately linked.

24–25   The war against the 'burzhoois'. Above and below: members of the 'propertied élite' are conscripted to clear snow while their Red Guards watch, Petrograd, 1918.

means of popular organization but a way of mastering the linguistic symbols of power itself. Among the lower classes, in general, there was a sort of groping understanding that language was a key to power and success which hitherto the privileged alone had enjoyed; and that to defend their own interests against them they had to attain a linguistic parity with the old social élites. For example, in the spring of 1917 leftist soldiers frequently complained to the Petrograd Soviet that 'smooth-talking democratic officers' were beating them in the elections to the newly established soldiers' committees. Many of them called for 'soldier orators who are equal to the cunning intelligentsia in this war of words'.[42] The workers' use of legalistic language not only gave them this linguistic parity with their employers and officialdom but, even more importantly, it also gave their resolutions (at least in their own eyes) the moral force of 'law'. By dressing up their economic demands and moral visions in the form of 'constitutions', they sought to make them binding on their employers.

Exclusive Dialects of Class

The universal language of human rights which many workers spoke in the early months of 1917 was not set to last. Lurking beneath their rhetoric of citizenship, there had always been a visceral hatred of the rich, a contempt for the law and desire for revenge by the mass of the workers. That hostility was voiced more explicitly as the economic crisis of the summer and the autumn strained labour's relations with management and the Kornilov uprising reinforced suspicions of the bourgeoisie. Factory committees saw themselves increasingly as fighting capitalist 'sabotage'.[43] Their inclusive spirit of the spring, when foremen and officials had joined the committees, gave way to a new class militancy and exclusiveness, with foremen and officials excluded from their factory meetings as 'class aliens'. The boundaries of 'the working class' became more narrowly defined by those types of worker who swung to the Left and its rhetoric of militant struggle: factory clerks and specialists (*spetsy*) were consigned to the camp of the 'burzhoois'; cleaners, street traders and tram conductors were excluded from 'the working class', an identity increasingly defined by economic conflict on the factory floor.

This discourse of class exclusion and class conflict was a change of idiom rather than a new language altogether. The earlier discourse of human rights had of course been a class language too, albeit one in which the morally and politically inclusive aspects of that language had been to

---

42. TsGASP, f. 1000, op. 74, d. 13, l. 133.
43. Smith, *Red Petrograd*, pp. 148, 174–5, 179 and *passim*.

the fore and its more class-exclusive aspects had remained concealed. But the political and economic conflicts of the summer encouraged many workers to adopt a more exclusive attitude to class and a more class-based attitude to politics.

One sign of this was the common understanding of the word 'democracy' (*demokratiia*) in 1917. It began as a universal political concept – one including 'all the people' in a 'democratic republic' (*vsenarodnaia demokraticheskaia respublika*). But it soon became an exclusive social term – one dividing 'the labouring people' from 'the bourgeoisie'. This transformation was a sign of the growing domination of the class discourse in the political language of 1917. The common people's understanding of 'democracy' was intimately linked with their social expectations and self-identity. If they often thought of class in terms of democratic rights, then they also thought of democracy in terms of social class.

A class-based understanding of 'democracy' – making it synonymous with 'the common people' – was not unique to Russia at this time. British socialists had often used the term in this social sense at the end of the nineteenth century. Thus in 1896 Ernest Belfort Bax, a leading member of the Social Democratic Federation, wrote to its paper *Justice* attacking an article by Ramsay MacDonald, in which Bax clearly used the word 'democracy' as a synonym for the labouring masses: 'Out of dread of allowing the democracy to fulfil a political function, Mr MacDonald would perpetuate an official body whose sole purpose is to serve as a bulwark of hide-bound red-tape reaction.' Such usages coexisted for a long time with what we would regard as the normal definition of democracy – as a system of government or ideological grouping – and indeed they appear to have become something of a conscious archaism in the way they were employed by many socialists to imply good old-fashioned radical virtue.[44] In any case in Britain, as in most of Western Europe, the trend appears to have been towards the modern usage of the term 'democracy'. It was increasingly understood as a governmental system, the opposite of which was 'dictatorship'.

But in Russia in 1917 the social understanding of the word 'democracy' was not just dominant but dictatorial: no other construction of the term was allowed to challenge it. 'Democracy' was almost universally understood to mean 'the common people' – and its opposite was not 'dictatorship' but the 'bourgeoisie' or indeed the whole of privileged society.

This peculiar – one might even say revolutionary – interpretation of the word 'democracy' appears to have stemmed from common usage: *demokratiia* was practically interchangeable with the words *narod* ('the people') and *trudiashchikhsia* ('the toilers') in the language of the street. This irritated lexicographers. 'The democracy is the whole of the people, poor and rich, men and women,' argued N.A. Arsen'ev in his *Short Political Dictionary for Everyone*. 'But now it is only the poor and common people, the workers and the peasants, who are described as the democracy: and this is wrong.'[45] Nevertheless, despite its origins in common usage, this class-based understanding was also found among the educated classes. In its *Dictionary of Political Words and Activists*, Liberated Russia, the liberal publishing house established by the Duma in 1917, defined democracy as 'all those classes who live by their own labour: workers, peasants, officials and the intelligentsia'.[46] Kerensky, in his famous speech to the Petrograd Soviet on 2 March, also used the word in this social sense when he claimed that, as a member of the government, he would be 'a hostage of democracy'. Kerensky was even more explicit in his address to the Soviet on 29 March: 'In the name of the Provisional Government of the country I greet and bow before the democracy: the workers, soldiers and peasants.'[47] Tsereteli also used the word in this social sense. Even in his *Memoirs*, written many years after 1917, he counterposed 'the democracy' against 'the bourgeoisie'.[48] The practice even spread to foreign diplomats. British military observers in Russia frequently distinguished between the 'bourgeois' and the 'democratic' parties.[49] Even George Buchanan, the British Ambassador to Petrograd in 1917, described 'the bourgeoisie' and 'the democracy' as two entirely separate political camps.[50]

This socialization of the word 'democracy' highlights the growing domination of the idiom of class in the political discourse of 1917. The Western language of democracy was, on its translation into Russian politics, redefined in terms of a language of class. It was this that ultimately undermined the attempt by the Russian democratic leaders to impose the ideals of 1789 on to the realities of 1917. There was no real cultural or social foundation for the liberal conception of democracy in Russia, at least not in the midst of a violent revolution, and the liberals themselves were ambivalent about the need to address their message to the urban masses.[51] Workers were capable of understanding the language of political democracy,

45. N.A. Arsen'ev, *Kratkii politiciheskii slovar' dlia vsekh*, Moscow, 1917, p. 9.
46. *Tolkovnik politicheskikh slov i politicheskikh deiatelei*, Petrograd, 1917, p. 22.
47. A.F. Kerensky, *The Kerensky Memoirs: Russia and History's Turning Point*, London, 1965, p. 411; *Petrogradskii sovet rabochikh i soldatskikh deputatov v 1917 godu*, pp. 77–8.
48. *Pervyi den' vserossiiskogo uchreditel'nogo sobraniia*, Petrograd, 1918, pp. 36, 45; I.G. Tsereteli, *Vospominaniia o fevral'skoi revoliutsii*, Paris, 1963, kn. 1, pp. 61, 121; kn. 2, pp. 194, 394, 402.
49. PRO (London), War Office, 158/964.
50. G. Buchanan, *My Mission to Russia and Other Diplomatic Memoirs*, London, 1923, vol. 2, p. 128.
51. See W.G. Rosenberg, 'Representing Workers and the Liberal Narrative of Modernity', *Slavic Review*, 1996, vol. 55, no. 2, pp. 245–69.

but they did not choose to think of democratic power in the language of 'constitutions' and 'parliaments', 'citizenship' and 'the rule of law'. They chose instead to think of it in terms of 'us' and 'them' – the 'democracy' against 'the bourgeoisie' – and in terms of which side would prevail against the other. As Lenin had once put it, the power question was a question of *kto kogo?* ('who whom?'). The workers talked of 'our revolution', 'our victory' and 'our liberty' after February 1917.[52] They understood the word 'democracy' to be synonymous with 'democratic organizations' (e.g. the soviets, factory committees, etc.), 'democratic forces' (i.e. those in favour of socialism) and the 'revolutionary democracy' (which meant the same thing).

In their view the tasks of the democracy and of the social revolution essentially amounted to the same: the political rejection of the 'bourgeois' state. During the course of 1917 the resolutions of the workers and the soldiers increasingly condemned the Provisional Government as a 'bourgeois' government. Its policies were deemed inimical to the interests of 'the democracy' (i.e. to their own social revolutions). The crucial turning-point was the Kornilov Affair, when Kerensky and his 'bourgeois ministers' were widely suspected of having been involved in the military plot against 'the revolution' and the red flag. Thousands of resolutions passed at factory and garrison meetings in the wake of the crisis called almost unanimously on the Soviet parties to end their coalition with 'the bourgeoisie' and establish their own 'democratic' government. The social conflict between 'the democracy' and 'the bourgeoisie' was thus linked in the language of these resolutions with the political conflict between the soviets and the Provisional Government; and any member of Kerensky's cabinet, even if in party terms a socialist, was portrayed as a 'bourgeois minister'.

From this point on, the democratization of the sphere of government was conceived from below as the purging of its 'bourgeois' elements: no 'bourgeois' party could be 'democratic'. The Democratic Conference, convened by the Soviet leadership to reform the government in the wake of the Kornilov Affair, specifically excluded the Kadets on this basis, even though the main question at the conference was whether to involve them in the reformed government. Workers' and soldiers' resolutions in the autumn of 1917 clearly understood Soviet power to mean the establishment of a purely democratic government, or what was called then in Soviet circles 'the dictatorship of the democracy'. The workers of the Dietmar factory in Kharkov, for example, called on the All-Russian Soviet, 'as the only organ representing the will of the entire people', to assume power.[53] A general meeting of the Pipe Works in Petrograd called for all power

52. V. Stankevich, *Vospominaniia, 1914–19 g.*, Berlin, 1920, p. 33.
53. *Izvestiia Iiuga*, 2 Sept. 1917.

to be transferred to the soviets 'for the defence of the people's liberty'.[54] This popular association of the soviets with democracy played a vital role in the events (and the later myth) of October, enabling the Bolsheviks to bring out their supporters on rumours that Kerensky was planning to launch a 'counter-revolution' by attacking the garrison and preventing the opening of the Soviet Congress. After their capture of the telephone exchange on the night of 24 October, the Kronstadt sailors passed a resolution to imprison the Junkers they had taken with it in the Kronstadt naval base. Their aim was 'to punish the Junker-Kornilovites for going against the will of the democracy'.[55]

This was much more than a group of revolutionaries appealing to 'democracy' to justify their actions. It was a deeply and widely held belief – not just among workers but among the peasants and the soldiers too – that the common people were the 'real' people, 'the democracy', and that, consequently, the only democratic forms of government were those public bodies, like the soviets and committees, that advanced the interests of social revolution in the factories, the regiments and the villages. Nothing could be further from the liberal conception of democracy – based upon the ideals of 1789 – which informed the political discourse of the educated classes in 1917. Where the educated classes spoke of civic rights and duties, the masses took the view that what had taken place was a social revolution in which the old élites were to be the losers and themselves the winners. Here was the crucial political divide between the common people and the privileged class: each spoke a different language of democracy.

The soviets were conceived as the democratic organs of this social revolution. They represented the workers, soldiers and peasants, but not the bourgeoisie; and in this respect their very title was symbolic and important. For many workers, in particular, the Soviet ideal of democracy was preferable to the Constituent Assembly precisely because it excluded any bourgeois representation. 'The less bourgeoisie, the more democracy.' The Bolsheviks were careful to exploit this perception of the Soviets.

The Bolshevik discourse of class was in fact extremely flexible, which was perhaps a key to its appeal among those workers who swung, albeit briefly, towards them in the autumn and the winter of 1917. On the one hand, the Bolsheviks were distinguished from the other socialist parties by the exclusivity of their rhetoric of class. They spoke of the soviets in a language of class that set them, as the organs of the 'proletariat', in opposition to 'the bourgeoisie' and the so-called 'bourgeois' concepts of democracy. For example, in their 'Declaration of the Rights of the Working

54. *Zvezda*, 4 Sept. 1917.
55. TsGASP, f. 131, op. 4, d. 31, l. 6.

People' (which they presented as an ultimatum to the Constituent Assembly and subsequently passed at the Third Soviet Congress in January 1918) the Bolsheviks deliberately echoed the language of *The Rights of Man* in order to underline the point that the interests of the 'proletariat' and 'the working class' were henceforth to be considered above the principles of citizenship. But, on the other hand, the Bolsheviks were also known to speak of class in more inclusive and even populist terms. In their early propaganda, for example, especially in the provinces, they frequently referred to the soviets (and to Sovnarkom) as a 'people's government' – one that represented all the 'labouring people', or the 'toiling people', including the poor peasants and the soldiers – rather than as a government of the working class.[56]

This was indeed a major reason why the discourse of class became so dominant during 1917. It was flexible enough to contain within its many dialects a wide range of different identities, moral visions of 'the people' or 'democracy', political ideals and socio-economic grievances. Yet at the same time it was meaningful enough to unite the diverse groups who identified with it, from the semi-peasant soldier to the textile worker, from the tram conductor to the factory clerk, in a common feeling of exclusion from society and, perhaps more importantly, in a common struggle for human rights.

56. TsGAIPD, f. 1, op. 1, d. 225, l. 42; d. 226, l. 30; d. 239, l. 67; Gosudarstvennyi Arkhiv Kurskoi Oblasti (Kursk), f. 474, op. 2, d. 8, l. 11; f. 1893, op. 1, d. 1, l. 3.

5

The Language of
the Revolution in the Village

The Provisional Government was a government of persuasion. Not having been elected by the people, it depended largely on the power of the word to establish its authority. It was a government of national confidence, self-appointed during the February Revolution with the aim of steering Russia through the wartime crisis towards democracy, and as such its mandate had to be *created* by propaganda, cults and festivals, fostering consensus and national unity. There was little else the government could do, since it lacked the power to enforce its will by any other means. And yet many of its liberal leaders also saw a virtue in this necessity. They rejected the traditions of the Tsarist state, emphasized the need to govern by consent, and, in the words of Prince G.E. Lvov, the Prime Minister, placed their faith in the 'good sense, statesmanship and loyalty of the people' to uphold the new democracy.[1]

Their optimism was based on the assumption that the primary duty of the February Revolution was to educate the people in their civic rights and duties. Like the French revolutionaries of 1789, they understood their task as nothing less than the creation of a *new political nation*. The peasants, above all, who made up more than three-quarters of the population, had to be transformed into active citizens. They had to be brought out of their cultural isolation and integrated into the national political culture. Upon that hung the revolution's fate – and not just because it depended on the peasants to fulfil their civic duty by supplying foodstuffs and soldiers for the nation, but even more importantly because, as they formed the vast majority of the electorate, it required them to vote as citizens, free from the domination of their former masters (landowners, priests and monarchist officials), in the elections to the Constituent Assembly and the other institutions of the nascent democracy.

1.   A.F. Kerensky, *The Kerensky Memoirs: Russia and History's Turning Point*, London, 1965, p. 228.

The 'darkness' of the peasants – and its inherent dangers for the revolution – was the constant refrain of democratic agitators in the countryside during 1917. 'The peasants do not understand anything about politics,' wrote one soldier from Penza province to the Petrograd Soviet on 25 April. 'Although there were deputies [i.e. Soviet agitators], the peasants soon forgot what they had told them about freedom, a republic, and a monarchy.'[2] As one propagandist concluded:

> The peasant is still very easily deceived by monarchist officials and other dark forces in his midst. He has never been acquainted with the most elementary political questions, he has never received the education of a citizen. But the peasants, whose votes will decide the political and socio-economic structure of the Russian state, have to become citizens, with an understanding of the different forms of rule and an ability to make rational choices between different political points of view, immediately![3]

Language was the key to this cultural integration of the peasantry. The dissemination of the revolution's rhetoric to the countryside – the development of a national discourse of civic rights and duties – would create the new political nation dreamed of by the leaders of democracy. Here again there were clear parallels with France. For just as in France there was an enormous gulf between the written culture of the revolution and the patois oral culture of the peasantry, so in Russia there was an equal divide between the political language of the towns and the terms in which the peasants couched their own moral and political concepts.

The terminology of the revolution was a foreign language to most of the peasants (as indeed it was to a large proportion of the uneducated urban populace) in most parts of Russia.[4] Of course there were important variations. The younger, richer and better educated peasants tended to be more politically aware, as did those living closest to the towns or in regions with a well-developed network of party and peasant organization (e.g. in parts of the north, the middle Volga, or western Siberia).[5] But in general the peasants and their spokesmen in 1917 were painfully aware of the linguistic gulf that separated them from the revolution in the towns. 'We can't understand many of your words,' complained one peasant to the SR leaders of the Kurgan' peasant congress during a debate on the

---

2. TsGASP, f. 7384, op. 9, d.209, l. 17.
3. E.N. Medynskii, *Revoliutsiia i vneshkol'noe obrazovanie. S prilozheniem konspektov besed s krest'ianami nad temami sviazannymi s revoliutsiei*, Moscow, 1917, pp. 4–5.
4. In the Ukraine, the Baltic lands and the Caucasus, where the urban élites were foreign to the native peasantry, this was literally so. But my concern here is exclusively with Russia.
5. For a discussion of these variations see O. Figes, *A People's Tragedy: The Russian Revolution, 1891–1924*, London, 1996, pp. 92–5, 182–4.

structure of the state: 'you have to speak in Russian.'[6] Imported words (e.g. 'republic', 'constitution', 'federation', 'democracy', 'regime', 'annexation', and even 'revolution') were misunderstood and mispronounced by peasants. Thus the word 'republic' (*respublika*) appeared as *rezh' publiku* ('cut the public'), *despublika* and *razbublika* in various peasant letters; 'regime' (*rezhim*) became *prizhim* ('suppress'); 'constituent' (*uchreditel'noe*) was transformed into *chereditelnoe* (on the basis that the Constituent Assembly would decide everything 'in its turn', or *cheredom*); 'revolution' (*revoliutsiia*) was pronounced and written as *revutsia, levoliutsiia* and *levorutsia*; the 'Bolsheviks' (*bol'sheviki*) were confused with a party of *bol'shaki* (peasant elders) and of *bol'shie* (big people); while 'annexation' (*anneksiia*) was thought by many peasant soldiers to be a small Balkan kingdom neighbouring *kontributsiia* (the word used at this time for 'indemnity') and at least on one occasion was confused with a woman called *Aksinia*. 'Who is this Aksinia?' one peasant asked another who had heard about her from an 'oratater' (*oratel'* instead of *orator*). 'God knows who she is. They say that because of her there will be a great harm, and that if there is Aksinia there will be another war against us after we have made peace with the Germans.' 'Ooh she must be bad: over one woman there is war again!' (*Ish' ved' kakaia vrednaia: ot odnoi baby i opiat' voina!*)[7]

Equally, the new institutions of the state appeared strange and alien to many of the peasants. One group of wounded peasant soldiers in a Petrograd hospital wrote through a scribe a series of petitions to the Tauride Palace in September. Each one started with the clumsy words: 'I have the honour humbly to ask the Tauride Palace not to refuse me an extraordinary pension as a wounded veteran of the war . . . ' None of the petitions was addressed to an official body – indeed the palace was empty by this time, the Duma having closed its offices and the Soviet having moved to the Smolny – and it seems the soldiers had no idea of who was in the building. The Tauride Palace – perhaps because of the connotations of the word 'palace' or perhaps because it had become a symbol of the revolution (which frequently appeared in propaganda posters) – simply meant to them the seat of power.[8]

Such misunderstandings were a major hindrance to the democratic cause in the countryside. Its propaganda had to cross a huge linguistic

6.   *Pervyi kurganskii krest'ianskii s'ezd (8–9 aprelia 1917 g.)*, Kurgan', 1917, p. 3.
7.   TsGASP, f. 7384, op. 7, d. 11, l. 57; op. 9, d. 254, l. 217; f. 1000, op. 74, d. 13, l. 147; A.M. Selishchev, *Iazyk revoliutsionnoi epokhi. Iz nabliudenii nad russkim iazykom poslednikh let (1917–1926)*, Moscow, 1928, p. 215; A. Okninskii, *Dva goda sredi krest'ian'. Vidennoe slyshannoe, perezhitoe v Tambovskoi gubernii s noiabria 1918 goda do noiabria 1920 goda*, Riga, 1936, p. 32; RGVIA, f. 162, op. 2, d. 18, l. 12; *Volia naroda*, 26 May 1917, no. 23, p. 2.
8.   RGIA, f. 1278, op. 10, d. 18, ll. 206, 209, 211, 213, 215, 217, 219, 222, 224, 226, 228, 229, etc.

gulf to communicate with the peasantry. The first pamphlets for the rural population were mostly reprints of editions published during the 1905 Revolution. According to a valuable report by the Temporary Committee of the Duma during May, they had been written 'in a language which the people do not speak ... They needed translators.' The report concluded that this 'played a major role in the rapid alienation of the peasantry from the intelligentsia'.[9]

A related problem was the peasants' inclination to believe naively every printed word. Long starved of an open press, they were hungry for *any* printed news, especially about the war and the latest events in the capital, and as a result they tended to believe that whatever was printed must be true. The Duma report thought that as a rule

> The less literate a peasant is, the more he believes in the written word. He has a conviction that if something is printed in a book then it is the truth. He reads one newspaper – and that is one truth; then he reads another – where there is another, even if it is directly contrary to the first. He sits there and tries to work it out 'freely' – until his head begins to spin.[10]

Such credulity could make the peasant vulnerable to demagogues, as Kerensky warned in his famous 'rebellious slaves' speech to the soldiers' delegates at the end of April, when he spoke of those who 'even now take every printed word for truth'.[11] One may suppose that among the peasants there was some extra persuasive power in the newspaper of the Bolsheviks because it was called *Pravda* or 'The Truth'. For during 1917 the Bolsheviks' opponents started up a rival paper by the name of 'The People's Truth' (*Narodnaia pravda*).

Oral forms of propaganda faced the same problems. Too many agitators spoke in terms the peasants could not understand, especially in the early months before they had been trained for their rural trips. Too many talked *at them* in long and boring speeches rather than engaging them in lively conversations. The educative purpose of the peasant congresses was similarly lost, especially in the early months, because of the tendency of the congress leaders, most of whom were SR *intelligenty*, to speak in abstract terms way above the heads of the peasant delegates. At the Kurgan' peasant congress during April, for example, the SR leaders of the congress became embroiled in a long debate about the relative merits of various federative principles.

9.   Ibid., d. 4, ll. 257–8. The report was compiled from information provided by local correspondents in more than a dozen provinces for the period between the start of March and the end of April.
10. Ibid., l. 257.
11. R.P. Browder and A.F. Kerensky (eds), *The Russian Provisional Government, 1917. Documents*, 3 vols, Stanford, 1961, vol. 2, p. 915.

The peasant delegates became restless, and at last one intervened: 'I have been listening for two hours and can't understand: is this an assembly for peasants or for speech-making? If this is a peasant assembly, then the peasants ought to speak.' There was a general hum of approval so that, whilst insisting on the need to discuss such important questions, the SR leaders felt obliged to explain the meaning of a federation to the delegates in terms that were more comprehensible to them. They chose to compare the federal division of the state to the division of the communal land. But this merely gave rise to more misunderstandings. One group of delegates said they did not want to 'divide Russia', while another suggested 'taking away the land of the nobles and dividing it between the peasants', only to be told, 'that is not the question'.[12] The all-too-frequent consequence of such abstract debates was that the peasant delegates forgot what had been said. As the Duma report put it:

> There are occasions when a deputy returning from Petrograd, where he has been deluged by noisy rhetoric and the storm of party arguments and debates, replies to the question about what he had heard there: 'I have forgotten! I've forgotten everything I heard. I heard so much that in the end I could remember nothing.' He has become confused and forgotten all. And his fellow-villagers put him into jail because they have paid him to travel to the city and he has told them nothing.[13]

Bridging the Linguistic Gulf?

The democratic intelligentsia set out with the passion of civic missionaries to break down these linguistic barriers and communicate the gospel of their revolution to the peasantry. It was like another 'Going to the people' – the propaganda mission of the Populists in the 1870s – only now the government was on their side. Dictionaries were published to explain the revolution's strange vocabulary.[14] And there was a whole new range of pamphlets for the people telling them what they should know to become citizens.[15] The new rural press also took upon itself the political education

---

12. *Pervyi kurganskii krest'ianskii s'ezd*, p. 3.
13. RGIA, f. 1278, op. 10, d. 4, l. 249.
14. See e.g. *Tolkovnik politicheskikh slov*, Petrograd, 1917; *Karmannyi slovar' revoliutsionnera*, Petrograd, 1917; N.G. Berezin, *Novyi sotsial'no-politicheskii slovar'. Sputnik svobodnogo grazhdanina*, Odessa, 1917. Over a dozen such dictionaries were published, with a total print run of half a million copies, between March and October.
15. See e.g. N. Petrovich, *Chto nyzhno znat' krest'ianinu*, Kiev, 1917; Petrovich, *Krest'ianskaia pamiatka*, Moscow, 1917; S. Zaiats', *Kak muzhiki ostalis' bez nachal'stva*, Moscow, 1917; I. Shadrin, *Blizhaishchie zadachi (krest'ianinu-grazhdaninu)*, Kazan', 1917; A. Os'minin, *Chto dolzhno dat' narodu uchreditel'noe sobranie*, Petrograd, 1917.

of its peasant readers. Many papers had a column such as 'Letters from the Village', or 'Answers to Your Questions', in which issues raised by peasants were explained. Most of these were technical concerns to do with the land and property, yet they often touched on politics as well. Many of the SR papers, in particular, also published so-called letters 'From a Soldier' which were thinly disguised propaganda. The 'soldier' (a party activist in the ranks) would call on his peasant 'brothers' to help in the defence of their freedom and their farms by giving up their harvest surplus to the government. Such appeals were often couched in religious terms: 'Your conscience says it's sinful to think about yourself while your brothers spill their blood . . . Make a sacrifice, as we soldiers are doing to defend you. We are just to say this.'[16]

There was also a small number of newspapers specifically intended for the political education of the peasants, such as the tabloid *Narodnaia gazeta* ('The People's Newspaper') put out twice a week in the Kerenskii district of Penza province between May and September. 'The aim of our newspaper,' its editors declared, 'is to help the people understand the events of the war, national and local political life, and to enable every citizen to play a conscious role in the construction of a new life.' It printed explanations of political terms and articles with titles such as 'What is freedom and why has it been given to us?' or 'What is socialism and will it arrive soon?'[17]

The supply of this literature could not keep up with demand. Of course there were places where the peasants were indifferent to politics, and where any propaganda was torn up for cigarette paper. But in general there was a huge demand, at least in the early weeks of the revolution, for news and explanatory literature. The war had opened up the peasants' world and made them more aware that their own daily lives were closely connected with national and international affairs. The publications of the peasant unions and provincial peasant assemblies often had to be reprinted several times. Hand-printed and mimeographed copies were also distributed in huge quantities. A second stenographic edition of the 1905 All-Russian Peasant Union Congress, published in the spring of 1917, carried on its title page a warning from the Main Committee of the Union that there were so many of these unofficial versions that it could not be held responsible for them.[18] The Petrograd Soviet, in particular, but also the Duma and the government, received hundreds of peasant appeals for political literature. As the Duma report put it, the phrase 'we are dark people' (*my temnye*), which the peasants had used ironically, now contained a message of 'sincere

16. *Izvestiia vserossiiskogo soveta krest'ianskikh deputatov*, 20 July 1917, p. 8.
17. *Narodnaia gazeta*, 28 July 1917, p. 2.
18. *Uchreditel'nyi s'ezd vserossiiskogo krest'ianskogo soiuza*, Moscow, 1917.

regret: there is so much the peasants want to know but cannot understand'. It cited the moving words of one peasant from Pskov: 'There are no words to explain the shame and pain that engulf a man when he realizes that even what has been given to him is too hard for him to understand, and is like a stone instead of bread.'[19]

In addition to pamphlets and newspapers the peasant leaders appealed for agitators, often specifically to help them counteract the influence of the local priests or monarchist officials, or to help them dispel rumours undermining confidence in the revolution.[20] The demand for such people was increased by the flight of the rural intelligentsia from the countryside during 1917.[21] Impoverished, demoralized and threatened by the violence of the peasant revolution, many teachers, vets and doctors fled to the towns. Yet these were the very people who in former years had read the newspapers to the peasants, explained to them the meaning of the news, interpreted decrees, and acted as their scribes to the authorities. Wounded soldiers and deserters from the army were arriving in the village all the time and they brought their own 'translations' of the new decrees and urban languages, but these did not serve and often worked against the political needs of the Provisional Government.

A wide range of public bodies – from working-class organizations to sailors' and soldiers' delegations – despatched agitators to the countryside. Teachers' bodies were particularly active.[22] One of their main professional journals carried a regular article entitled 'For the Aid of Teachers in Their Conversations with the Population on Current Affairs', in which they were advised on how best to engage the attention of their peasant audience.[23] Many of the provincial peasant congresses, and even some of the district ones, organized their own teams of rural propagandists to acquaint the peasants with their resolutions or to counteract the influence of local monarchists.[24] In Perm, Nizhegorod, Vladimir, Saratov and Viatka the provincial zemstvos and public committees trained and paid for 'lectors' and 'translators' (*perevodchiki*) from the local intelligentsia to go to the peasants and explain to them the main issues of the day.[25] In Moscow, Petrograd and Kaluga there was a religious-oriented group called the Union for the Free Person which set up lecture and discussion circles for the

19. RGIA, f. 1278, op. 10, d. 4, l. 258.
20. See e.g. TsGASP, f. 7384, op. 9, d. 176, l. 184; d. 209, l. 10.
21. On this see O. Figes, *Peasant Russia, Civil War: The Volga Countryside in Revolution, 1917–1921*, Oxford, 1989, pp. 35, 147–51.
22. See N.N. Smirnov, *Na perelome: rossiiskoe uchitel'stvo nakanune i v dni revoliutsii 1917 goda*, St Petersburg, 1994, pp. 243–50.
23. *Dlia narodnogo uchitelia*, 1917, no. 8, pp. 29–32; 1917, no. 10, pp. 29–31; etc.
24. See e.g. TsGASP, f. 1950, op. 1, dd. 10, 13.
25. RGIA, f. 1278, op. 10, d. 4, l. 257.

peasantry.[26] Democratic priests and seminarians also doubled up as propagandists, the priests often using the church service to preach about the 'Christian mission of the revolution' to their peasant worshippers. For example, the chaplain of the 105th Orenburg Regiment gave a speech in the church of Slipki village on Trinity Sunday (21 May) in which he compared the revolutionaries to Jesus Christ, the 'liberator of the poor and oppressed peasants and the proletariat' from their 'enslavement' to the 'Roman Tsars'.[27] Finally, there was a Society for the Political Education of the Army and Wide Sections of the Population, set up by the zemstvos and cooperatives in several provinces, which trained volunteers (mainly teachers and students) for propaganda work among the peasantry and sent them out to the villages and army units to explain to them the duties of a citizen.[28]

All these missionaries faced the same problem: how to talk to the peasants about politics so that they would listen and understand. It was an old problem, going back at least to the 1870s and the 'Going to the people', but it was now more urgent since upon it hung the fate of the democracy.

Many books and articles were published on this problem during 1917. E.N. Medynskii's *How to Conduct Conversations on Political Issues* was perhaps the best known of these manuals, selling 50,000 copies in its first edition, and up to 40,000 more in two further editions of 1917.[29] Close behind came his *Revolution and Education Out of School*, which sold up to 70,000 copies in its two editions of the same year.[30] Both gave advice on how to talk with peasants on political issues. The agitator should speak in the language of the peasants and avoid using foreign words. It was important not to give a 'dry and official speech' but to have a 'conversation' with the audience and to ask them questions from time to time. The agitator was to illustrate his arguments with examples drawn from peasant daily life. The war, for example, might be compared with a village fight, in which one side (Russia) fights fairly and the other (Germany) unfairly. To explain the advantages of a republic over a monarchy the speaker might say:

'Would it be good if you could not judge the chairman of your cooperative or your *volost* elder? If he spends your money, or loses it, or rules the *volost* badly – he is always right. You cannot replace him or take him to court.

26.   *Otchet deiatel'nosti soiuza vospitaniia svobodnogo cheloveka za 1917–18 (pervyi) god*, Petrograd, 1918.
27.   RGIA, f. 806, op. 5, d. 10313, l. 131.
28.   *Biulleten' obshchestva politicheskogo prosveshcheniia armii i shirokikh sloev naseleniia*, 1917 no. 1, pp. 1–3; no. 2, pp. 1–4.
29.   E.N. Medynskii, *Kak vesti besedy po politicheskim voprosam: metodicheskie ukazaniia, konspekty i spiski literatury dlia lektorov, uchitelei i pr.*, Moscow, 1917. Medynskii (1885–1957) later became a well-known Soviet educationalist.
30.   Medynskii, *Revoliutsiia*.

"Do not dare to touch me, to judge me is a sin," he says to you. The same happens with a monarchy. The Tsar, however bad, is always right.'[31]

One can detect the same philosophy in the rhetoric of the democratic leaders. They made a conscious effort to explain the abstract concepts of the democracy in simple concrete terms. The February Revolution was often portrayed as an enormous *physical* effort – comparable to the peasants' own back-breaking toil. 'The Russian people has pulled itself free . . . [and] thrown off the heavy chains of Tsarist slavery . . .'[32] Notions of statehood and civic duty were couched in metaphors from peasant daily life. The post-revolutionary state was depicted as a 'beautiful new house' whose construction, like a village house, required the participation of all its inhabitants.[33] The purpose of the Constituent Assembly was explained by analogy with the cooperatives, which were normally organized at a 'constituent assembly' of their members where the administration was elected and the rules of the society defined.[34] Where there were no cooperatives, and the word 'constituent' (*uchreditel'noe*) was not understandable by the peasants, agitators used the word *narodnoe* ('people's') instead. Thus one peasant leader in Olonets province ended a speech with the rallying cry: 'Long live land and freedom and the People's Assembly! [*narodnoe sobranie*].'[35] The word *narodnyi* was also substituted for other foreign words (e.g. 'democratic' and 'national').[36] Similarly, the 'nationalization' of the land was frequently explained as the transfer of the land to the 'people's' ownership.[37]

Family metaphors for society – which were a staple of the political rhetoric of the nineteenth century – featured prominently in the language of the democratic leaders for the peasantry. The family itself was the central institution of peasant life, the village community was bound by kin relations. 'The Russian people wants to be and must be a single family of brother-labourers,' wrote the peasant propagandist Alexander Os'minin[38] in his

---

31. Ibid., p. 23; Medynskii, *Kak vesti besedy*, pp. 4, 7.
32. G. Korelin, *Gotovtes' k uchreditel'nomu sobraniiu*, Kerch, 1917, p. 2.
33. See e.g. the speeches of Uspenskii and Nabatov in *Zhurnal shatskogo uezdnogo s'ezda krest'ianskikh deputatotv, 23–25 iiulia 1917 goda*, pp. 2, 5.
34. Shadrin, *Blizhaishchie zadachi*, p. 7.
35. TsGASP, f. 446, op. 1, d. 15, l. 26.
36. *Tikhvinskii uezdnyi krest'ianskii s'ezd 29–30 aprelia 1917 g.*, Tikhvin, 1917, p. 6.
37. S.P. Rudnev, *Pri vechernykh ogniakh. Vospominaniia*, Kharbin, 1928, pp. 96–9.
38. Os'minin is a fascinating figure in the history of the February Revolution. A peasant from Osvishi village in Tver province, he fought at the Front for 30 months and rose to the rank of sergeant. On 7 March 1917 he was sent by his village to the capital with a gift of bread and salt and 60 roubles for Rodzianko, chairman of the Duma, in gratitude for 'the blessing of the people's victory' (RGIA, f. 1278, op. 10, d. 11, l. 332). There he became involved in politics – figures of his type were in high demand. He wrote for the newspapers *Trud i volia* and *Soldatskaia mysl'* before becoming editor of *Soldatskoe slovo*, a paper oriented towards peasant soldiers like himself. It is thought that he joined the SRs and became a leader of the soldiers' veteran organization.

brochure for the first-time rural voter.[39] Two fundamental ideas of the democracy were contained in this metaphor: that the people's victory as a brotherhood was incompatible with their domination by patriarchal figures like the 'father Tsar'; and that its success depended on the expression of that brotherhood as a sense of duty to the nation as a whole. The peasants' obligation to supply the army was often couched in these familial terms of national unity. 'If the village does not give its harvest,' declared the *Izvestiia* of the Peasant Soviet, 'then the ones to suffer will be the poor people and the soldiers, the brothers of the peasantry by blood and destiny.'[40] The need for the officers and soldiers to unite was similarly described in familial terms – as in this telegram to the Soviet: 'The soldiers and the officer-citizens of the 16th Irkutsk Hussar Regiment, united in a single compact family, send their heartfelt greetings to the Soviet of Workers' and Soldiers' Deputies in celebration of 1 May.'[41] Last but not least, the democratic leaders also used the metaphor of the family to assert their status as 'the best sons of the nation' because they had 'sat in Tsarist jails and suffered for their brothers, the peasantry'.[42]

How effective was this rhetoric? How far, and in what forms, did the peasants understand the political concepts of the democratic revolution in the towns? It is always difficult to know what peasants think. They may speak in one language to each other, address outsiders in another, and, as far as they are able, write or dictate petitions to the authorities in a third 'official' language.[43] Peasants often adopt the language of a politically dominant urban culture without necessarily believing in its values – indeed they may do so to pretend conformity to it, to legitimize their own aims and actions, or to ridicule and subvert it. In short, behind the public discourse of any peasantry there may be (and often is) what J.C. Scott has called a 'hidden transcript', carried through the language of village songs and jokes, rumour and gossip, largely impenetrable to the outside world.[44] In 1917 the peasants would write humble petitions to the Provisional Government, prefacing them with stock phrases of religious thanks, deferential greetings and heartfelt declarations of loyalty – and then go on to demand the release of their sons from the army or the right to confiscate the landowners' land. Or they would pretend that 'we are dark people' – echoing the urban myth about the peasantry – to explain and justify their neglect or contravention of the law. But it would be mistaken to conclude from this that the peasants were indifferent towards

39. Os'minin, *Chto dolzhno dat' narodu*, p. 15.
40. *Izvestiia vserossiiskogo soveta krest'ianskikh deputatov*, 22 Aug. 1917, p. 1.
41. TsGASP, f. 7384, op. 9, d. 158, l. 29.
42. Shadrin, *Blizhaishchie zadachi*, pp. 10–11.
43. See M. Bakhtin, *The Dialogic Imagination*, Austin, 1981, pp. 295–6.
44. J.C. Scott, *Domination and the Arts of Resistance: Hidden Transcripts*, New Haven, 1990.

– and remained untouched by – the new democratic political culture spreading towards them from the towns. The peasants had their own forms of politicization, their own *prise de conscience politique*, in which certain aspects of the public discourse might be adopted to articulate their own political ideals and traditions, while other aspects of it might be consciously ignored because they could not be 'peasantized'.

The remainder of this chapter will attempt to sketch the political worldview of the peasants – their construction of the state and the nation, their ideas of citizenship and equality – in so far as these may be inferred from their village resolutions and petitions, private letters and recorded conversations, and the statements of peasant delegates at provincial assemblies. Of course the reader should bear in mind that sometimes these records have come down to us through non-peasant intermediaries – scribes, officials, schoolteachers and other spokesmen for the peasants – and hence may be couched in a language that reflects the intelligentsia's construction of the peasantry ('dark', 'dependent', 'pious', etc.) rather than the discourse of the peasantry itself. But in the absence of any other sources, and with the proviso that those used below are approached critically, it seems appropriate to proceed.

Peasant Monarchical Attitudes

The idea that the peasant was at heart a monarchist remains one of the most enduring myths of Russian history.[45] There were of course peasants who were monarchists. Yet throughout Russia in 1917 the peasantry, in general, either rejected the monarchy or were indifferent to others doing so. As a Duma report wittily concluded:

> The widespread myth that the Russian peasant is devoted to the Tsar and that he 'cannot live' without him has been destroyed by the universal joy and relief felt by the peasants upon discovering that in reality they *can* live without the Tsar, without whom they were told they 'could not live'. The scandal of Rasputin, which is known in even the remotest villages, has helped to destroy the status of the Tsar. Now the peasants say: 'The Tsar brought himself down and brought us to ruin.'[46]

Not all the peasants were equally decided. Many were afraid to speak their minds until the land captains and police were removed – which in some provinces (e.g. Mogilev and Kazan) was not completed until April–

---

45. The most recent statement of the view is in R. Pipes, *The Russian Revolution, 1899–1919*, London, 1990, pp. 118–19.
46. RGIA, f. 1278, op. 10, d. 4, ll. 241–2.

and even then they were hesitant in case the revolution was reversed.[47] Many of the older peasants were confused by the downfall of the Tsar.[48] 'The church was full of crying peasants', one witness recalled. '"What will become of us?" they constantly repeated – "They have taken the Tsar away from us?"'[49] Some of these older peasants had venerated the Tsar as a god on earth. They crossed themselves whenever his name was mentioned, took their hats off when entering a room in which his portrait, which they considered an icon, hung. Many at first saw the overthrow of the Tsar as an attack on religion – a fact exploited by many priests and monarchist officials in their counter-revolutionary propaganda. Even among the more rural workers the Tsar's removal could give rise to religious doubts. The American Frank Golder talked with one such worker, 'an old muzhik', in mid-March, who 'said it was a sin to overthrow the Emperor, since God had placed him in power. It may be that the new regime will help people on this earth, but they will surely pay for it in the world to come.'[50] The patrimonial conception of the Tsar – as the 'master [*khoziain*] of the Russian land' – also found expression in these fears. 'How can Russia survive without its master?' one old Tambov peasant asked.[51]

But generally the news of the Tsar's abdication was welcomed joyously. 'Our village,' wrote one peasant, 'burst into life with celebrations. Everyone felt enormous relief, as if a heavy rock had suddenly been lifted from our shoulders.' Another wrote: 'People kissed each other from joy and said that life from now on would be good. Everyone dressed in their best costumes, as they do on a big holiday. The festivities lasted three days.'[52] Many villages held religious processions to thank the Lord for their newly won freedoms, offering up prayers for the new government. The revolution thus attained the status of a religious cult, while those who had died fighting for freedom (*bortsy za svobodu*) were venerated as modern saints. The villagers of Bol'she-Dvorskaya *volost* in Tikhvinsk district, for example, held a 'service of thanksgiving for the divine gift of the people's victory and the eternal memory of those holy men who fell in the struggle for freedom'.[53] To reciprocate this sacrifice many villages sent donations of

47. Ibid., l. 241.
48. Many propagandists commented on this generational divide. See e.g. TsGASP, f. 1950, op. 1, d. 10, ll. 7–8; f. 7384, op. 9, d. 176, ll. 177–80; d. 209, l. 5; TsGAIPD, f. 1, op. 1, d. 228, l. 46.
49. F. Iusupov, *Pered izgnaniem, 1887–1919*, Moscow, 1993, p. 187.
50. *War, Revolution, and Peace in Russia: The Passages of Frank Golder, 1914–1927*, ed. T. Emmons and B. Patenaude, Stanford, 1992, p. 50.
51. Okninskii, *Dva goda*, p. 28.
52. *1917 god v derevne: vospominaniia krest'ian*, Moscow and Leningrad, 1929, pp. 40, 64.
53. TsGASP, f. 8558, op. 1, d. 5, l. 30.

money, often amounting to several hundred roubles, to the authorities in Petrograd for the benefit of those who had suffered losses in the February Days.

What is striking here is the extent to which the peasantry identified with the ideas and the symbols of the republic. There was, of course, a precedent here. The establishment of a republic had been a basic demand of the peasant unions and the rural socialists ever since the 1905 Revolution. And events since then ('Bloody Sunday' and the suppression of the peasant disorders during 1905–7; the gross mismanagement of the war campaign and its criminal wastage of human life; the scandal of Rasputin and the rumours of treason at the court) had already shaken many of the peasants' old belief in the Tsar's benevolence and the sacred sources of his power. None the less, it is still remarkable how far and how fast the idea of the republic took root among certain sections of the peasantry. The most educated peasants and those living closest to the towns readily adopted the rhetoric and metaphors of the new republican propaganda in their petitions to the authorities. The form of the republic was heatedly debated at most provincial peasant congresses. Hundreds of villages passed formal resolutions in favour of a republic, and sent them to the authorities. Some of them took part in the 'festivals of freedom' and the 'peasant days', sponsored respectively by the Provisional Government and the Peasant Soviet, where the symbols and the public rituals of the nineteenth-century republican tradition – the singing of the 'Marseillaise', the construction of memorials to those who had died in the struggle against the monarchy (there was at least one case of a 'Tree of Liberty') – played a major role in the celebrations.[54]

For many peasants, however, the idea of the republic remained confused with the idea of the monarchy. They conceived of the state as embodied in a monarch, and projected their ideals on to a 'peasant king', or some other authoritarian liberator, come to deliver their cherished land and freedom. Here, at least in part, were the popular roots of the cults of Kerensky, the 'people's champion', and of Lenin too. This monarchical republicanism mirrored in some ways the philosophy and practice of the village assembly, where there was a strange mix between the principles of democratic self-rule by open debate and patriarchal rule by the village elders. During 1917 this was reflected in the way that many peasants believed the new democratic institutions ought to operate. Thus it was common for the peasants to declare that the Constituent Assembly should 'take complete power in its hands' or 'become the master [*khoziain*] of

54. RGIA, f. 794, op. 1, d. 17, l. 23; f. 1278, op. 10, d. 4, l. 83; *Izvestiia vserossiiskogo soveta krest'ianskikh deputatov*, 14 March 1917, p. 3; 15 March 1917, p. 4.

the Russian land' in the manner of an autocrat.[55] Two old peasants were heard in conversation in a railway carriage during the autumn, and although this version, printed in the press, may have been exaggerated to amuse the reader, it conveys the spirit of their words:

> [*First peasant*]: 'The Constituent Assembly, brother, will be the master; and because we the peasants will be voting, it will be a peasant one [*budet muzhitskim*]. The peasant cannot stand disorder. Our business is a serious business: we feed everyone. And for our work we need peace and order. We have not had that. There have been too many changes . . .'
>
> [*Second peasant*]: 'Too many! We don't like changes! Under the Tsar everything was normal, but now it is hard to keep up with the changes.'
>
> [*First peasant*]: 'Our rulers today – they have thought of everything, but they don't have any real strength. They are unable to rule the people strictly as they ought to do. But the Constituent Assembly – that, my friend, will be the real master. It will put everyone in their place. Do not disobey! Do not shout! Wait for us to give you your land and freedom! Great deeds cannot be achieved in a single day. The peasantry has waited a long time for their land and freedom. It has to be done properly – not just for us but also for our children and grandchildren – and for that we need a master's hand [*khoziaiskaia ruka*].'[56]

The need for a 'master's hand' to maintain order and defend their interests was a frequent theme in the peasants' statements on politics. This authoritarianism was, at least in their view, quite compatible with the democratic goals of the revolution. So much for the notion of most historians that the Russian peasant was at heart an 'anarchist' and rejected the need for a strong authority. On the contrary, many peasant resolutions spoke out in support of a 'firm power' (*tverdaia vlast'*) to end the disorder in the country and force the other classes to accept their revolution on the land.[57] The SR and sociologist S.S. Maslov, paraphrasing what the peasants had told him during 1917, claimed that they distinguished between the need for a strong government at the national level and the right of self-rule in the localities:

> There can be no order without a stable power. A stable power needs a single person in whose hands are concentrated force and many rights. Such a person ought to be a president but under no circumstances a Tsar.

55. *Tret'ii s'ezd vserossiiskogo krest'ianskogo soiuza v Moskve*, Moscow, 1917, p. 11; *Gubernskii s'ezd krest'ianskikh deputatov tomskoi gubernii, sostoiavshchiisia v g. Tomske 14–22 sentiabria 1917 g.*, Tomsk, 1917 p. 27.
56. *Delo derevni*, 3 Nov. 1917, p. 2.
57. *Sel'skii vestnik*, 5 July 1917, p. 4.

A president is elected by the people, he is temporary and can be super-vised, but a Tsar is like a *volost* elder who would rule the *volost* all his life and on his death would pass on his power to his children. With such an elder one could not live. The Russian state should be unified, but it must not oppress the people – let everyone think, believe and speak as they wish, as their mother and father taught them. Local matters must not be left to bureaucrats from Moscow or Petrograd. The people should be given complete freedom to organize their own local affairs.[58]

But some peasants also advocated running local government on the same authoritarian lines as it had been run under the Tsarist regime, albeit now in the revolutionary interests of the people. At the Tambov provincial peasant congress in mid-September one delegate argued:

The Soviets do not need the sort of power which the Bolsheviks are foisting upon them – the power to appoint and mix ministers: that is not power but powerlessness. No, give them the power to make people listen, as they once listened to the [provincial] governors. Surely if we are not fully organized for power and cannot use it, then it will be the cause of our downfall. Our enemies will say – they are good for nothing!

Another peasant took up the same theme: 'What was the strength of the old regime? It had autocrats at every level – Nicholas, the governor, and the policeman. Let us arrange things so that today there is a people's autocracy [*samoderzhavie narodnoe*]!'[59]

Peasant Notions of Citizenship

During the course of 1917 the word *grazhdane* spread throughout the countryside as a term of peasant self-identity. Village resolutions and peti-tions tended increasingly to begin with the words, 'We the citizens' (*My grazhdane*) of such and such a village, rather than the old phrase, 'We the peasants' (*My krest'iane*).[60] Delegates to peasant congresses referred to each other as 'citizens' during the debates. This new self-identification was no doubt a source of pride for many peasants. It was a badge of equality with the other classes of society, a society from which they had

58. S.S. Maslov, *Rossiia posle chetyrekh let revoliutsii*, Paris, 1922, p. 149.
59. *Delo derevni*, 20 Sep. 1917, p. 2. The phrase *samoderzhavie narodnoe* was sometimes used in propaganda – and so may have been picked up by him in this way. It appears, for example, in the programme of the Russian Social Democratic Labour Party (A. Nishchenskii, *Polnyi sbornik programm bsekh politicheskikh partii Rossii*, Lumiaki, 1917, p. 7).
60. Sometimes a village resolution might begin: 'We the citizens of peasant origin' (*My grazhdane iz krest'ianskikh proiskhozhdenii*).

always been excluded by a comprehensive range of laws discriminating against them. The abolition of the old class system of legal estates (*sosloviia*), a legacy from serfdom which guaranteed the privileged position of the landed nobles, had long been a demand of the peasant movement. The announcement of the Provisional Government's plans to abolish the *sosloviia* ('on the principle of equal rights for all citizens')[61] was hailed by many peasants – and especially by those in the army, where the privileges of the noble officers was still a source of bitter resentment among the soldiers – as a new emancipation. As one soldiers' resolution put it (with a rhetorical flourish that gave expression to their euphoria), the abolition of the estate system 'will bring our freedom to full liberation [*raskreposhcheniia*] from the heavy yoke of slavery, from the eternal prison, and the shameful servitude in which we have lived.'[62]

But within the village what did 'citizenship' mean? Clearly, it did not mean equal rights for everyone: the peasant revolution was itself class-based and directed *against* groups outside 'peasant society' (landed nobles, townsmen, the intelligentsia, etc.). The peasants' language of citizenship was different from that of other classes. One noble officer understood this well when he wrote to his father on 11 March:

> Between us and the soldiers there is an abyss that one cannot cross. Whatever they might think of us as individuals, we in their eyes remain no more than *barins* [masters]. When we talk of 'the people' [*narod*] we have in mind the nation as a whole, but they mean only the common people [*demokraticheskie nizy*]. In their view what has taken place is not a political but a social revolution, of which we are the losers and they are the winners. They think that things should get better for them and that they should get worse for us. They do not believe us when we talk of our devotion to the soldiers. They say that we were the *barins* in the past, and that now it is their turn to be the *barins* over us. It is their revenge for the long centuries of servitude.[63]

One way to review this question is in terms of who was given land and voting rights within the village community (*mir*). Generally, the peasants drew up their own circle of 'insiders' and assigned a certain set of rights and duties to each different subgroup of the community according to their perceived social value. Peasants who farmed with their own family labour – and former landowners who turned themselves into 'peasants' by doing the same – were assigned an equal share of the communal land and full voting rights at the village assembly (*skhod*). The younger peasants,

61. *Izvestiia*, 12 March 1917, p. 4.
62. TsGASP, f. 7384, op. 7, d. 11, l. 32.
63. 'Iz ofitserskikh pisem c fronta v 1917 g.', *Krasnyi arkhiv*, 1932, 50–1, p. 200.

in particular, gained a larger influence at the assembly – partly because the astronomic rate of household partitioning in 1917 created a large number of young household heads (with rights to attend the assembly), and partly because the prestige of the younger peasants increased as a result of their service in the army and the growing need for literate village leaders after the collapse of the old regime and the flight of the rural intelligentsia. Peasant women, too, gained rights at the *skhod*, often as the heads of households in the absence of their husbands on military service. But it was not just the peasants who were given land or rights at the assembly. Non-farming groups deemed of value to the village (e.g. craftsmen who manufactured goods demanded by the peasants, democratic priests and teachers, agronomists and vets, and sometimes landless labourers) were also deemed to be citizens, with a right to share in the benefits of the community. On the other hand, those who were a burden on the village's resources (e.g. migrants and townspeople without relatives in it) might be given temporary aid 'as human beings' but were rarely given land or rights at the *skhod* as 'village citizens'.[64]

It was common for the peasants to define their own tightly knit community in familial terms. The 'peasant family' (*krest'ianskaia semia*) was a stock phrase in their rhetoric, and within the village they addressed each other as if they were kin. At one level, then, the familial metaphor for society used by the democratic leadership found an echo in the traditional language of the peasantry. But it would be mistaken to conclude from this that the official usage of the metaphor – to define a notion of civic rights and duties – was also adopted by the peasantry. On the contrary, the peasants used the family metaphor to reinterpret these rights and duties so that the traditions and the interests of the village were not undermined by them.

Take, for example, the question of elections, where the peasants were to exercise their civic rights. The peasants did not vote as individuals but as families or whole communities (the household or village elders decided how to vote and the rest of the peasants followed suit, or alternatively the household or the village decided collectively how to vote). This sort of 'herd voting', to adopt the phrase of O.H. Radkey, was widely noted in the three main elections of 1917: to the *volost* zemstvos, the *volost* soviets, and the Constituent Assembly.[65] There were obvious reasons to

64. See O. Figes, 'Peasant Farmers and the Minority Groups of Rural Society: Peasant Egalitarianism and Village Social Relations during the Russian Revolution (1917–1921)', in E. Kingston-Mann and T. Mixter (eds), *Peasant Economy, Culture and Politics of European Russia, 1800–1921*, Princeton, 1991, pp. 378–401.
65. RGIA, f. 1278, op. 10, d. 4, ll. 247–8; *Sel'skii vestnik*, 23 Sept. 1917, p. 4; 30 Sept. 1917, p. 3; Rudnev, *Pri vechernykh ogniakh*, pp. 83–5; Figes, *Peasant Russia*, pp. 64-6; *Delo naroda*, 19 Dec. 1917, p. 3; O.H. Radkey, *Russia Goes to the Polls: The Election to the All-Russian Constituent Assembly, 1917*, Cornell, 1989, pp. 65–71.

vote in this way. It was very hard, if not impossible, to arrange a secret ballot in the Russian village, where voting had always been done in the open (either by shouting or standing in sides) and where, in any case, everybody knew how everybody else was intending to cast their vote. In this context it was more important for the villagers (or household members) to maintain their unity by voting all together than it was for them to exercise their voting rights as individual citizens and yet run the risk of becoming divided on party lines. Unity had always been the main priority at the village assembly – its resolutions were by custom passed unanimously – and it was enforced by the patriarchs. Equally, most peasants were quick to condemn the fighting between the socialist parties, which, to extend the familial metaphor, they blamed for the 'war of brothers' (*bratoubiistvennaia voina*), an old term for civil conflicts which the peasants adopted to refer to the civil war.[66]

On the issue of taxation, where they were to exercise their civic duties, the family concept of society was similarly interpreted by the peasants to suit their own best interests. Nearly all the peasants recognized the need to give food to the army, where their sons and brothers were fighting for the defence of the motherland, but very few agreed with the need to give food to the towns. Despite the efforts of the urban propagandists, they felt no kinship with the workers, whose strikes and eight-hour days they held responsible for the problems of the army and the growing shortages of manufactured goods.[67]

Peasant Constructions of Power and the State

'For hundreds of years the Russian peasant has dreamt of a state with no right to influence the will of the individual and his freedom of action, a state without power over man.' Thus wrote Maxim Gorky in 1927.[68] His view of the peasantry as anarchists has been shared by many historians since. Indeed, the idea that the peasants wanted nothing to do with the state, that their only aim was to free themselves completely from its influence and to rule themselves in their own villages, has become the dominant conception of the rural revolution in the Western historiography of 1917.

It is true that among the peasantry there was a marked preference for localist solutions to the social problems of 1917 (land and food distribution

66. Figes, *Peasant Russia*, pp. 175–6, 309.
67. RGIA, f. 1278, op. 10, d. 4, l. 255; TsGASP, f. 446, op. 1, d. 1, ll. 11–12; *Sel'skii vestnik*, 9 July 1917, p. 4.
68. M. Gorky, 'On the Russian Peasantry', in R.E.F. Smith (ed.), *The Russian Peasantry 1920 and 1984*, London, 1977, p. 12.

above all), and that this formed part of a general peasant drive towards autonomy from the state.[69] But it would be mistaken to conclude from this that the peasants were indifferent to the structures of the state or that they did not want a state at all. The peasant idea of autonomy was not the same thing as anarchy: it was a demand for a state in their own image, one that would enforce their own agenda of the revolution and compel the other classes to submit to it. Judging from the fat files of their letters and petitions lying in the archives from 1917, the peasants had a lot to say about the power question. The First World War had politicized the village – literally so during 1917, as the peasant soldiers, revolutionized by their military service, returned home. Thousands of villages passed formal resolutions on the future structure of the state. Many of these mandates were imbued with a solemn rhetoric, such was the seriousness with which they were viewed, and nearly all contained a long list of political demands. The villagers of Vyshgorodetsk in Pskov province, for example, signed a petition to the Soviet, entitled 'Our Demands', in which they called for the establishment of a democratic republic, universal suffrage, more rights of local self-government, school education in the local tongue, equal rights for women and all national groups, court reforms, progressive taxes, and the prohibition of all vodka sales.[70] Such resolutions hardly suggest a parochial peasantry with its back towards the outside world and preoccupied with its own village affairs, as so often depicted in the literature on 1917, although one cannot rule out the possibility that their content was dictated by the village intelligentsia. Nor can one conclude that the peasantry was focused narrowly on its own affairs from the long and heated debates about the power question which so often dominated peasant congresses, and even less from the high turn-out of peasant voters in the elections to the Constituent Assembly. This was not a peasantry indifferent to the state but, on the contrary, one that, for the first time in its history, was becoming aware of its power to reshape it.

Following the February Revolution the Provisional Government and the Petrograd Soviet received hundreds of peasant greetings and declarations of support. Many of these were couched in religious terms. The villagers of Tetrin in Arkhangel'sk province wrote to express their 'devout gratitude' to the Provisional Government for Russia's liberation from 'the sinful Tsarist regime' and to 'pray to it to lead Russia on to the just path of salvation and truth'.[71] A group of peasant soldiers from the 11th Army was even more explicit in its religious greeting to the leaders of the Soviet:

69. On this see Figes, *Peasant Russia*, chs 2 and 3.
70. TsGASP, f. 7384, op. 9, d. 255, l. 11.
71. RGIA, f. 1278, op. 10, d. 4, ll. 192–3.

'You have been blessed by Jesus our Saviour and are leading us to the dawn of a new and holy fraternal life. May the Lord help you!'[72] Many peasants saw the February Revolution in religious terms, or at least gave that impression in their correspondence with its official bodies.[73] They described the old regime as sinful and corrupt, praised the revolutionary 'freedom fighters' (*bortsy za svobodu*) as Christ-like saviours of the people, and projected their religious hopes and ideals on to the new government. The words *pravda* (truth or justice) and *pravitel'stvo* (government) are – uniquely to the Russian language – derived from the same root. These two concepts were intimately linked in the Russian peasant mind: the only true form of government (and the only one the peasants recognized) was the administration of *pravda* (meaning the giving of land and freedom to the peasantry). By embracing it in these religious terms the peasants sought to imbue the new order with their own ideals of government. As the peasant propagandist Os'minin concluded: 'We are standing for the people to become the masters of their own lives, for our country to become a single family of brother labourers, without rich or poor – in short for the Kingdom of God to come to our land.'[74] Such millenarian language echoed traditional religious ideals as well as socialist rhetoric.

The peasantry projected its own ideals of social justice on to the new order – and in this way they inverted (or perhaps subverted) the whole state structure to suit peasant goals. Thus in the peasants' view any public body sanctioning their revolution on the land had the status of an organ of the state with the power to pass its own 'laws'; whereas the laws of any other body, including the Provisional Government, that opposed their revolution should not be recognized at all. This is neatly illustrated by the All-Russian Peasant Congress during May, and the peasant assemblies convened in most central Russian provinces during the spring.[75] Despite the warnings of the Provisional Government, which had pledged to protect the gentry's property rights until the convocation of the Constituent Assembly, most of these assemblies gave what the peasants took to be a legal sanction for their confiscation of the gentry's land. The peasant delegates, in the words of one observer at the All-Russian Congress, 'did not clearly understand the difference, firstly, between a declaration of some principle and the implementation of it as a law, or, secondly, between a resolution by the Congress, expressing its opinion, and a law by the

---

72. TsGASP, f. 7384, op. 9, d. 255, l. 24.
73. On the religious dimension of the revolution among other classes see B.I. Kolonitskii, 'The "Russian Idea" and the Ideology of the February Revolution', in T. Hara and K. Matsuzato (eds), *Empire and Society: New Approaches to Russian History*, Sapporo, 1997, pp. 41–71.
74. Os'minin, *Chto dolzhno dat' narodu*, p. 15.
75. On the peasant assemblies in the Volga provinces see Figes, *Peasant Russia*, pp. 40–6.

government, which has a binding force.'[76] The peasants seemed to believe that their own assemblies' resolutions already carried the status of 'laws', and that in order to 'socialize' the land it was enough for a large peasant assembly to pass a resolution to that effect. Their expectations transformed their assemblies into pseudo-governments promulgating 'laws' by simple declaration – 'laws' which then took precedence over the statutes of the Provisional Government. As one of the government's provincial commissars complained, 'The peasantry has got a fixed opinion that all civil laws have lost their force, and that all legal relations ought now to be regulated by peasant organizations.'[77]

It was precisely in this sense that the peasants came to see their local soviets as sovereign state organs, implementing and legitimizing their own revolution on the land, as the Bolsheviks encouraged them to do through the slogan 'All Power to the soviets!' In the peasant view their soviets were the only legitimate organs of state power in the countryside, and if they resolved to seize the gentry's land against the orders of the Provisional Government, they did so with the idea that they were acting with the sanction of a national state authority (the All-Russian Soviet Assembly) and as such their actions were 'legal'. A strong soviet, with the coercive means to enforce this peasant revolution and compel the other classes to submit to it, was thus seen by the peasants as a necessity, at both the local and the national level. Nearly all the peasant soviets had their own Red Guard or armed detachment, not to mention police and judicial institutions, precisely for this purpose.

Similarly, the peasants tended to regard the Constituent Assembly as a national body giving legal force to their own revolution on the land. They saw it as 'the spokesman of the peasants' will', as the 'deliverer of land and freedom', which, by 'getting all the people to agree' with it, would make their revolution binding and irreversible.[78] At times the peasants expressed the naive belief that as long as the assembly had a wise old peasant at its head, like some elder at a giant 'people's *skhod*', or that as long as it contained enough peasants who were known and trusted by their fellow villagers, then it could not fail to bring them land and freedom.[79] There was in this an element of peasant chauvinism to parallel the chauvinism of the workers. It was reflected in the standard rhetoric about

76. V.Ia. Gurevich, 'Vserossiiskii krest'ianskii s'ezd i pervaia koalitsiia', *Letopis' revoliutsii*, 1923, no. 1, p. 191. See similarly the Duma report in RGIA, f. 1278, op. 10, d. 4, l. 248 ('the peasants take as a law any resolution in the newspaper . . . And usually they take to be "the most correct law" those parts of the parties' resolutions . . . in which their own ancient ideals are expressed').
77. L. Trotsky, *The History of the Russian Revolution*, London, 1977, p. 882.
78. TsGASP, f. 446, op. 1, d. 1, ll. 2, 5, 8; f. 7384, op. 9, d. 255, l. 11.
79. See e.g. TsGASP, f. 8558, op. 1, d. 5, l. 24; *Zhurnal shatskogo uezdnogo s'ezda*, p. 7; *Gubernskii s'ezd krest'ianskikh deputatov tomskoi gubernii*, p. 25.

the peasants being the *narod*, the real toiling people that kept the country fed, the '160 million peasants' in whose name their leaders claimed to speak.

Finally, in relation to this theme of the peasants' reconstruction and inversion of the state, it was common for them to propose remedies to national problems which they might have applied in their own village. So, in April 1918 the peasants of Trost'ian *volost* in Samara province suggested resolving the industrial crisis by a repartition of all town property, just as the repartition of the land had 'resolved' the crisis in agriculture.[80] Similarly, many peasants believed that the war with Germany could and should be resolved like a village brawl.[81]

The Peasants and the Language of Socialism

There were four aspects of the 'Russian peasant ideology' that could loosely be described as 'socialist' in content: the belief that all the land should be held collectively and that every person had a right to work it using his own labour; the custom of the land commune (in most parts of Russia) of redistributing the plots of land in accordance with household size; the welfarism of the village (e.g. provision for widows and orphans); and the not infrequent custom of collective labour for communal ends (e.g. the building of irrigation schemes or the harvesting of communal grain stores). Yet this does not mean that the peasantry was ripe for 'socialism' in the usual understanding of that term. The peasants may have assimilated some of the ideas of the socialist movement in the towns, but they added to them a peasant gloss, informed by the egalitarian values of their own political culture, and the result was a strange hybrid creation.

The socialists in Russia had always found it hard to get across their abstract ideas to the peasantry. As one Populist concluded from the failure of the 'Going to the people' in the 1870s, the peasants 'were left cold by socialism, and yet they debated heatedly those questions which affected their immediate concerns and which did not go beyond their customary ideas of a better peasant life'.[82] Most were easily confused by the abstract jargon of the socialists – all their talk of 'classes', of successive 'stages of development', and their 'ism' this and their 'ism' that. At the Shatsk district peasant congress in July 1917 one muddled peasant, obviously outraged by the exploitation of the capitalist system, argued that no socialist should be elected to the Constituent Assembly 'because socialism grew

80. GAKO, f. 81, op. 1, d. 119a, l. 171.
81. *Sel'skii vestnik*, 13 April 1917, p. 3.
82. O.V. Aptekman, *Obshchestvo 'zemlia i volia' 70-kh gg.*, Petrograd, 1924, p. 178.

from capitalism'.[83] Even those peasants who had learned to speak this 'scientific' language, mostly in the army, and who liked to speak it as a sign of 'education', sometimes betrayed a ridiculous confusion about the meaning of its words. The memoirist Okninsky, in his remarkable account of rural life in Tambov province during the civil war, recalls the visit of some Soviet propagandists in the summer of 1920. Among them was a young local peasant from the Red Army who, to the delight of the villagers, also gave a speech, from which Okninsky quotes:

> Comrades! Can you tell in diameters what you know of the internal size of our victorious Red Army? I am sure that diametrically-perpendicularly you cannot say anything about its internal size. Our victorious Red Army on a scale always beats our enemies in parallel. To understand the axiom, you ought to think not in straight lines, like women, but perpendicularly like men. Then two radiuses will be equal to a diameter . . .

As the peasant spoke, his fellow villagers were increasingly amazed: 'See how clever he has become! All those words! Where did he learn them! He is completely educated!'[84]

The socialists' theoretical language of class was almost entirely alien to the peasants – and was soon transformed by their use of it. The word 'burzhooi' – which, as we shall see in Chapter 6, was roughly synonymous with 'bourgeois' in the propaganda of the socialists yet had no set class connotations for the urban masses and was used by them as a general form of abuse for virtually *any* perceived social enemy – became in the language of the village a term for all forces hostile to the peasantry. Many peasants used it to describe *all* townsmen, thought to be hoarding the manufactured goods so badly needed in the countryside. Some confused 'burzhooi' with *barzhui* (the owners of a barge) and *birzhye* (from the word *birzh* for the Stock Exchange) – perhaps on account of this association with the towns.[85] But by far the most common peasant understanding of the term 'burzhooi', at least during 1917, was as a supporter of the monarchy who was perhaps plotting for its restoration, along with the power of the gentry on the land. For example, two peasants from Viatka province wrote in May to the Peasant Soviet claiming that in their district 'no new laws have been introduced because all the "burzhooi" support the old regime and do not permit our village committees'.[86] In Penza province the word *borzhuki* (a misspelling of 'burzhooi') was used by the peasants 'for all

83. *Zhurnal shatskogo uezdnogo s'ezda*, p. 7.
84. Okninsky, *Dva goda*, pp. 247–8.
85. I. Nazhivin, *Zapiski o revoliutsii*, Vienna, 1921, p. 15; GARF, f.551, op. 1, d. 106, l. 2; TsGASP, f. 7384, op. 9, d. 255, l. 25.
86. *Izvestiia vserossiiskogo soveta krest'ianskikh deputatov*, 20 May 1917, p. 4.

monarchists', whom they said had committees called *khameteti* – a compound of *komitety* (committees) and *khamy* (hooligans).[87]

Later, in the summer of 1918, when the Bolsheviks attempted to divide the 'rural poor' against the 'kulaks' or the 'rural bourgeoisie', this language of class was equally rejected by the peasantry. The committees of the rural poor (*kombedy*), which were supposed to ignite this class war in the village, spectacularly failed to get any of the peasants, let alone the poorest, to think of themselves as 'proletarians' or of their richer neighbours as a 'bourgeoisie'. In most villages the peasants thought of themselves as a community or 'family' of farmers (*krest'ianskaia sem'ia*), tied together by their common links to the village and its land, and the notion of a separate body for the village poor, especially when the whole village was united behind the soviet, seemed both strange and unnecessary. The villagers of Kiselevo-Chemizovka in the Atkarsk district of Saratov, for example, resolved that a *kombed* was not needed, 'since the peasants are almost equal, and the poor ones are already elected to the Soviet . . . so that the organization of separate committees for the poor peasants would only lead to unnecessary tensions between the citizens of the same commune'.[88] Most villages either refused to elect a *kombed*, thus leaving it to outside agitators, or established one which every peasant joined on the grounds that all of them were equally poor. The following resolution, from the Serdobsk district of Saratov province, was typical of this linguistic subversion: 'We the peasants of Commune No. 4 welcome the committees of the rural poor, for in our commune no one speculates and no one is rich. We are all middle peasants and poor peasants and we will do all we can to help the poor peasants.'[89]

'Socialism', recalled the writer Ivan Nazhivin in his entertaining *Notes on the Revolution*, appeared to the peasants 'as some mystical method – mystical because it was unclear to us and we could not imagine what it might consist of in practical terms – of dividing all the property and money of the rich; according to our village tailor, this would mean that every peasant household would be given 200,000 roubles. This, it seems, was the biggest number he could think of.'[90] Nazhivin meant this as a condemnation of the socialists, and of the naive peasants who believed them. Yet there is no doubt that the propaganda of socialism was most effective when communicated, if not explicitly in religious terms, then at least in terms of the peasantry's traditional community values, which they saw as 'just' and 'willed by God'. If socialism became the dominant political

87. Ibid., 20 Oct. 1917, p. 4.
88. Cited in G.A. Gerasimenko and F.A. Rashitov, *Sovety Nizhnego Povolzh'a v Oktiabr'skoi Revoliutsii*, Saratov, 1972, p. 266.
89. GARF, f. 393, op. 3, d. 340, l. 70.
90. Nazhivin, *Zapiski*, p. 14.

language of 1917, then it was largely because it provided the peasants with an idiom in which to formulate their own revolutionary ideals. The old peasant conception of the 'toiling people' (*trudovoi narod*) gave the socialist parties an ideological *point d'appui* for the dissemination of a class-based rhetoric of politics – a rhetoric that increasingly undermined the language of democratic citizenship promoted by the Provisional Government as this came to be seen by the peasantry as a language signifying the defence of the gentry's landed rights.

It was a well-established practice of the socialists to couch their propaganda in religious and peasant terms. The Populists of the 1870s, like other socialists, had often used the ideas of Christian brotherhood to preach socialism to the peasantry. And the same theme was taken up by the socialist parties in 1917. Pamphlets for the peasants presented socialism as a sort of religious utopia: 'Want and hunger will disappear and pleasure will be equally accessible to all. Thieving and robbery will come to an end. In place of compulsion and coercion there will be a kingdom of freedom and fraternity.'[91]

It was the Bolsheviks, however, who made the most political capital out of socialism's religious resonance. Even Menshevik S.G. Strumilin, in a pamphlet for the rural poor, compared socialism to the work of Christ and claimed that it would create a 'terrestrial kingdom of fraternity, equality and freedom'.[92] The cult of Lenin, which took off in August 1918 after he had been wounded in an assassination attempt, carried explicit religious overtones. Lenin was depicted as a Christ-like figure, ready to die for the people's cause, and, because the bullets had not killed him, blessed by miraculous powers.[93] Even the Red Star, the emblem of the Red Army, had religious connotations deeply rooted in peasant folklore. A Red Army leaflet of 1918 explained to the servicemen why the Red Star appeared on the Soviet flag and their uniforms. There was once a beautiful maiden named *Pravda* (Truth) who had a burning red star on her forehead which lit up the whole world and brought it truth, justice and happiness. One day the red star was stolen by *Krivda* (Falsehood) who wanted to bring darkness and evil to the world. Thus began the rule of *Krivda*. Meanwhile, *Pravda* called on the people to retrieve her star and 'return the light of truth to the world'. A good youth conquered *Krivda* and her forces and returned the red star to *Pravda*, whereupon the evil forces ran away from the light 'like owls and bats', and 'once again the people lived by truth'.

91. *Chto takoe sotsializm?*, Minusinsk, 1917, p. 9.
92. S. Petrashkevich (Strumilin), *Pro zemliu i sotsializm. Slovo sotsial-demokrata k derevenskoi bednote*, Petrograd, 1917, pp. 1–2.
93. See N. Tumarkin, *Lenin Lives! The Lenin Cult in Soviet Russia*, Cambridge, Mass., 1983, pp. 82–95.

The leaflet made the parable clear: 'So the Red Star of the Red Army is the star of *Pravda*. And the Red Army servicemen are the brave lads who are fighting *Krivda* and her evil supporters so that truth should rule the world and so that all those oppressed and wronged by *Krivda*, all the poor peasants and workers, should live well and in freedom.'[94]

The democratic revolution in the towns spoke a foreign language to the peasantry. Its leaders were acutely aware of the problem – many even thought that the whole success of their democratic mission would depend on finding a common discourse with the peasantry – and they went to great lengths to explain their ideas in terms they thought the peasants might understand. To some extent they succeeded with that small section of the literate peasantry amongst which the urban culture of democracy was most developed. But in their communication with the peasant masses these ideas were soon translated (almost beyond recognition) into specific peasant forms. The idea of the republic had the potential to become a monarchical idea in the village, a demand for order and a 'master's hand' to direct the revolution, shaped less by the democratic culture of the towns than by the patriarchal culture of the peasantry. The new language of citizenship was reinterpreted to suit the peasants' own revolutionary and social needs. The idea of the state and its coercive power, far from being negated by the peasants, was reconstructed and inverted by them to serve their own interests and moral and religious ideals of social justice. Finally, the language of socialism was similarly understood in these religious terms.

Language, then, was still a fundamental problem for the democratic mission in the village, even after eight months of trying to construct a new national political culture. The leaders of the February Revolution had initiated a public discourse of democracy, to which the peasants had been exposed through newspapers, pamphlets and oral propaganda, but the peasants' 'hidden transcripts' of this public discourse gave a different meaning to many of its terms. Whereas the main purpose of this discourse had been to break down class distinctions, resolve social conflicts, and create a nation of citizens, the way it had been received by the peasantry merely served to reinforce these social divisions. Language, more than ever, defined the peasants' self-identity and united them against the educated classes of the towns.

---

94. R. Stites, *Revolutionary Dreams: Utopian Vision and Experimental Life in the Russian Revolution*, Oxford, 1989, p. 110; Tumarkin, *Lenin Lives!*, pp. 71–2.

6

Images of the Enemy

All revolutions are at times portrayed as a Manichaean struggle between good and evil, light and darkness, the future and the past. Revolutions 'make the world anew' – in the words of the 'Internationale' – putting truth and justice in the place of evil, freedom in the place of oppression, fraternity in place of 'eternal bitterness'. The breakthrough to this 'brilliant future' is at such times presented as a last heroic struggle, the 'final and decisive battle' of the revolution, for which the people must unite to defeat their enemies, the 'dark forces' of the past.

Such contrasting images can serve as a focus of unity. As such they are powerful instruments which are bound to be developed by the propagandists of any revolutionary government. Indeed, the idea of 'the enemy' is necessary for all leaders of a revolution, in so far as it alone (or more than anything) enables them to rally the people behind them. Where there are no obvious enemies, revolutionary leaders have invented them. As Lynn Hunt has argued in the case of revolutionary France, the obsession with conspiracy was largely created and certainly exploited by the leaders of the revolution as they tried to cope with 'the novelties of mass politics'.[1] Certainly, it is difficult to see this obsession becoming systematic, or leading to a culture or politics of terror, without the direction of the revolutionary élites whose discourse defined these enemies. However, it can happen too that the popular image of the enemy takes on an existence of its own, sometimes even against the intentions of its creators, and in cases such as this the demonology is likely to be shaped by cultural traditions and pressures from below.

Enemies of the People – Enemies of the Old Regime

One of the specificities of pre-revolutionary Russia was the existence of a revolutionary underground. It was a counter-system to the official state

1. L. Hunt, *The Political Culture of the French Revolution*, London, 1984, pp. 42–3.

with its own subculture which created and carried its political traditions. Central to this subculture – and to its mythology of struggle for the people's cause – was its pantheon of heroes and enemies. The overcoming of these enemies was perceived as the key to the breakthrough from the darkness of the present to a bright new world. It was the function of the revolutionary subculture to prepare each new generation of recruits, 'fighters for the people's freedom', for the last decisive battle. It was a 'sacred battle of revenge'. But who were the enemies to be defeated?

Common to the whole of the revolutionary tradition was the idea of the enemy as the 'dark forces'. It had its origins in the chiliastic-Christian tradition – in the image of the Last Judgement – which could give it a special resonance. In the narrative of the revolutionary tradition, in songs and texts, the Tsar was the main image of the enemy: the 'tyrant', the 'Tsar-vampire', the 'Tsar-plutocrat'. Next came his servants: 'judge-executioners' (*sud'i-palachi*); 'heartless bureaucrats'; 'corrupt priests', etc. Increasingly, however, the demonic image had a social dimension. First it just divided the rich from the poor: 'bigwigs' (*bogachi*), 'kulaks' and the 'bosses'. But the enemies became more sophisticated as they were defined by the terminology of the socialist tradition. They were the 'power of capital', the 'bourgeoisie' and the 'burzhooi'.

The image of the enemy was awful to behold. He was disgusting in every way – morally, aesthetically, hygienically – so that just to touch him was to invite mortal danger. This is how he was presented in cartoons and other images, in verses and in songs, and the political message was quite clear: there could be no talk of compromise with him. Sometimes the demonic imagery was zoological. The enemies of the people were portrayed as subhuman ('predators', 'vermin' and 'parasites') so that the use of violence and terror against them was seen not merely as a justified recourse but as necessary too. The rich were the 'spiders' and the poor the 'flies' in left-wing revolutionary metaphors. The capitalists were 'packs of dogs', 'wolves', 'snakes' and 'gangs of cruel wild beasts' in workers' songs. And at the core of this violent imagery – indeed at the heart of the whole conception of the revolution which it in turn expressed – was the idea of a Manichaean struggle, a huge social purge, to rid the world of these predators. The 'Workers' Marseillaise', the most popular song of the February Revolution and effectively the national anthem during 1917, called for nothing less than their complete destruction, or exorcism, in order to create a better world:

> To the parasites, to the dogs, to the rich!
> Yes and to the evil vampire-Tsar!
> Kill and destroy them, the villainous swine!
> Light up the dawn of a new and better life!

Other revolutionary songs also equated the physical destruction of the old élites with the coming of the 'new life':

We will wipe out the manufacturers,
Just like dust along the ground,
And in place of hatred and poverty,
We will place fraternity and liberty
                    ('Mashinyshka')

The French diplomat De Robien, who witnessed a performance of revolutionary songs in Petrograd in the spring of 1917, wrote with irony: 'The tenor demanded the heads of all the nobles, the soprano the head of the Tsar. As for the bass he would not spare anyone at all.'[2] There was a further irony in that many of these songs were published in collections – with titles such as *Songs of Terror, Songs of Hatred and Vengeance*, or *Songs of National Fury* – compiled by editors with relatively moderate views. *The Red Flag: Songs of the Revolution – Songs of Hatred*, for example, published in Tiflis in 1917, had portraits of Lvov and Kerensky on the cover, suggesting it was put out by loyal supporters of the Provisional Government.

This revolutionary subculture, with its demonic imagery, was the laboratory of the civil war in the sense that it first developed the symbols of the enemy around which the war was fought.

If the image of the enemy was important for the political culture of the revolutionary underground, then it was just as vital for the ideology of the old regime. In the imagination of its Tsarist defenders, Russia was like a besieged fortress surrounded by enemies – her 'external' and 'internal' enemies were connected in their minds – and it was crucial to wage a constant battle against them for the very survival of the dynasty.

The Grand Duke Alexander Mikhailovich recalled in his memoirs:

I needed a great deal of inner strength to overcome the xenophobia which had been instilled into me by my teachers of Russian history . . . The French were blamed for the numerous treacheries of Napoleon, the Swedes were to pay for the damage inflicted on Russia by Karl XII during the reign of Peter the Great. It was impossible to forgive the Poles their ridiculous vainglory. The English had always been 'crafty Albion'. The Germans were guilty on account of Bismarck. The Austrians bore responsibility for the policies of Franz Josef, the monarch who did not keep a single promise to Russia. My 'enemies' were everywhere. The official understanding of patriotism demanded that I sustain in my heart the fire of a 'sacred hatred' for everyone and everything.[3]

2. L. de Robien, *The Diary of a Diplomat in Russia (1917–1918)*, London, 1967, p. 28.
3. Grand Prince Aleksandr Mikhailovich, *Kniga vospominanii*, Moscow, 1991, pp. 77–8.

Among supporters of the old regime it was commonplace that Russia had two allies: its army and its navy. This xenophobia was spoken *sotto voce* in official circles but loudly broadcast by the propaganda of the Black Hundreds. According to the latter, the history of Russia was a constant struggle with a hostile outside world. Yet Holy Russia was also too naive, in their view, and this made her vulnerable to foreign conspiracies.

But for the Tsarist patriots Russia was also threatened by the Enemy Within: the nihilists and revolutionaries. The image of the internal enemy too was tinged with the colour of xenophobia: domestic problems were explained by foreign conspiracies. The revolutionary movement was deemed to be the work of foreigners, who incited the Russians to sedition. The revolutionaries within Russia, according to this view, were the ethnic foreigners, whose demonic image combined external and internal enemies. First it was the Pole – and then it was the Jew. 'Polish agitators have educated our domestic revolutionaries,' declared M.N. Katkov.[4] Even as late as 1881, the conservative D.I. Ilovaiskii still considered the Pole the main national enemy, followed by the Jew.[5] But from that point on the Jews became the regime's main enemy. There were widespread pogroms against Jews in retribution for the murder of the Tsar. And in the following decades the extreme Right was constantly 'exposing' a secret international Jewish (Jewish-Masonic) conspiracy. 'It is as if all the enemies of Hell are conspiring against Russia,' declared one Russian nationalist. The Black Hundreds saw themselves as heroic knights fighting the last battle between Christ and the Antichrist.[6]

The defenders of autocracy did not limit their attacks to the Jewish Left. They also argued that democracy in general, and the constitutional movement in particular, were 'great lies of the Jews' – threatening to destroy the sacred union between Tsar and people. The founder of the Union of the Russian People, Dr Alexander Dubrovin, for example, published a best-selling tract in 1907 called *The Secret of Our Destiny* in which he described his nightmare vision of a future Russian democracy: in the seat of power sat a Jewish president surrounded by his Jewish ministers. Another Union member, Georgii Butmi, similarly portrayed the constitutional movement as a conspiracy by the Jews, who were out to gain greater freedom for themselves so that they could more easily pursue their ultimate objective which was to enslave the Russian people and the world.[7]

4. *Mikhail Nikiforovich Katkov i ego istoricheskaia zasluga (Po dokumetam i lichnym vospominaniiam N. A. Liubimova)*, St Petersburg, 1889, p. 227.
5. Cited in, O. Budnitskii, 'V chuzhom piru pokhmel'e (Evrei i russkaia revoliutsiia)', *Vestnik evreiskogo universiteta v Moskve*, 1996, no. 3 (13), p. 21.
6. D.I. Raskin, 'Ideologiia russkogo pravovo radikalizma v kontse XIX – nachale XX v.', in R.Sh. Ganelin (ed.), *Natsional'naia pravaia prezhde i teper': Istokiko-sotsiologicheskie ocherki*, St Petersburg, 1992, pt. 1, p. 21.
7. See D. Rawson, *Russian Rightists and the Revolution of 1905*, Cambridge, 1995, p. 70.

Closely linked to its anti-Semitism was the Right's hatred of the intelligentsia. As they saw it, the intelligentsia was entirely foreign to Russia. It was dominated by the Jews – and by Western socialist ideologies alien to the Russian peasant's Christian spirit of humility and threatening to destroy the sacred links between the people and the Tsar. 'Our intelligentsia,' wrote Katkov in 1878, 'is straining itself to breaking-point, attempting to show itself as un-Russian as possible and supposing that this constitutes its Europeanism.' The faith of the simple people united with the Tsar was contrasted with the anti-national lifestyle of the intelligentsia in the works of many other conservatives.[8] V.P. Meshcherskii despised the intelligentsia, condemning it as a 'union of the Jews and Poles', formed to destroy the Russian aristocracy.[9] The Black Hundreds were even more violent in their imagery. B.V. Nazarevskii, a founding member of the Russian Monarchist Party, wrote in 1906: 'a huge pile of manure calling itself "the intelligentsia" has been dumped on our capitals, and from this pile the splendid flower of revolution grows'.[10] Language such as this, widely read in pamphlet form, no doubt helped to incite the attacks on people with an educated appearance during the pogroms of 1905–7.[11]

The subculture of the revolutionary underground and the official culture of the Tsarist system were two entirely separate political systems, each with its own demonology of the other. This political-cultural clash was the prehistory of the revolution and civil war. At the same time, however, the two systems had some things in common. They were structurally similar, and used a similar demonic lexicon (the 'dark forces', the 'holy battle', etc.). Some of their images – of the bourgeoisie and the Jews, for example – were ambivalent enough for them to be shared by both sides at times.

The Right was often just as hostile to capitalism as the Left. It associated capitalism with foreign elements and a cosmopolitanism alien to Russia. Banks, with their international connections, were their main target and, needless to say, this had strong anti-Semitic overtones.

Meanwhile, the demonization of the Jew was not exclusive to the political culture of the Right. The Left was not averse to using anti-Semitism for revolutionary purposes. In the 1870s and 1880s some Populists even wel-

8. *Moskovskie Vedomosti*, 28 April 1878. On the anti-intelligentsia position of Katkov, see Iu.B. Solove'v, *Samoderzhavie i dvorianstvo v kontse XIX veka*, Leningrad, 1973, p. 183.
9. Solove'v, *Samoderzhavie i dvorianstvo*, pp. 296–7.
10. B. Nazarevskii, *Biurokratiia i intelligentsiia*, Moscow, 1906, pp. 6–7.
11. Certain government documents, such as the manifesto of 18 Feb. 1905, could be taken as incitement to settle scores with 'the intelligentsia'. On anti-intelligentsia pogroms, see L.K. Erman, *Intelligentsia v pervoi russkoi revoliutsii*, Moscow, 1966, pp. 172–4, 197–8, 227; S.J. Seregny, *Russian Teachers and Peasant Revolution: The Politics of Education in 1905*, Bloomington and Indianapolis, 1989, pp. 150, 176–8; S.A. Stepanov, *Chernaia sotnia v Rossii (1905-1914 gg.)*, Moscow, 1992, pp. 62–3.

comed the prospect of pogroms as a sign of the beginning of a protest movement by the peasantry. In the main, however, anti-Semitism was frowned upon as ignorant, a capitulation to Tsarist propaganda, in the political culture of the Left.

Spontaneous protest movements by the peasants and the workers could draw from both demonologies. Attacks on Jews often played a part in the revolutionary violence of the crowd. The word 'pogrom' itself could mean both an attack on the Jews and an assault on property in general. The Tsarist regime, in stirring up the one, had to be careful not to let it spill over into the other. And the left-wing leaders of a strike or demonstration were painfully aware that in certain regions, such as the mining districts of the Don basin and Ekaterinsolav in the Ukraine, they were likely to be transformed into a pogrom. Charters Wynn has shown this in his book on strikes and pogroms in the Donbass region at the end of the nineteenth century.[12] In other words, the labourers and peasants who took part in pogroms against the Jews in 1905 or 1917 also (and sometimes simultaneously) attacked manor houses, factories and taverns, plundered shops and offices, or conducted themselves in what the élites termed a 'hooligan' manner against society: vandalizing property, mugging well-dressed passers-by, being drunk and acting rudely. In sum, these attacks against the Jews were part of a general plebeian assault on the whole social order, in which Jews were targeted not so much as Jews, a separate ethnic group, but as the propertied, or simply as the closest and most vulnerable of the educated classes, whom the attackers saw none the less as a part of the élite.

Dark Forces

The image of the enemy was transformed by the First World War. The situation necessitated it: total war demanded total enemies. This was the war to end all wars – the last and holy battle – in the language of both Right and Left. But on both sides the demonic hierarchy was transformed by war. Left-wing defensists put the national enemy above the political one, while the German replaced the Jew as the main enemy for many on the Right.

The German was the main external enemy, while the German within Russia (ethnic Germans, Russians with German-sounding names, the pro-German circles of the court and government) became the main internal one. German subjects of the Tsar were constantly harassed by the authorities.

12. C. Wynn, *Workers, Strikes and Pogroms: The Donbass–Dnepr Bend in Late Imperial Russia, 1870–1905*, Princeton, 1992.

Thousands were arrested and sent into internal exile in Siberia, while their property was confiscated. Others were dismissed from their jobs or expelled from societies and clubs. 'Germans are bad for Russian industry' became a popular wartime expression and there were many manufacturers who ordered the dismissal of every German.[13] The use of the German language, and of Germanic expressions in Russian, was prohibited in many institutions. German works were removed from the repertoire of theatres, concert halls and opera houses. German place-names were Russified. St Petersburg was renamed Petrograd, although some left-wing intellectuals, particularly those, like the Bolsheviks, who saw themselves as 'Internationalists', thought this smacked of chauvinism and, ironically, continued to use the old Imperial name for the city. The Bolshevik leaders of the city continued to call themselves the Petersburg Committee until the beginning of the 1920s. People with German surnames applied to the Imperial Chancellery to change them. Many emphasized their Russian patriotism and identity in their new surnames: Romanov, Novorusskii ('Newrussian'), and Shmidt-Slavianskii ('Schmidt-Slavic').[14] Some people even changed their first names. The archaeologist Wilhelm Wilhelmovich Struve, for example, changed his name to Vasilii Vasilevich.

Russia's wartime Germanophobia became entangled in its spy-mania. Military failures were explained by foreign conspiracies in the capital. Even the Tsarina, herself the main subject of these conspiracies, suspected officials at the Stavka of treachery and informed Nicholas of this.[15] Generals and officers with foreign-sounding surnames were in a particularly difficult position. Some, such as General Rennenkampf, responded by displaying patriotic zeal. According to some of his officers, when they were interrogated by their German captors as prisoners of war, Rennenkampf demanded that his officers with German names swear a special oath of loyalty. Such was the mood of despondency following the defeats of 1915 that most people naturally assumed there were German spies in the High Command. During that autumn Moscow cabbies claimed that everybody knew the generals were traitors and that, without them, Russian troops would have been in Berlin long ago.[16]

This spy-mania had a revolutionary impact on the army and society. Rumours of betrayal by the country's leaders became ever more widespread. The public was totally convinced of the 'treachery' of Sukhomlinov, the

13. *Izvestiia sluzhashchikh v pechatnykh zavedeniikh*, 1917, no. 39, p. 475.
14. A.M. Verner, 'What's in a Name? Of Dog-Killers, Jews and Rasputin', *Slavic Review*, 1994, vol. 53, no. 4, pp. 1046–70.
15. *Perepiska Nikolaia i Aleksandry Romanovykh. t. III: 1914–1915 gg.*, Moscow, 1925, pp. 212, 223, 243.
16. V.P. Semennikov (ed.), *Dnevnik b. velikogo kniazia Andreia Vladimirovicha*, Leningrad, 1925, p. 100.

Minister for War, as it was of that of many other generals and officials.
If the Tsarina was initially suspected merely of sympathizing with the
Germans, then she was accused later of direct collaboration with the
enemy. Such rumours got through to the army, demoralizing all the ranks.
Soldiers at the Front said openly that the Empress was supporting all the
'spying Germans'. They spoke bluntly of the pointlessness of fighting as
long as the Germans were 'ruling Russia'. Some were encouraging their
comrades not to fight – 'How can we fight if Riga is full of spies?', – and
by the end of 1916 there were even refusals to attack.[17]

Senior politicians and Allied diplomats believed in these German conspiracies – and this gave them added credibility. The speeches in the Duma
by the liberal Miliukov, the monarchist Purishkevich, and the radical
Kerensky, each implying treason in the court and government, had the
combined effect of making everyone, whatever their political orientation,
believe in the conspiracies. They were all united – as a 'national opposition'
– by this belief. The ban on the publication of these speeches in the press
merely added to their popularity. Handwritten transcriptions were passed
around. They reached the remotest provinces and, despite the efforts of
the military censors, spread into the army at the Front. With each reproduc-
tion the speeches became more sensational, and in some versions people
added their own specific grievances against the regime.

The British Ambassador was so sure of the influence of pro-German
forces at court that he stated directly to the Tsar: 'Their agents are working
everywhere. They are pulling the strings and those, who normally give
advice to Your Majesty in the selection of your ministers, are being used
as blind instruments.'[18] Buchanan's warning provoked the Tsar's anger –
and indeed it was hardly diplomatic. But English diplomats and officers
assumed that the 'German party' was ruling Russia and would detach it
from the Allied war campaign.

Revolutionary propaganda played on this Germanophobia. Indeed, the
rallying of popular national sentiment against the foreign dynasty had
been a feature of the opposition movement since at least the Decembrists
in the early nineteenth century. The German origin of so many Romanov
empresses was used to confirm, as it were, the anti-national essence of
the dynasty – the 'Gottorp-Holstein' Tsars. In the depiction of the Left,
in particular its Slavophile and populist versions, the regime meant the
imposition of a 'German way of life' that was alien to and rejected by
ordinary Russians.

All the left-wing parties made the most of these conspiracies in their

17. A. Wildman, *The End of the Russian Imperial Army*, Princeton, 1980, pp. 116–17.
18. Sir George Buchanan, *My Mission to Russia and Other Diplomatic Memoirs*, London, 1923, vol.
2, p. 47.

wartime propaganda. A leaflet put out by the Petersburg Committee of the Bolsheviks announced: 'What was predicted a long time ago by the leaders of the working class has come to pass: the autocratic government has committed a monstrous crime – the betrayal of the Russian people . . . It has done a deal, and has sold out the Russian army to the German bourgeoisie.'[19]

This was not just a question of the Left borrowing the arguments of 'patriotic' propaganda. It was a coincidence of mentalities. Revolutionary texts and chauvinistic propaganda were equally obsessed with enemy conspiracies. Both projected the image of a 'bright future' on the other side of a Manichaean struggle: where the revolutionaries declared their battle with the social enemy to be 'final and decisive', the militarists proclaimed the war to be a final 'war to end all wars'. Some even tried to justify the war as a struggle to 'defeat militarism', envisaging a millennium of heaven on earth after victory, an idea paralleled by left-wing fantasists, such as the Symbolist Valery Briusov in his poem 'The Last War', in which he envisages the 'miracle' of 'eternal peace'.[20]

The revolutionary potential of anti-German sentiment was clearly illustrated by the riots in Moscow, at the height of the German breakthrough on the Eastern Front, in 1915. German shops and offices were burned and looted. Piano stores were attacked, Bechsteins and Blüthners hurled from windows on the second floor. Anyone suspected of being 'German' – which often meant no more than having a foreign-sounding name, or being the owner of an expensive shop – was a potential target for the mob. Crowds tried to attack the residence of the Grand Duchess Elizaveta Fedorovna, the sister of the Empress, as rumours spread that she was concealing foreign spies and princes. Stones were thrown into her carriage and she was spat at. The police were in no doubt that what was going on was a 'revolution', or at least the start. And in a sense the police were right.

Anti-German violence and attitudes were equally clearly to be seen in the February Days. Crowds demanded the head of the 'German Tsarina'. Officials and residents with German-sounding names were arrested and some even killed. The writer D.V. Filosofov, who lived in Petrograd, wrote in his diary on 1 March: 'At 10 o'clock in the evening Nuvel' called. Soldiers had gone round to his place and dragged him and his brother out on to the street, under arrest, because they have a "German surname". On the street the two of them explained that their family was French. The soldiers said, "Well then, go home." A member of the State Council,

19. A.G. Shliapnikov, *Kanun semnadtsatogo goda. Semnadtsatyi god*, Moscow, 1992, t. 1, pp. 160, 170, 173.
20. V.Ia. Briusov, *Sobranie Sochinenii*, Moscow, 1973, t. 2, pp. 140–1.

[Baron] Ikskul [von Hildenbrandt], who happened to be staying with them, was also arrested because of his surname and dragged with a beating to the Duma, where they let him go.'[21] Soldiers singled out their officers with foreign-sounding names. Some regiments organized kangaroo courts where such officers were tried and (usually) convicted of treason, sometimes executed, for trying to restore the 'old regime' by 'opening up the Front to the enemy'. Such was the popular association of all evil or misfortune with 'the Germans' that, later in the summer, there were soldiers who explained the failure of the offensive as an act of betrayal by the 'German' officers. Some even accused General Kornilov, the Supreme Commander, of working for the Germans: they were convinced that he had not escaped from the Austrian prisoner-of-war camp, as Kornilov and his supporters claimed, but that he had in fact been 'despatched by the Germans' to sow discord in Russia.[22]

The February Revolution identified itself and was perceived as a patriotic revolution. Anti-German and anti-monarchist attitudes were closely interwoven in the new democratic consciousness which its leaders sought to cultivate as the basis for Russia's national renewal. Condemning the monarchy as 'German' was a way of defining and legitimizing the public's revolutionary anger as the patriotic mood of 'the nation', as if all the country's problems were due to the evil influence of foreigners and could be solved by getting rid of them. In this sense the anti-German riots of 1915 were the true 'dress rehearsal' for 1917 – as a national revolution.

If the February Revolution was able to unite so many diverse (and even hostile) forces, that was largely due to its own self-definition in opposition to a common enemy. That enemy was defined extremely vaguely – as the 'dark forces'. Yet the term 'dark forces' could mean many different things, according to the politics of those who deployed it; and indeed it had been used for many decades both by government and revolutionary propagandists. Even the Grand Duke Nikolai Mikhailovich, in a letter to the Tsar in November 1916, complained of 'the constant intrusion of dark forces into everything'.[23] Fear of the 'dark forces' (Black Hundred, monarchist, Rasputinite and German) temporarily united diverse political groups (constitutional monarchists and republicans, liberals and socialists) behind February as a national revolution. During the February Days people in the crowd in Petrograd told foreign correspondents that what they wanted, and were fighting for, was victory over Germany: 'Now we have

21. D.V. Filosofov, 'Dnevnik', *Zvezda*, 1992, no. 2, p. 190.
22. OR IRLI, f. 185, op. 1, d. 1935, l. 70.
23. V.S. Diakin, *Russkaia burzhuazia i tsarizm v gody pervoi mirovoi voini (1914–1917)*, Leningrad, 1967, pp. 251–3.

beaten the Germans here, we will beat them in the field.'[24]

Many commentators at the time saw the February Revolution in similar terms. The philosopher S.L. Frank regarded it as the 'expression of Russia's instinct for national self-preservation'. P.B. Struve spoke to friends about the 'patriotic necessity' of the revolution.[25] Others saw the overthrow of the Tsar as 'revolution in the name of victory', a 'miracle to save the nation from catastrophe', a 'blow against conspiracies and treachery'. N.A. Berdiaev, another from the Vekhi group of anti-Marxist philosophers, wrote shortly after February: 'The Russian Revolution is the most patriotic, the most national, the most popular revolution of all time.'[26]

Others who had taken part in 'the events' described them as a collision between 'the Russian nation and its enemies' – 'the betrayers of the national cause'.[27] The Committee of the 9th Finland Infantry Regiment sent this greeting to the Soviet: 'We hail the great historic fact of the fall of the monarchy and with it, the evil domination of Russia by the Germans . . .'[28] Similar attitudes were expressed in private letters at the time. 'I congratulate you,' wrote one soldier to his family, 'on the new Russian and not German government.' A survey of soldiers' letters by the military censor noted: 'The opinion is often expressed that the overthrow of the old regime is the salvation of Russia from the Germans, whose victory would have been assured by the former treacherous ministers.'[29]

This idea of the revolution as a victory over 'the enemy within' was sometimes mixed with the theme of the Resurrection. The newspaper *Soldat-grazhdanin* (Soldier-Citizen) printed a hymn on 24 March:

Much blood, torment, suffering and tears
Have been borne by the patient people of Russia, –
The cup of tolerance has overflowed!
The internal enemy is crushed, and the country has arisen
She has woken from a nightmarish dream,
Bringing glory to her resurrection.[30]

Victory over the 'internal enemy' was nearly always seen as the most important condition for a victory over the 'external enemy'. In the spring

24. H. Pitcher, *Witnesses of the Russian Revolution*, London, 1994, pp. 24, 43.
25. S.L. Frank, 'Demokratiia na rasput'e', *Russkaia svoboda*, 1917, no. 1, p. 13; Frank, *Mertvye Molchat*, Moscow, 1917, p. 9; Frank, *Biografiia P.B. Struve*, New York, 1956, p. 108.
26. N. Berdiaev, 'Psikhologiia perezhivaemogo momenta', *Russkaia svoboda*, 1917, no. 1, p. 6; Berdiaev, *Narod i klassy v russkoi revoliutsii*, Moscow, 1917, p. 12; Berdiaev, *Vozmozhna li sotsial'naia revoliutsiia*, Moscow, 1917, p. 2.
27. RGA VMF, f. r-95, op. 1, d. 103, l. 114.
28. GARF, f. 1778, op.1, d. 80, l. 55.
29. RGVIA, f. 2003, op. 1, d. 1496, ll. 18, 39.
30. D. Semenov, 'Pala staraia vlast'!', *Soldat-grazhdanin*, Moscow, 24 March 1917.

of 1917, when nearly everyone was agreed on the need to revive the war campaign, if only for the defence of the revolution, it was a commonplace that if the Kaiser won the war the first thing he would do would be to restore his cousin, 'Bloody Nicholas', to the Russian throne, subjugating Russia to Germany again. Furthermore, since all the revolution's enemies at home were presumed to be the tools of Germany, continuing the war to victory was deemed to be the best way of counteracting them. Military propaganda used such reasoning, and many soldiers reasoned the same way, at least in the spring of 1917. 'It is not enough that we have defeated the internal enemy, we must also smash the external enemy,' declared one military newspaper: 'he is feeding on our bread, wearing our boots, but this will not happen any more, as long as the entire people rises up and does whatever it is called to do to help our Great and Valiant Army.'[31]

The launching of a new offensive was widely perceived as a necessary proof that February was indeed a national and patriotic reawakening. What united the liberals and the moderate socialists was the idea that this was a 'national revolution', not just a revolt against the old regime, and that through the defence of their liberties in battle the Russians would develop a civic consciousness. That was the sense of Kerensky's famous ('rebellious slaves') speech at the Congress of Delegates from the Front.[32] The image of the 'German enemy' – the last bastion of 'autocracy' in Europe – was essential to this call for a new type of Russian civic patriotism. The Allies, by contrast, were presented as the champions of democracy, with high-profile visits by the Allied socialists (such as Albert Thomas and Arthur Henderson) to urge the Russians on before the summer offensive. The launching of the offensive was to prove disastrous, however, by polarizing Russian society, and those who opposed it on the Left increasingly presented the military campaign as a conspiracy by the British capitalists.

Little has been written about Anglophobia in 1917. This is perhaps because it developed in the First World War in the relative obscurity of the German prisoner-of-war camps for soldiers captured on the Eastern Front. As early as 1914 there were plans in the German High Command to fund exiled Russian revolutionaries to publish anti-Tsarist propaganda for distribution among the Russian prisoners of war.[33] But some commanders objected to the plans (stirring anti-monarchism was to play with fire) and

31. V. Rozov, 'K russkim soldatam', *Voennaia Gazeta: Dlia russkikh voisk vo Frantsii*, 1917, no. 27, p. 5; A. Maksimov (ed.), *Tsarskaia armiia v period mirovoi voiny i fevral'skoi revoliutsii. (Materialy k izucheniiu istorii imperialisticheskoi i grazhdanskoi voiny)*, Kazan, 1932, p. 150.
32. For an analysis see O. Figes, *A People's Tragedy: The Russian Revolution 1891–1924*, London, 1996, p. 411.
33. See B.I. Kolonitskii, 'Emigratsiia, voennoplennye i nachal'nyi etap germanskoi politiki "revoliutsionizirovaniia" Rossii (avgust 1914 – nachalo 1915 g.)', *Russkaia emigratsiia – laboratoriia liberal'noi i revoliutsionnoi mysli*, St Petersburg, 1997, pp. 197–216.

so the Germans focused their efforts on pacifist and anti-English propaganda instead. The plan was to stay clear of their prisoners' commitment to Russia and the Tsar but to make them see there was no point in fighting on if Russia's war was being fought for English interests.

The newspaper *Russkii vestnik* (Russian Herald), published by the German government for Russian prisoners of war, waged the fiercest campaign against Russia's Allies, the 'English vampires' above all. Russia was portrayed as England's lackey. One cartoon showed a Russian peasant soldier returning to his hut, only to discover a Highland Grenadier lying on his bed. The caption read: 'Get back to the Front, Ivan, I shall make sure you get kids.'[34] The German domestic press was equally obsessed with the British domination of Russia, portraying 'British agents' as the country's real rulers.[35]

German aeroplanes dropped propaganda leaflets to the Russian soldiers at the Front. The message was the same – that they were spilling blood for British interests. It was not without effect. 'England is to blame for the continuation of the war,' one soldier wrote home from the Front in 1915. 'She wants complete victory. Her towns have not been destroyed by the war. She suffers less than any other country, just pays out capital, but doesn't think of us.' The same sentiments were expressed in soldiers' letters during 1916: 'If the English had not joined in, we would have had peace long ago. England is to blame for everything. If there is a God in the sky, then this little island will not escape punishment'; 'They say that England is prepared to fight until the last drop of Russian blood, and that England just gives Russia money to go on fighting. But is that a gift?'[36]

German propaganda played on stereotypes of England and the English found in Russian culture even before the Crimean War.[37] On the one hand was the Anglophilia of the Russian liberals and constitutional monarchists – on the other the Anglophobia of the Russian Right. For the former, England was the home of liberty; for the latter, an 'Empire of Evil' – its agents directed the Tsarist ministers, its Freemasons the revolutionaries.[38] Such beliefs continued in the First World War, along with the traditional Germanophilia of the Russian Right, and indeed in some ways as a disguised form of the latter. Anglophobia was the acceptable face of Germanophilia in right-wing circles during the war. The articles of P.F. Bulatsel', in his journal *Rossiiskii grazhdanin*, for example, were particularly popular. Bulatsel' spun the theory that the English controlled

34. See B.I. Kolonitskii, 'Berlinskaia gazeta "Russkii vestnik" (1915–1919 gg.)', *Knizhnoe delo v Rossii vo vtoroi polovine XIX – nachale XX veka*, St Petersburg, 1996, vyp. 8, pp. 132–43.

35. The paranoid mood of wartime was clearly reflected in the reports of British informers, which spoke in the most exaggerated terms of the 'German domination' of Russia.

36. Maksimov (ed.), *Tsarskaia armiia v period mirovoi voiny*, pp. 31, 71–2.

37. N.A. Erofeev, *Tumannyi Al'bion: Angliia i anglichane glazami russkikh (1825–1853 gg.)*, Moscow, 1982, pp. 247–303.

38. Raskin, 'Ideologiia russkogo pravogo radikalizma', pp. 15–16, 18–19.

Russia, even claiming that King George was the head of the dreaded English Masons.[39] These ideas found a ready audience in the wake of the military defeats of 1915, which many Russians blamed on the failure of the Allies to support the Russian armies. The growing dependence of the Russian government on Allied, and especially British, financial aid supported these conspiracy theories.

The February Revolution provided the Germans with a new propaganda opportunity. They presented it as an English putsch to ensure the continuation of the war. The Allies had installed the liberals in power to forestall a social revolution against the war. *Russkii vestnik* warned: 'The masses won't be satisfied with fine liberal phrases and if Chkheidze and the Social Democrats do not give them any more than the Kadets and Octobrists, they will kick them out and rise up against the English vampires.'[40] England was thus portrayed as a conservative power – 'the most reactionary country in the world'[41] – whose purpose was to restrain the Russian Revolution in order to continue with the war.

The German aim was clear: to stir a broader Russian revolution that would end the war (hence their support for the Bolsheviks). Many soldiers at the Front found out about the events of the February Days from German leaflets. The fact that their officers had tried to keep them in the dark – and ordered the destruction of the leaflets – reinforced suspicions of a conspiracy.[42] The German leaflets claimed that the English were responsible for the overthrow of the Tsar, who had been on the point of concluding peace with Germany.[43] However, once they realized the pointlessness of trying to persuade the Russians to support their former Tsar, the Germans switched the emphasis of their propaganda. The leaflets they gave out to the Russian soldiers during the Easter fraternizations blamed the British for the war. John Bull was the reason why the Russian soldiers were not going home. They might have been liberated from the Tsar but the British Ambassador Buchanan was still in Petrograd and in effect controlling the government. While he ruled over Russia 'like a Tsar' and 'drank the Russians' blood', the Russians could have neither peace nor liberty.[44]

To judge from soldiers' letters in 1917, the Germans were comparatively successful in their propaganda campaign to divide the Russians from their Western Allies. It became a commonplace of left-wing opposition to the war, especially of what Allan Wildman called the 'trench Bolshevism' of

39. *Rossiiskii grazhdanin*, 1916, no. 37, 16 Oct.; RGIA, f. 776, op. 10, d. 2159.
40. *Russkii vestnik*, 13 (24) March 1917.
41. *Russkii vestnik*, 1 (14) April; 26 Aug. (8 Sept.) 1917.
42. E.N. Burdzhalov, *Vtoraia russkaia revoliutsiia: Moskva, front, periferiia*, Moscow, 1971, p. 131.
43. A.W.F. Knox, *With the Russian Army*, London, 1921, vol. 2, pp. 600–1.
44. K.K. Zvonarev, *Agenturnaia razvedka*, t. 2., *Germanskaia agenturnaia razvedka vo vremia voiny 1914–1918 gg.*, Moscow, 1931, p. 138.

the soldiers at the Front, that the war was being fought for British capitalist interests. 'Recently it has become a widely held view that Britain is to blame for the war,' declared one Russian journalist in the summer of 1917.[45] The Bolsheviks, in particular, made much of the Allied imperialist war aims, as if that was the only reason why the war was still being fought to the bitter end; and in the wake of the April crisis, sparked by Miliukov's assurance to the Allies that Russia would fulfil its imperialist commitments, many soldiers were inclined to believe the propaganda of the Bolsheviks. Certainly, the reluctance of the Russian soldiers to take part in the summer offensive was, at least in part, informed by the feeling that they were being asked to fight for Allied interests rather than for Russian ones.

There were occasions when the Russian High Command, let alone the lower-ranking officers, confirmed the soldiers' suspicions. On the eve of the summer offensive General Brusilov went on a tour of the Northern and Western Fronts to strengthen the soldiers' will to fight. Addressing a group of particularly Bolshevized soldiers near Dvinsk, the Commander-in-Chief claimed that the Germans had destroyed 'one of the French people's finest properties, the beautiful vineyards that produce champagne'. This of course merely alienated and enraged the soldiers, who began to shout at Brusilov: 'Shame on you! You want to spill our blood so you can drink champagne!' Brusilov became afraid and summoned his protectors to surround him. When the shouts had died down he called on one of the most vociferous soldiers to step forward and state his views. The soldier, a young, red-bearded peasant, stood next to the Commander, leant on his rifle with both arms, and, looking askance at Brusilov, delivered a speech in which he claimed that the soldiers had 'had enough of fighting', that 'for three long years the Russian people had spilled their blood for the imperialist and capitalist classes, not just in Russia but in France and England too', and that 'if the general wanted to go on fighting for champagne then let him go and spill his own blood'. The troops cheered; Brusilov was lost for words, and began to leave; and as he did so the soldier read out the declaration of the soldiers' committee calling for the conclusion of an immediate peace. 'We shall not fight any longer for the British or the French imperialists!'[46]

The Bourgeois Enemy

Anti-bourgeois attitudes had a long tradition in Russia. They were to be found in diverse political and cultural traditions, from the Black Hundreds

45. E.S. Gorskii, *Voina i mir*, Odessa, 1917, p. 4.
46. BA, Pronin Collection, Box 1, 'Miting gen. Brusilova'.

to the socialists; and at all levels of society, from the court and the landed nobility to the workers and the peasantry, at the beginning of the century. For different reasons, all these groups were mainly hostile to the emerging industrial bourgeoisie, the usurers and the merchants, who were transforming Russia on capitalist lines. Aristocrats looked down on the bourgeoisie as parvenus and condemned them for threatening the traditional order. 'All the capitalists are foreigners and Jews, who desire the downfall of the monarchy,' explained the Grand Duke Alexander Mikhailovich in a letter to the Tsar.[47] The Black Hundreds frequently denounced 'the mighty gang of bourgeois-capitalists' in their propaganda.[48] But, then, so did the revolutionaries.

Hostility towards 'the bourgeoisie' was an important feature of the revolutionary crowd in 1905–6. But it was unfocused – and could be directed against any member of the propertied élite: employers, officers, landowners, priests, merchants, Jews, students, professionals or anyone well dressed, or foreign looking or apparently well-to-do. In other words, a dominant cultural dimension (the 'uncultured' poor against the 'cultured' rich) lay at the heart of this 'class' or social violence, as Joan Neuberger has argued in her stimulating study of 'hooliganism' in St Petersburg between 1900 and 1914.[49] This created a dilemma for the revolutionary intelligentsia: if they encouraged this hostility to 'the bourgeoisie', it could turn the lower classes against them as well.

The radical intelligentsia juxtaposed their own cultural values with the 'philistinism' or 'petty-bourgeois' style of the commercial bourgeoisie. Berdiaev was speaking for the whole of the radical intelligentsia when he wrote: 'The aversion to everything that is denoted by the term "bourgeois", not just in the social but the spiritual sense, was always my motive force.'[50] This rejection of 'bourgeois' values was central to the intelligentsia's self-identity – as a cultural mission of enlightenment – and it can be seen in the works of Ivanov-Razumnik, D.S. Merezhkovsky and many others who defined its role.[51] It was also expressed in the cultural codes of dress and behaviour by which the intelligentsia defined itself. For example, Moscow students, at the beginning of the century, would use the term 'bourgeois' for anyone among their fellow students who wore leather gloves, or who hung paintings by their dormitory beds.[52]

But however hard they tried to set themselves apart from the bourgeoisie,

47. Grand Duke Alexander Mikhailovich, *Kniga vospominanii*, Moscow, 1991, pp. 77–8.
48. Raskin, 'Ideologiia russkogo pravovo radikalizma', p. 24.
49. J. Neuberger, *Hooliganism: Crime, Culture and Power in St Petersburg, 1900–1914*, Berkeley, 1993.
50. N.A. Berdiaev, *Samopoznanie*, Leningrad, 1991, p. 118.
51. R.B. Ivanov-Razumnik, 'Chto takoe intelligentsiia?', *Intelligentsiia. Vlast'. Narod: Antologiia*, Moscow, 1993, pp. 73–80; D.S. Merezhkovskii, 'Griadushchii ham', ibid., pp. 81–104.
52. P. Ivanov, *Studenty v Moskve: Byt. Nravy. Tipy*, Moscow, 1918, p. 233.

the intelligentsia might remain 'burzhoois' in the common people's mind. As long as they wore spectacles, warm overcoats and boots, they might remain the targets of the crowd. Indeed, during the First World War, the 'intelligentsia' was often singled out in soldiers' condemnations of the 'burzhoois'. 'If I could go back to Russia,' wrote one soldier from the Front, 'then I'd not just bash the heads of our internal enemy but would fight a war against the intelligentsia. If only I could get home, I'd sort out that old windbag – the intelligentsia.'[53]

The February Revolution was perceived by many who took part in it as an 'anti-bourgeois' uprising. As an appeal to the soldiers by the factory committee of the Russian Society for Munitions Manufacture put it during March,

> Comrades, we are very pleased that you have understood us and that you now fully realize that there is an enemy of the people. You have seen that this enemy cannot be found among the workers, either of this factory or of any other, for the workers and the soldiers represent one whole, one army of labour, which the bloodthirsty capitalists, together with Nicholas and Rasputin, have so mercilessly and so pitilessly exploited and oppressed, building their own happiness on our misery.[54]

Crowd violence against the 'burzhoois' (including the intelligentsia) was much in evidence in the February Days. Armed gangs looted shops and liquor stores, broke into the houses of the well-to-do, and robbed and raped their inhabitants. Well-dressed passers-by were mugged in the streets. Even wearing spectacles or a white starched collar was enough to mark one out as a 'burzhooi'.[55]

Much of this violence was spontaneous and arose from below. But it was encouraged and to some extent legitimized by the anti-capitalist rhetoric, and the language of class conflict, articulated by the socialists. The 'burzhooi' was the main enemy in the socialist demonology of 1917. Take, for example, the best-selling pamphlet by Wilhelm (not to be confused with Karl) Liebknecht called *Spiders and Flies*.[56] It went through over

53. Maksimov (ed.), *Tsarskaia armiia v period mirovoi voiny*, pp. 49, 60, 64, 73, 83, 94, 98, 101, 110, 111, 113, 114, 117, 119.
54. TsGAIPD, f. 1, op. 1, d. 18, l. 1.
55. S. Jones, *Russia in Revolution, Being the Experience of an Englishman in Russia during the Upheaval*, London, 1917, p. 119; GARF, f. 102, op. 341, d. 57, ll. 24–9; f. 5849, op. 2, d. 33, ll. 4–5; V. Bulgakov, 'Revoliutsiia na avtomobiliakh (Petrograd v fevrale 1917 g.)', *Na chuzhoi storone*, 6, Berlin and Prague, 1924, pp. 14–17.
56. Right-wing pamphleteers before 1914 used the image of the spider to depict the Jew 'sucking the blood of the harmless flies [the Russian people] it has caught in its web' (see L. Engelstein, *The Keys to Happiness: Sex and the Search for Modernity in Fin-de-Siècle Russia*, Ithaca, 1992, pp. 322–3). On the long history of arachnophobic imagery see Paul Hillyard's superb study *The Book of the Spider: From Arachnophobia to the Love of Spiders*, London, 1994. Thanks to Marina Warner for this reference.

twenty editions and was published by Bolshevik, SR and Menshevik presses, including G.V. Plekhanov's publishing group, Edinstvo. The brochure, which was widely distributed in the revolutionary underground, divided Russia into two warring species:

> The spiders are the masters, the money-grubbers, the exploiters, the gentry, the wealthy, and the priests, pimps and parasites of all types! . . . The flies are the unhappy workers who must obey all those laws the capitalist happens to think up – must obey, for the poor man has not even a crumb of bread. The spider is the factory-owner earning five or six roubles every day from each of his workers and impertinently giving them a paltry wage as if it were a kindness.[57]

The concept of the class war as a Darwinian struggle became commonplace in 1917.[58] *Spiders and Flies* probably did more than any other book to educate the Russian masses in class consciousness. A participant in the revolution subsequently recalled that

> I always had an excellent memory and always earned high marks at school. But I began to see things more clearly in 1915, after I had read *Spiders and Flies* by the truly ardent revolutionary Karl [sic] Liebknecht. It ignited the spark of revolutionary protest within me. And what had I been before my 'encounter' with this torchbearer of reason? A country lad, the son of a poor woman.[59]

Liebknecht's pamphlet had a similar effect on many readers in 1917:

> The brochure was most interesting. It exposed the bourgeoisie and its role in capitalist society. The exposition was so popular that, after a brief explanation, even a semi-literate soldier understood: the bourgeoisie holds all the nation's wealth in its hands and has *de facto* power. Through merciless exploitation it sucks out the juices of the toilers like a spider. The brochure was very useful for soldiers in the trenches. It helped to raise their consciousness and became, as they say, our first political textbook.[60]

Obviously, such a perception did not depend on which press – Bolshevik, Menshevik, SR – had published the pamphlet.

S.R. Dikshtein's *Who Lives by What* (*Kto chem zhivet*), also went through

57. V. Liebknecht, *Pauki i mukhi*, Samara, 1917, p. 4.
58. See e.g. *Protokoly vladimirskogo gubernskogo s'ezda krest'ianskikh deputatov, sosotoiavshchegosia 14–18 maia 1917 g.*, Vladimir, 1917, p. 31 and *passim*.
59. L. Beliaeva, 'Gotov ruchat'sia za nego golovoi (Beseda s I. S. Shkapoi)', *Literaturnaia gazeta*, 23 Nov. 1988.
60. S. Dundukov, 'Burnoe vremia', *V bor'be za Sovetskuiu vlast'*, Minsk, 1967, p. 42.

several editions – no fewer than eleven in 1917 – and was published by Bolshevik, Menshevik and SR presses. Both Liebknecht's and Dikshtein's pamphlets were among the most popular publications of the Russian revolutionary underground, and several generations of young revolutionaries were raised on them. It is not surprising that they were reprinted in much greater numbers when legal circumstances made this possible in 1917.

The various expositions of party programmes, published most often by party committees and organizations, similarly deepened the anti-bourgeois orientation of mass consciousness. *What the Socialist Revolutionaries Are Fighting For* (*Za chto boriutsia sotsialisty-revoliutsionery*), which went through at least seven editions in 1917, announced that

> people who previously enjoyed equal rights in everything have been divided into classes: a class of property-owning capitalists; and a class of toilers that has been deprived, or practically deprived, of property and that has been forced to feed a small group of effete parasites. As a result of this state of affairs, people who have worked indefatigably their entire lives live in dirty hovels, in need, suffering from hunger and cold, while the parasites, the capitalists and property-owners, enjoy all the best of life without lifting a finger.[61]

It seems that the moderate socialists' propaganda contained a deep contradiction. On the one hand was their strategic goal – the negation of capitalism. On the other, the tactical task of the moment: reaching agreement with 'the country's vital forces', which meant coalition with the 'bourgeoisie'.

The socialists, however, often conducted concrete political campaigns as if they were class-based, anti-bourgeois acts. On the eve of the local elections in Kiev, for example, they distributed the leaflet *Burzhooi Get'* (*Get' burzhuev*), which called upon people to vote for the Ukrainian slate.[62]

It was not only the socialist parties which conducted anti-bourgeois propaganda. The Union of Evolutionary Socialism, founded in part by N.O. Losskii, propounded an ethical socialist ideal.[63] The Union's position, 'Through a people's Great Russia – to socialism', won support among the Provisional Government's propaganda officials, who financed the publication of brochures carrying a corresponding message.[64] All sorts of organizations

61. *Za chto boriutsia sotsialisty-revoliutsionery*, Tver, 1917, pp. 3–4.
62. *Kievlianin*, 27 July 1917.
63. N.O. Losskii, 'O sotsializme', *Vestnik partii narodnoi svobody*, 1917, no. 8, pp. 3–5; V.P. Buldakov, 'Politicheskie manevry kontrrevoliutsii v 1917 godu: K voprosu ob izuchenii neproletarskikh politicheskikh obrazovanii', *Neproletarskie partii Rossii v gody burzhuazno-demokraticheskoi revoliutsii i v period nazrevaniia sotsialisticheskoi revoliutsii: Materialy konferentsii*, Moscow, 1982, p. 166.
64. RGIA, f. 1278, op. 10, d. 14, 1. 315.

propagandizing the ideals of Christian Socialism appeared.[65] Advocates of a radical reform of the Church utilized 'anti-bourgeois' rhetoric in their arguments: 'Is it not a disgrace when the overfed bourgeois, with their fat bellies and fine garments, talk of a world-wide Christian brotherhood and pray for peace on earth?'[66]

Several clergymen of the Orthodox Church also took a position hostile to the bourgeoisie. A.A.Vvedensky, the future founder of the Soviet-sponsored 'Living Church', wrote on behalf of the 'socialist clergy':

How great a love for the Church we have seen from even the most inveterate Bolsheviks! We have appeared in factories, in military units, on cruisers and so on. We have not made unfeasible promises, but we have said that the Gospels and the holy fathers are not deaf to societal evils, that Christianity has long condemned capitalism, and that [Christianity] 'stands behind the sorrowful and those left out'. I would dare to maintain that many [Bolsheviks] have come to terms with the Church . . . The struggle on behalf of the poor is the basic principle of socialism, and it is our own Christian struggle.[67]

It stands to reason that the author of those lines was one of the most radical clergymen, and it is not surprising that he was elected to the Petrograd Soviet by the 'democratic clergy'.[68] But it is indicative that even the editor of the Holy Synod's newspaper was fairly sympathetic to the sort of critique of capitalism levelled by the socialist parties.[69] Subsequently, the local council of the Russian Orthodox Church created a special 'Commission on Bolshevism in the Church'. From its sessions came the admission that 'Bolshevism has captured a significant number of clergymen'.[70] This was not so much a case of the clergy having joined the party, as of their

65. See *Katekhizis khristianina ili sotsialista*, Ekaterinoslav, 1917, p. 15; A.A. Mudrov, *Khristos sotsialist, ili khristianstvo i sotsializm*, Ekaterinoslav, 1917, p. 15; *Soiuz novykh khristian-sotsialistov*, Kiev, 1917, p. 16; and *Evangelie khristianskogo sotsializma*, Tver, 1917, p. 8. In August 1917 the creation of the 'Socialist Church Party' ('tserkovnosotsialisticheskaia partiia') was announced. See Kh.M. Astrakhan, *Bol'sheviki i ikh politicheskie protivniki v 1917 godu*, Leningrad, 1973, p. 366.
    Various concepts of 'national' socialism were formulated: 'Today's capitalist system is the reason for our sorrows,' declared P. Al'berg, asserting further that Wilhelm II was the 'Antichrist' and Marx was a 'false prophet' and 'the Antichrist's helper'. See Al'berg, *Da zdravstvuet chestnaia rabota! Kto rabotaet, tot dolzhen byt' syt!*, Riga, 1917, pp. 6, 8. See also *Partiia russkikh natsional'nykh sotsialistov: Osnovy partii*, Moscow, 1917, pp. 1 ff.
66. N.A. Rtishchev, *Kto iz nas burzhui?*, Moscow, 1917, p. 20.
67. A. Vvedenskii, 'O sotsializme,' *Vserossiiskii tserkovno-obshchestvennyi vestnik* (Petrograd), 5 Aug. 1917. Some theologians held a similar point of view: 'We have Christians, and then there are the greedy priests who try to play with socialism and even declare themselves Social-Democrats.' Curiously, this tract went on to say, 'Don't we know instances where worker-Bolsheviks called themselves sincere Christians?' See G. Prokhorov, *Sotsializm, khristianstvo i khristianskii sotsializm*, Petrograd, 1917, p. 54.
68. *Vechernee vremia* (Petrograd), 5 Aug. 1917.
69. B. Titlinov, 'Politicheskie partii v svete khristianstva', *Vserossiiskii tserkovno-obshchestvennyi vestnik*, 3 Aug. 1917.
70. RGIA, f. 833, op. 1, d. 33, l. 29.

general radicalization. In the language of 1917, 'Bolshevism' was used by the non-Bolsheviks to mean any extreme form of radicalism.

The 'fashion for socialism' was widespread during the February Revolution. Attesting to its further spread is the appearance of a wide variety of socialist organizations, even a Socialist Union of Deaf-Mutes, during 1917 in all walks of society. Demands were made of non-socialist groups to define their attitudes to socialism, as if there were something wrong or suspicious in their not being socialist. The executive organ of the Kadet Party, for example, received a letter which in part read:

Why are the Kadets not socialists? Why do they say nothing about this? What other ways for a better life or better economic arrangement are there besides socialism? Only capitalism or socialism? Or is there something else? Do tell us. After all, you are not socialists yet you admit that we cannot go on like this. How, then, should things be?[71]

Examining this cult of socialism, the historian A.A. Kizevetter took note of 'a general aspiration of a huge mass of Russians to declare themselves, no matter what, to the amazement of foreigners, to be absolute socialists'.[72] There were, of course, various models of socialism, and various ideas of how to achieve it in Russia at this time. But they all contributed to the development of anti-bourgeois attitudes. Such was the domination of socialist ideas, moreover, that many non- and anti-socialists were obliged to mimic it for political survival in the hostile climate of 1917. Bourgeois groups and parties adopted 'the protective colour of socialism', or conducted propaganda 'with a socialist stamp'. As A.S. Izgoev ironically noted, even the Stock Exchange newspaper, *Birzhevye vedomosti*, 'did not deny itself the pleasure of making wounding comments about "the bourgeoisie" and of poking fun at "bourgeois" ways'.[73] The journal of the Inter-District Group (Mezhraionka) wrote indignantly about the same phenomenon: 'The yellow boulevard press calls itself "non-party socialist". The financial newspapers reinvent themselves by adopting the protective colour of "realistic socialism", while the banks try to protect themselves by raising the red banner of the revolution over their buildings.'[74]

One of the most vivid examples of this sort of political mimicry can be found in Petrograd's *Malen'kaia gazeta* (Little Newspaper), widely read even before February. It was a lively urban chronicle (covering the criminal scene for the most part), with a religious moralizing tone and a stance as the defender of the 'little man' against 'the mighty' and 'the rich'. The

71. GARF, f. 579, op. 1, d. 876, l. 2.
72. A. Kizevetter, 'Moda na sotsializm', *Russkie vedomosti*, 25 June 1917.
73. A. Izgoev, 'O burzhuaznosti', *Vestnik partii narodnoi svobody*, 1917, no. 1, pp. 8–9.
74. *Vpered* (Petrograd), 1917, no. 1, p. 1.

respectable poor and lower-middling folk of Petrograd saw it as 'their' newspaper. The political line of *Malen'kaia gazeta* was emphatically chauvinist, anti-Semitic and militarist. After the February Revolution, however, the paper's publishers, with a fine sense of the changing political fashion, decorated the paper with the words beneath its title: 'The paper of non-party socialists.' 'Our ideal,' it informed its readers, 'is the ideal of labouring humanity. The first stage toward this lies in the ideals of the proletariat, the liberation of labour.'[75]

Malen'kaia gazeta stood on an anti-Bolshevik platform. But several ultra-right-wing publications even welcomed the October insurrection. The Black Hundred organ *Groza*, for example, declared on 29 October:

> the servant of the English and the bankers, the Jew Kerensky, who impudently took the title of Commander-in-Chief and Minister-President of the Orthodox Russian Kingdom, has been swept out of the Winter Palace ... The regiments [of the garrison] refused to obey the government of the Yid-bankers, the treacherous generals and landlords, and the merchant-thieves.[76]

There were several attempts to instigate pogroms with anti-bourgeois propaganda of this sort. On 26 June leaflets of the 'Free Association of Anarchists and Communists' appeared in Kiev (possibly as forgeries by the Black Hundreds): 'Down with the Provisional Government, smash the bourgeoisie and the Jews.'[77] There were even occasions in 1917 when the Bolsheviks flirted with the idea of a pogrom against the bourgeoisie. And in a sense that is just what they would unleash with the slogan 'Loot the looters' during 1918 (on which more below). At a session of the Petrograd Soviet, Trotsky argued:

> Pogroms are a movement by the desperate masses, and the most politically backward masses at that ... A hatred naturally arises against those who are better dressed and richer; after all, the rich have twice the clothes and can get their food without ration cards. Their hatred is directed against those who are better educated, who have different beliefs, and so on. We understand them, and we regard them differently from the way we regard the bourgeois bastard who wants to shoot them.[78]

Perhaps not surprisingly, the Germans tried to make use of the Russian

75. *Malen'kaia gazeta*, 15 June 1917.
76. *Groza* (Petrograd), 29 Oct. 1917.
77. *Kievlianin*, 27 June 1917. (*Rabochii put'*, 18 Oct. 1917.)
78. *Rabochii put'*, 18 Oct. 1917. On the anti-Semitic attitudes of certain sections of the Red Guards see D.V. Filosofov 'Dnevnik', *Zvezda*, 1992, no. 3, p. 160.

soldier's anti-bourgeois attitudes. *Russkii vestnik*, the Russian-language newspaper published in Berlin, regularly denounced the 'English vampires', even before 1917. After the revolution such denunciations were given a more anti-bourgeois tone. 'The Russian people has not freed itself in order to replace Tsarism with the capitalist yoke of the English and their friends,' the German paper proclaimed in late April. It continued in this vein throughout the spring, writing in early June that 'the government officials in Petrograd are paying in blood, the blood of their compatriots, to receive money which in turn flows into the pockets of English and French capitalists'.[79] The paper printed similar letters from Russian soldiers: 'We do not want millions of people like us to perish because of the whims of our capitalists.'[80] Austro-Hungarian propaganda used many of the same arguments. The Vienna-based Russian-language newspaper, *Nedelia*, wrote that 'Russian soldiers are being forced to sacrifice their lives for the fantastic plans of the Entente; in reality they are fighting for England's mercenary aims and on behalf of French capitalists.'[81]

Here anti-bourgeois attitudes were linked with popular xenophobia, Anglophobia in particular, as analysed above. The plebeian image of the 'burzhooi' was not free of elements of xenophobia: the 'burzhooi' was not properly 'Russian', he was cosmopolitan (depicted in cartoons in a morning suit and top-hat). In pre-revolutionary Russia hostile attitudes towards the bourgeoisie were often expressed in terms of opposition to the domination of foreigners in Russian business life. This was reflected in working-class popular culture.[82] In this sense, the intersection between the Anglophobic propaganda of the Germans and the anti-capitalist propaganda of the Bolsheviks was significant. Both sought to persuade the Russian masses that the war was being fought for the capitalist interests of Russia's Allies, England above all.

Efforts by supporters of the Coalition to counteract this anti-bourgeois propaganda attest to the prevalence of such sentiments in 1917. One example is a pamphlet by the Petrograd Union of Trade and Industry.[83] The cover picture, ironically, showed a revolutionary soldier with his rifle, and a worker with a hammer, itself an indication of how widespread the symbols of the socialist culture had become. This type of propaganda was in the main counter-productive. It often happened, for example, that

79. *Russkii vestnik* (Berlin), 26 April (9 May) 1917; 1 (14) July 1917.
80. Ibid., 15 (28) March 1917.
81. *Nedelia* (Vienna), 2 (15) April 1917.
82. See A.P. Prusakov, 'Fol'klor moskovskikh rabochikh v predoktiabr'skoe desiatletie', *Sovetskaia etnografiia*, 1970, no. 4, pp. 109–10.
83. L. Nemanov, *Burzhuaziia i proletariat*, Petrograd, 1917, p. 32. See also other brochures from this press: V.S. Ziv, *Chto poteriaiut russkie rabochie i krest'iane ot pobedy Germanii?*, Petrograd, 1917; and M. Dobrov, *Chto takoe burzhuaziia*, Petrograd, 1917.

entrepreneurs refused to refer to themselves as 'bourgeois', preferring to be part of the 'trade and industry class'. At other times, to deflect this propaganda, the supporters of the bourgeoise offered moralistic tracts – in which any greedy person, regardless of social class, was portrayed as 'bourgeois'. In either case the negative connotations of the term 'bourgeois' were not only left unquestioned but were even implicitly confirmed. Condemnations of the 'bourgeoisie' became so widespread in 1917 that they were found even in the publications of the Kadets, the 'bourgeois' party *par excellence*. 'Many of the worst kind of "burzhoois",' declared one well-known liberal critic, 'are really more concerned for their own bellies than they are for the "cultural valuables" for which they profess to have so much concern. And it must be said that the concern for culture and the nation professed by people such as these, who do not have faith other than in themselves and their own beneficial interests, is far more dangerous than the "fanaticism" of "Pravda".'[84]

The fact, moreover, that the thematic subject of the 'bourgeoisie' began to appear in folklore, satire and parodies testifies to the broad diffusion of anti-bourgeois attitudes.[85] As Arthur Ransome, then in Russia, wrote: 'Much time is spent in discussing who is a "bourgeois" (the Russians use the French word) and who not. To be a "bourgeois" is the greatest imaginable disgrace. When boys quarrel in the street and one of them wishes to hurl a deadly insult at his opponent he shouts "Bourgeois!" That is a slur which really can only be washed out with blood.'[86]

In their anti-bourgeois propaganda, various parties and organizations defined the 'bourgeoisie' in many different ways. In the popular understanding, moreover, 'the bourgeoisie' was something often very different from the definition of it given by the parties. Often, for example, all property-owners, even those just living comfortably, were called 'bourgeois'. The term was also used to describe a person's occupation or status rather than their class: the soldier considered officers to be 'bourgeois'; soldiers at the Front regarded soldiers in the rear as 'bourgeois'; and the infantry looked upon artillerymen as 'bourgeois'. Then again, the naval officer who was angry with the demands of his sailors would call them 'bourgeois' too.[87] Even the Bolsheviks, after they came to power, were perceived as 'burzhoois'.

In the countryside the peasantry used the word 'burzhooi' to describe all hostile forces, as already discussed in Chapter 5. The most common peasant understanding of the term was as a supporter of the monarchy

84. D. Filosofov, 'Zolotye sny', Rech', 1 April 1917.
85. 'Iz dnevnika Burzhueva', Revel'skoe utro, 28 April 1917; Voina kukharki s burzhuem na Tverskom bul'vare, Moscow, 1917.
86. Pitcher, Witnesses of the Russian Revolution, p. 120.
87. RGA VMF, f. R-21, op. 1, d. 14,1. 39.

and the gentry on the land. The movement on the land was frequently described in peasant resolutions as a 'struggle against the burzhoois'. 'Burzhooi forests' were felled by the peasants; 'burzhooi property' was destroyed. 'Hatred for the burzhooi' was also sometimes cited as the immediate cause for the destruction of estates.[88]

Peasant soldiers used the language of an 'anti-burzhooi' revolution, a fact acknowledged by the military censor of the Kazan district in the first week of August 1917: 'Holding fast to time-honoured convictions, based upon centuries of hatred for the noble landowner, the naive peasants do not realize that only a tiny proportion of the landowners, most of whom were ruined a long time ago, in fact belong to the bourgeoisie; there are many more merchants in the bourgeoisie, and even more foreigners, Germans and others.'[89] In other words, the military censor did not repudiate the language of the 'anti-bourgeois' revolution. Nor did he deny that it was applicable to the landed nobility. He merely objected that relatively few of the landowners were rich enough to be considered properly 'bourgeois'.

The understanding of the term 'burzhooi' in this general sense – i.e. as an enemy of the common people – exacerbated social and cultural conflicts. 'Who isn't called a "burzhooi" these days?', asked one pamphleteer. 'Workers call all non-workers "burzhoois"; peasants – all "gentlemen", including anyone dressed in city clothes.'[90] The term helped to reveal and articulate an anti-Western, anti-urban, anti-intelligentsia, mood: 'Don't you believe the newspapers,' a peasant admonished a schoolteacher. 'The bourgeoisie writes them.'[91] Physical appearances often determined who were perceived as 'burzhooi'. 'There are some who think that anyone who wears a hat and has a "seigniorial face" is a burzhooi', declared one political pamphlet. 'The word "burzhooi" is given to anyone whose clothes are clean or who wears a starched collar and cuffs,' concluded another. 'Many people are called bourgeois because they are educated, live in a clean way or wear a gentleman's suit instead of a worker's blouse, even though financially they barely make ends meet and live solely through their own labour,' proclaimed a third. And another: 'soon it will be dangerous to wear a starched collar, a tie and hat or a decent suit without being called "burzhooi" '.[92] Socio-cultural conflicts of this sort arose every day:

The masses do not see an abstract 'bourgeoisie' or social class, but real, living people whom they call *burzhooi* [bourgeois], *barzhooi* [barge-

88. *1917 god v derevne: Sb. vospominanii krest'ian*, Moscow, 1929, pp. 66–7, 85, 174; O. Figes, *Peasant Russia, Civil War: The Volga Countryside in Revolution 1917–1921*, Oxford, 1989, p. 54.
89. Maksimov (ed.), *Tsarskaia armiia v period mirovoi voiny*, p. 139.
90. N.A. Kabanov, *Chto takoe burzhui*, Moscow, 1917, p. 1.
91. *Ezhemesiachnyi zhurnal*, 1917, no. 11–12, p. 149.
92. Dobrov, *Chto takoe burzhuaziia*, p. 3; Kabanov, *Chto takoe burzhui*, p. 3; and D.N. Vvedenskii, *Nasha revoliutsiia i khristianstvo*, Rannenburg, 1917, p. 3.

owners: from *barzhui*] and *birzhooi* [stockbrokers: from *birzhye*], and they vent their anger not against some imaginary class called the 'bourgeoisie', but against real people they meet on the streets, in trams and trains.[93]

Social and cultural attitudes like these informed political identities. Analysing the results of the June City Duma elections in Moscow, which the SRs won, Kizevetter wrote:

The shawls and peaked caps voted against the fur hats, regardless of what sort of world-view – bourgeois or non-bourgeois – filled those hat-covered skulls . . . To be sure, the masses have mastered the 'prevailing' terminology of 'socialist' and 'burzhooi', but while using these terms quite boldly and confidently they have infused them with their own meanings that have nothing in common with the programmes of the SDs [Social Democrats] or SRs.[94]

The term 'burzhooi' , in this sense, became an expletive. 'From 1 March a new swear-word has appeared in party newspapers,' the well-known publicist A. Iablonovskii wrote: 'Burzhooi. It seems that this word, with its abusive connotations, means something between "scoundrel" and "swine", and its wide usage is explained, apparently, by its polemical convenience.'[95]

The term, moreover, was also used as a type of ethical category. 'A genuine "burzhooi" is not burzhooi because he is rich, owns a factory, is educated, or is not a socialist,' wrote one publicist, 'but because he places his own interests and those of his type above everybody else.'[96] As another pamphlet on the subject concluded:

A burzhooi is someone who thinks only of himself, of his belly. It is someone who is aloof, who is ready to grab anyone by the throat if it involves his money or his food. A burzhooi is a person who leads an egotistical, meaningless and aimless life, unilluminated by the vivid and wonderful goals of any valuable or spiritual labour . . . Such people, regardless of their class identity – be they rich merchants, kulaks or a skilled worker whose only interest is his weekly wage – are all equally burzhoois.[97]

93. Dobrov, *Chto takoe burzhuaziia*, p. 15.
94. A. Kizevetter, 'Itogi moskovskikh vyborov', *Russkie vedomosti*, 28 June 1917. On the use of the term 'bourgeoisie' in the newspaper polemic of 1917 see L. McReynolds, *The News under Russia's Old Regime: The Development of a Mass Circulation Press*, Princeton, 1991, p. 270.
95. *Russkoe slovo*, 22 March 1917.
96. Kabanov, *Chto takoe burzhui*, p. 1.
97. N. Kadmin, *Chto takoe burzhui?*, Moscow, 1917, p. 10.

In this view, egotism and cupidity were also signs of being 'burzhooi'. This was precisely the plane on which the polemics with the socialists were often conducted. In criticizing one Bolshevik leaflet a provincial newspaper wrote: 'You say that our Provisional Government is "bourgeois". But it consists of honest, intelligent citizens who fervently love their country.'[98]

Accusations of being 'bourgeois', moreover, were often a way of attaching political labels. The socialists considered all other parties to be 'bourgeois'. However, the term was also used in the polemics between socialist groupings. As Izgoev noted with malicious glee,

> The Social Democrats call the Socialist Revolutionaries a bourgeois party; the Socialist Revolutionaries do not recognize as true socialists either the Popular Socialists or those in their own party who call for the war to be continued until victory over the Germans. The Social Democrats also are riven by internecine strife: the Bolsheviks curse the Mensheviks for being bourgeois, while the Mensheviks try to prove that the Bolsheviks are a petit bourgeois party.[99]

The Moscow Soviet considered Plekhanov's group 'Edinsto' (Unity) to be part of the 'bourgeoisie', and called upon the people not to vote for it in local elections.[100]

The 'bourgeois' identity was so fluid that at times it was defined in a different way by different groups of soldiers, even within a single battalion. In April, for example, the 2nd Company from the Petrograd Electro-Technical Battalion listed *Edinstvo* as one of the socialist newspapers and contrasted it with 'bourgeois' papers to be boycotted; at the same time, however, the battalion's 3rd Company demanded that the 'bourgeois' *Edinstvo* be boycotted.[101]

Anti-bourgeois ideas were coloured by and spread as a hostile attitude towards the continuation of the war. The 'bourgeoisie' indeed was commonly regarded as principally to blame for the fact that the war had lasted quite so long – a fact which most socialists connected with the huge war profits of the industrialists. Thus, on 25 May, a meeting of the workers from the Moscow factory Dinamo adopted a resolution declaring that 'the cause of all the destruction is a war that no one needs but the greedy capitalists'.[102] Tellingly, the text of the resolution was put forward by the SRs – the

98. V., 'Revel'skie lenintsy', *Revel'skoe slovo*, 21 April 1917.
99. Izgoev, *Sotsialisty i krest'iane*, Petrograd, 1917, p. 5.
100. Belorussov, 'Soldatskii sotsializm', *Russkie vedomosti*, 22 June 1917.
101. See B.I. Kolonitskii, 'Rezoliutsii rabochikh i soldat o burzhuaznoi pechati (mart–aprel' 1917 goda)', *Vspomogatel'nye istoricheskie distsipliny*, vyp. 19, Leningrad, 1987, p. 235.
102. *Trud*, Moscow, 27 May 1917.

Bolshevik resolution (which we should assume was even more radical) having been rejected.

On the other hand, even 'Revolutionary Defensists' deployed anti-bourgeois arguments. On 19 April the Kolomna Garrison Soviet declared itself in favour of 'an end to the fighting only after that lair of global militarism – the German ruling classes – has been destroyed, and all the peoples of the world have reached the point of laying down their arms and liberating themselves from the excessive militarism that is ravaging so many nations in the interests of dynasties and capital'.[103] Tsereteli, in arguing for a continuation of the war, noted: 'we have declared to all the peoples of the world that this is what the Russian democracy has done, that it is the sole way out of this murderous situation in which, on behalf of the interests of a few bourgeois, millions of people must shed blood . . . Trying to end the possibility of war is senseless as long as personal property and bourgeois states, even the most democratic ones, still exist.'[104] Such declarations obviously facilitated the spread of anti-bourgeois sentiment: frustrations with the war, and the hardships it entailed, were taken out on the 'bourgeoisie'.

In socialist propaganda, 'bourgeois' was often counterposed to 'democracy' – a word whose common understanding in 1917 has already been discussed. Accordingly, the repression of the bourgeoisie was not considered to be contradictory to 'democracy', defined as the interests of the common people. In one and the same resolution the Slutskii Soviet, for example, demanded the restoration of a free press and the closing of the counter-revolutionary press.[105] Similarly, a resolution to the 'Central Soviet' from the workers at the Baltic Factory in Petrograd demanded that 'our socialist newspapers, regardless of party, be circulated freely and that no arrests are made'. At the same time, however, it wanted 'decisive measures to close all the counter-revolutionary newspapers of the hateful and the dirty bourgeoisie'.[106]

In practice, too, groups considered 'bourgeois' were placed beyond the pale of the democratic process, making repressive measures against them justifiable. On 7 September the Min'iarskii Soviet of Workers' Deputies urged postal workers to deliver only socialist newspapers; 'bourgeois' papers should be taken to the Soviet, which would 'sell them for wrapping paper, if possible'.[107] The Sobinsk Factory Soviet called for 'halting the import

103. GARF, f. 1778, op. 1, d. 83, l. 54.
104. *Rechi N.S. Chkheidze, M. 1. Skobeleva i I. G. Tsereteli, proiznesennye na s'ezde soldatskikh i rabochikh deputatov Zapadnogo fronta v gorode Minsk 8-go aprelia 1917 goda*, Petrograd, 1917, pp. 13, 15, 16.
105. GARF, f. 6978, op. 1, d. 247, l. 60.
106. TsGASP, f. 4598, op. 1, d. 247, l. 60.
107. *Bor'ba za Sovetskuiu vlast' na Iuzhnom Urale (1917–1918 gg.): Sbornik dokumentov i materialov*,

and sale of bourgeois newspapers', which were to be 'placed under strict control: subscribers will receive them after the lapse of one month'.[108]

Here one can see the emotional basis of the Bolshevik Decree on the Press. It was fundamental to the socialist conception of democracy propounded by the Bolsheviks that the state, not capital, should determine who had access to the public through the press; and that in a civil war which (they claimed) existed after October and was bound to last as long as the bourgeoisie survived, the state should ensure that only those who spoke for the common people's side should have access to the press. As the Bolshevik V.A. Avanesov put it while defending the decree in the Soviet Executive at its noisy session on 4 November:

> If the new government has had the strength to abolish private landed property, thereby infringing the rights of the landlords, it would be ridiculous for Soviet power to stand up for antiquated notions about liberty of the press. First the newspapers must be freed from capitalist oppression, just as we have freed the land from the landlords, and then we can promulgate new socialist laws and norms enshrining a liberty that will serve the *whole toiling people and not just capital*.[109]

Two points should be noted here. The comparison of the press question to the confiscation of the gentry's land served to subordinate what the Bolsheviks termed the 'bourgeois' principles of political freedom to the idea of the revolution as class war or social levelling through the expropriation of 'bourgeois' property. And when Avanesov said that the Bolshevik press laws would enshrine the liberties of the 'whole *toiling* people', he did not include in this the 'bourgeoisie' (the words 'and not just capital' were in this sense mendacious: it would have been more honest to omit the word 'just').

The Bolshevik conception of Soviet power specifically excluded the bourgeoisie. In this conception – and, as we have seen, in the popular conception to a large extent as well – the democratization of the sphere of government was understood to mean the squeezing out of all 'bourgeois' elements. This understanding became widespread within Soviet circles after the Kornilov crisis – and it formed the basis of the drive to Soviet power as a purging of all 'bourgeois' elements from the revolutionary organs of the state. It was on this understanding, for example, that the Kadets were excluded from the Democratic Conference: as a part of the

Cheliabinsk, 1957, p. 131.

108. *Sotsial-demokrat*, Moscow, 22 Sept. 1917.

109. *The Debate on Soviet Power: Minutes of the All-Russian Central Executive Committee of Soviets. Second Convocation. October 1917–January 1918*, trans. and ed. J.L.H. Keep, Oxford, 1979, p. 70.

'bourgeoisie', they were not deemed 'democratic'. It was also on this basis that the workers' and soldiers' resolutions called for Soviet power from September on. They clearly called for the establishment of a purely 'democratic' government, or, 'the dictatorship of the democracy'. Such a government was to represent the workers, the soldiers and the peasants, but specifically not the bourgeoisie. 'The less bourgeoisie, the more democracy.'

It stood to reason that the Bolsheviks and their allies wanted to advance this class conception of democracy. But they were not the only ones, and it deserves to be stressed that in the climate of 1917 many of the moderate socialist parties also called for the advance of democracy through discrimination against the 'bourgeoisie'. For example, the officers and soldiers of the 3rd Railway Battalion's headquarters sent a resolution to Kerensky in the autumn calling for a 'curbing of the bourgeois press, which is disseminating vile slander'.[110] *Golos soldata* (The Voice of the Soldier), the influential SR-Menshevik newspaper, proclaimed 'the need to stop the piles of bourgeois newspapers, which no one reads, from clogging up the postal system'.[111] That such groups should call for the suppression of the bourgeoisie, and base their arguments on the idea that this was to serve 'democracy', illustrates how far the socialist language of class conflict had come to dominate the democratic discourse in 1917.

Towards the Terror

In his memoirs General Denikin gives a good idea of what it meant to be a 'burzhooi' after October 1917. For the first time in many years he found himself among ordinary Russians as he sat in a third-class railway carriage, disguised as a Polish nobleman, on his way to join the 'counter-revolution' on the Don:

> Now I was simply a 'burzhooi', who was shoved and cursed, sometimes with malice, sometimes just in passing, but fortunately no one paid any attention to me. Now I saw real life more clearly and was terrified. I saw a boundless hatred of ideas and of people, of everything that was socially or intellectually higher than the crowd, of everything which bore the slightest trace of abundance, even of inanimate objects, which were the signs of some culture strange or inaccessible to the crowd. This feeling expressed hatred accumulated over the centuries, the bitterness of three years of war, and the hysteria generated by the revolutionary leaders.[112]

110. GARF, f. 1778, op. 1, d. 362, l. 311 (a resolution of the officers and soldiers of the staff of the 3rd Railway Battalion).
111. *Golos soldata*, Petrograd, 3 Oct. 1917.
112. A.I. Denikin, *Ocherki russkoi smuty*, Paris, 1921–6, vol. 2, pp. 147–8.

The future White army leader was not the only refugee from Bolshevik Russia to feel the wrath of the common people during that terrible winter of 1917–18. The memoir literature is full of similar accounts by princes, countesses, artists, writers and businessmen of the traumatic journeys they had to make through revolutionary Russia in order to flee the Bolshevik regime. They all express the same sense of shock at the rudeness and hostility which they now encountered from the ordinary people: weren't these the brothers and sisters of their nannies and their maids, their cooks and their butlers, who only yesterday had seemed so kind and respectful? It was as if the servant class had all along been wearing a mask of goodwill which had been blown away by the revolution to reveal the real face of hatred below.

This hatred of the 'burzhooi' was the emotional basis of the Terror, which developed from below as well as from above. For, however much one may condemn it, and however hard it may be to admit, there is no doubt that the Terror struck a deep chord in the Russian civil war mentality, and that it was based on a strange mass appeal. The slogan 'Death to the Bourgeoisie!', which was written on the walls of the Cheka interrogation rooms, was also the slogan of the street. People even called their daughters Terrora.[113]

How was this language of violence created, and what was its impact in generating terror? Was it that Russian popular culture was already brutalized before the revolution and, as a result of this long tradition of coercive rule, responded to the political divisions of 1917 with its own forms of spontaneous retribution against perceived enemies? That all the Bolsheviks did was to make this retribution possible and institutionalize it in the form of the Terror? Or was it that their discourse of violence and terror, the symbols of the enemy which they held up as something to be vanquished, legitimized and organized the violence from below?

It would seem from the evidence we have reviewed in this chapter that the basis of the Terror was already laid in the subculture of the revolutionary underground which was absorbed into the popular culture of the revolution during 1917. Many people were prepared to see the revolution as a life-and-death struggle between good and evil, the future and the past, which justified and indeed necessitated the suppression of its 'dark' enemies. This in turn became a fundamental aspect of the Bolshevik language of civil war. In 1919 the writer Bunin saw a placard on the building of the Cheka in Odessa with the words of the revolutionary song the 'Varshavianka':

---

113. B.I. Kolonitskii, '"Revolutionary Names": Russian Personal Names and Political Consciousness in the 1920s and 1930s', *Revolutionary Russia*, 1993, vol. 6.

On to the throne covered with the people's blood
We will pour the blood of our enemies.[114]

For Bunin there was a direct line from the culture of the revolutionary
underground to the Terror of the Bolsheviks. But it was more complicated.
The language of the underground took on a new function in 1917. It
was disseminated and appropriated in a multitude of different ways by
people in the streets hungry for a new political language to express their
emotions, their anger and ideals. Before 1917 they had been 'just' words
– symbols of ideals in the future tense:

. . .
It will be our last and decisive battle
        ('Internationale' before 1917)

During 1917, however, these same words were taken up by the people in
the very action of self-liberation from their enemies. They became the
slogans of their revolutionary banners, and were sung in the present tense:

. . .
It is our last and decisive battle
        ('Internationale' during and after 1917)[115]

Once the battle had commenced such words became a part of the action
itself. They ceased to be just symbols and became performative.

In the early days of the revolution the idea of the last battle had a
quasi-sacred appeal among those who placed their hopes in it. The symbols
of their songs promised them a release from the past and a breakthrough
into a new life. However, as their ideals failed to materialize and euphoria
gave way to disappointment and despondency, so people looked for explanations in the same songs and texts from which they had derived their
hopes. The answer came that the last decisive battle was still not won,
that the enemy still had to be annihilated. But who was the enemy now?
The Tsar had fallen, his supporters fallen too, the people's victory should
have been assured. So the tendency was to look for new and 'hidden'
enemies, for conspiracies and plots against the revolution. This, after all,
was to continue the logic of the February Revolution which had its own

114. I.A. Bunin, *Okaiannye dni*, Moscow, 1990, pp. 97–9.
115. Many revolutionary songs made this transition from the future to the present tense in 1917.
     See N.I. Mironets, 'Publikatsiia sbornikov revoliutsionnykh pesen v 1917–1922 gg.', in
     Arkheograficheskii ezhegodnik za 1987 god, Moscow, 1988, p. 68; N.S. Polishchuk, 'Otrazhenie
     samosoznaniia rabochikh v ikh pesennom repertuare', in *Rossiiskii proletariat: Oblik, bor'ba,
     gegemonia*, Moscow, 1970, p. 179; E. Kann-Novikova, *Vy zhertvoiu pali v bor'be rokovoi*, Moscow,
     1968, p. 84.

conspiracy theories. The 'burzhooi' was the perfect scapegoat – vague and undefined, combining as he did all the previous images of the enemy, both from the right-wing and left-wing traditions – capitalist, foreign, parasitical.

The Bolsheviks took over the symbolic system of the revolution, including its images of the enemy. But they used this symbolic system in a different way from the SRs and the Mensheviks of 1917 – stressing, unlike them, that its words were meant for action. The SRs and Mensheviks, aware of the violent potential of their symbols, attempted to restrict them to the domain of words: symbols just as symbols. But Lenin talked the language of civil war. In 'How to Organize Competition?', written in December 1917, he called for a 'war to the death against the rich, the idlers and the parasites'. Each village and town should be left to develop its own means of

> cleansing the Russian land of all vermin, of scoundrel fleas, the bedbug rich and so on. In one place they will put into prison a dozen rich men, a dozen scoundrels, half a dozen workers who shirk on the job . . . In another place they will be put to cleaning latrines. In a third they will be given yellow tickets [such as prostitutes were given] after a term in prison, so that everyone knows they are harmful and can keep an eye on them. In a fourth one out of every ten idlers will be shot. The more variety the better . . . for only practice can devise the best methods of struggle.[116]

The 'enemies' which Lenin identifies are the same as the enemies of the classical revolutionary tradition. But he invites a literal reading of these symbols and directly appeals for mass action to annihilate the people (indeed any people) identified by these labels as the enemy.

This literal reading and its application unleashed mass terror in a chaotic way. For in every village and in every town different scapegoats were found under these same labels. To some extent the Bolsheviks' ability to control these symbols of the enemy was a source of power, for in this way they could direct the mass terror against the 'counter-revolutionaries' of their choosing. Yet that terror was always bound to be chaotic because people read its symbols in their many different ways.

But a more important source of power was the symbolic victory which many perceived in the physical destruction of the 'burzhoois'. The Red Terror appealed to the plebeian desire for revenge – a desire which was at the heart of the social revolution of 1917. Through their 'war on privilege' the Bolsheviks were able to draw on the energies and revolutionary zeal of those numerous elements from the poor that derived a certain pleasure from seeing the rich and mighty destroyed, regardless of whether it brought

116. V.I. Lenin, *Polnoe sobranie sochinenii*, Moscow, 1958–65, vol. 35, p. 204.

about any improvement in their own lot. Indeed, if Soviet power could do little to relieve the misery of the poor, it could at least make the lives of the rich still more miserable than their own – and this was itself a cause for considerable psychological satisfaction. Without bread, land or peace, the Bolsheviks were increasingly obliged to base their claim to mass appeal on this psychology of retribution. In an editorial to mark the start of 1919, *Pravda* proclaimed:

> Where are the wealthy, the fashionable ladies, the expensive restaurants and private mansions, the beautiful entrances, the lying newspapers, all the corrupted 'golden life'? All swept away. You can no longer see on the street a rich *barin* [gentleman] in a fur coat reading the *Russkie vedomosti* [a liberal newspaper closed down after October 1917]. There is no *Russkie vedomosti*, no fur coat for the *barin*; he is living in the Ukraine or the Kuban, or else he is exhausted and grown thin from living on a third-class ration; he no longer even has the appearance of a *barin*.[117]

117. *Pravda*, 1 Jan. 1919.

Conclusion

Like all modern social revolutions, the Russian Revolution was a struggle for state power. Each side of this power struggle was defined by its own symbolic system – flags and songs, political phrases and slogans, pictures and emblems – which served to articulate its ideology and to rally its supporters to 'the cause'. These symbolic systems played a complicated role in the politics of 1917. They did more than just reflect the clash of ideologies. There were times when symbols were themselves the object of the struggle, times when they defined it, provoked it or contained it, and times when the struggle was entirely fought on a symbolic plain.

The February Revolution was, at one important level, a struggle for control of the symbols of the state. Far from being 'spontaneous', the insurrection in Petrograd was in fact organized around the capture of symbolic sites and the symbolic or physical destruction of Tsarist statues and monuments, prison buildings, emblems and flags. This destruction of the old state symbols was seen by many people as the physical destruction of the old regime itself. In the absence of any obvious counter-revolution – without a real enemy to fight against – the war against the Tsarist regime was fought against its symbols. Indeed in many towns, where there was a peaceful transfer of power during the February Days, the symbolic re-enactment of the revolution (replacing the old with new state symbols at 'festivals of freedom' and other ceremonies) served as a sort of substitute for it. Here there was no revolutionary struggle – only the symbolic representation of it.

Once the old regime and its symbolic system were destroyed, the competitors for power struggled to control the symbolic system of the revolutionary underground which dominated the political culture of the February Revolution. Russia may have been a pluralist democracy in 1917, truly the 'freest country in the world', but the symbolic language of the socialists had an absolute monopoly. No one doubted for a moment that the symbols of the revolutionary movement would become the emblems of the future state. During 1917, the red flag effectively became the national flag, and the 'Marseillaise' the national anthem, even though such matters were supposed to be decided by the Constituent Assembly. There was simply no alternative since the people flatly rejected the old national symbols, while the liberals had neither a symbolic tradition of their own nor an inclination to develop one in 1917 (there were no Kadet songs or banners). The symbolic system of the socialists, in short, was bound to fill the gap.

All the socialists shared a political language and symbolic tradition inherited from the European revolutionary movement and their own common subculture in the underground. The Bolsheviks were no exception, and even the symbolic system which they went on to develop after October was largely based on this common socialist tradition.

The political conflict between the rival socialist parties in 1917 was defined in many ways by the struggle to control this symbolic system. The prize was very great – for it alone was capable of mobilizing support among the masses. Sometimes these conflicts were intensified by the simultaneous struggle over symbols (for example, on 10 and 18 June, in the July crisis, or during the October Days, when the slogan 'All Power to the Soviets!' was itself a major cause of the heightened tension; or in the period after October, when the political conflict between the Bolsheviks and their socialist opponents was paralleled and exacerbated by the rivalry between the 'Internationale' and the 'Marseillaise'). At other times, however, the sharing of a symbolic system enabled the socialists to forget their differences and unite around the red flag and the 'Marseillaise' to fight against the 'counter-revolutionary' enemy (e.g. during the Kornilov crisis).

In some ways the symbolic language of the revolution served as a bridge to the past. It could reinterpret old mentalities in a new political discourse. This was the case, for example, with the cults of Kerensky, Kornilov and Lenin, which recast the monarchical psychology of the cult of the Tsar in a republican context. The traditionalism apparent in much of the peasantry's political discourse was another case in point. However, in the main, the symbolic language of the revolution served to create new meanings and to give expression to new life.

All the competing 'democratic' factions struggled to control this symbolic language, knowing that it was the key to power in the new mass democracy. Each strove to fix its public meanings and to assert the ascendancy of its own particular idiom, its own understanding of the symbols' connotations, within the dominant political discourse. Radicals spoke one language of democracy, patriots another, socialists a third; and within each language there were different dialects (constitutionalist, imperialist, defensist, populist or Marxist, and so on). The revolutionary struggle was articulated, at one level, as a competition between these symbolic systems, each of which had its own criteria for identifying the interests of 'the people' and its 'enemies'.

This was not just a fight between the parties to monopolize and control the symbols of the revolutionary underground – the battle over songs and anthems, party slogans and so on. It was also a much more fundamental struggle to define the values of the new society, for these were what the symbols of the revolution represented. This was clearly the significance of the public debate about 'democracy' in 1917. The liberals, the Populists and the Marxists all had their own understanding of the term, each of which involved a different moral vision of the new society; and within society itself there were many different conceptions of 'democracy'. Each interpretation had its own symbolic discourse (the idea of democracy as all the 'citizens', 'the labouring people', or 'the proletariat') which defined its social meanings and ideals.

The whole of society was affected by these competing discourses as it became more politicized during 1917. The values and traditions which these languages expressed helped individual people and collective groups to define themselves (as a 'citizen', a 'toiler', a 'peasant', a 'worker' and so on) as well as to decide their political outlook. However, in this act of communication the discourses themselves became dispersed, their connotations changed, as diverse people interpreted and used them for their own particular purposes and did so in a multitude of different ways.

This greatly complicated the politics of the revolutionary period, for a word signalled by the revolutionary leaders to encourage one thing among their followers might be understood to mean another by local activists or by society at large. The popular interpretation of the word 'burzhooi' is an obvious case in point. The Bolshevik leaders may have understood it to signify a class – whether defined sociologically as the bourgeoisie or politically as the enemies of the Bolshevik regime. But the popular perception of the 'burzhooi' (as any selfish or anti-social person, anybody showing signs of above-average wealth or education, anybody foreign or alien) meant that the Bolshevik campaign against this 'class enemy of the people' was likely to develop into a mass terror in which virtually anyone could be targeted: ex-landowners and officers, schoolteachers and clerks, 'kulaks' and creditors, or even the victims of a private vendetta. The Bolsheviks, while they may have welcomed it in many ways, could not direct this mass terror, which was consequently completely chaotic; nor could they control the public meaning of its slogan, written on the walls of the Cheka's interrogation rooms: 'Death to the burzhoois!' Indeed, there were cases where this slogan was used by an angry public to sanction acts of violence against the local Bolsheviks, who were frequently perceived to be the new 'burzhoois' on account of their well-dressed appearance and masterly ways.

This is not to conclude that language became an independent actor, divorced from the conflicts of society, during the revolutionary period. The social and political divide (between 'us' and 'them', the *verkhy* and the *nizy*, the mighty and the weak) was real enough without having to depend on language for its existence. But it is to say that the symbolic language of the revolution helped in many ways to determine these conflicts. Words and symbols acted as a code of communication to sanction or legitimize the actions of the people, to articulate their goals and grievances, to identify 'us' and 'them', the 'people' and their 'enemies', during the struggle. The signals of this code were infinitely varied and understood in many different ways. Yet there was a dominant discourse that unified these many idioms in a common language of social justice, and that was the language of the socialists. Theirs was not a discourse of compromise. It had been developed in the underground as a fighting language, a lexicon of battle, and it called upon the people to destroy their oppressors. Perhaps in the end that helps us to explain why the Russian Revolution was so violent.

Index